Lincoln
and the Civil War

IN THE DIARIES AND LETTERS OF

John Hay

President Lincoln and his two secretaries, John George Nicolay and John Hay, Nov. 8, 1863. Later Hay became the equivalent of Military Aide with the brevet rank of Lieutenant Colonel. The original of this photograph, which is usually reproduced without the background, is owned by Miss Nicolay, whose father had the details painted in, thus making an interesting contemporary record.

Lincoln
and the Civil War

IN THE DIARIES AND LETTERS OF

John Hay

Selected and
With an Introduction by
TYLER DENNETT

New Foreword by
HENRY STEELE COMMAGER

A DA CAPO PAPERBACK

Library of Congress Cataloging in Publication Data

Hay, John, 1838-1905.
   Lincoln and the Civil War in the diaries and letters of John Hay /
selected and with an introduction by Tyler Dennett: new foreword by
Henry Steele Commager.
     p.   cm — (Da capo paperback)
   Reprint. Originally published: New York: Dodd, Mead: 1939.
   Includes index.
   ISBN 0-306-80340-2 (pbk.)
   1. Hay, John, 1838-1905 — Diaries. 2. Hay, John, 1838-1905 —
Correspondence. 3. Lincoln, Abraham, 1809-1865 — Friends and
associates. 4. United States — History — Civil War, 1861-1865 —
Personal narratives. 5. Statesmen — United States — Diaries.
6. Statesmen — United States — Correspondence. I. Dennett, Tyler,
1883-1949. II. Title.
[E664.H41A3   1988]
973.7'092'4 — dc19   88-17072

This Da Capo paperback edition of *Lincoln and the Civil
War in the Diaries and Letters of John Hay* is an unabridged
republication of the edition published in New York in 1939,
here supplemented with a new foreword by Henry Steele Commager.
It is reprinted by arrangement with Dodd, Mead & Company.

Published by Da Capo Press, Inc.
A Subsidiary of Plenum Publishing Corporation
233 Spring Street, New York, N.Y. 10013

FOREWORD

John Milton Hay was a young man of many ambitions and talents who fulfilled all of them. From the improbably named town of Warsaw (originally Spunky Point), on the Illinois side of the Mississippi, he yearned for broader horizons and a New England education. He did in fact enroll at Brown University and graduated with high honors; his ventures in poetry earned him the designation "class poet," and he later published a book of *Pike County Ballads*. Law and medicine were family professions, and young Hay read law with his uncle in Springfield. There he encountered men of national distinction: Stephen Douglas, who had just defeated Abraham Lincoln for the Senate; Lyman Trumbull, an elder statesman in Washington; and the formidable David Davis, whom Lincoln was to appoint to the Supreme Court. Most important was Lincoln himself, whom young Hay came to know because his uncle's office was in the same building as that of Lincoln and Herndon, and Hay's friend, the German-born John Nicolay, was Lincoln's secretary. Thus Lincoln saw the aspiring lawyer daily and took a fancy to the boy; when he was elected to the Presidency he asked Hay, somewhat casually, to come along with him to the White House and share Nicolay's duties as "Secretary"—a term which covered a bit of everything.

After Lincoln's death, Hay abandoned the law for diplomacy, serving his country well in Paris, Vienna, Madrid and, eventually, in the most exalted of diplomatic posts, at the Court of St. James's. Almost inevitably he graduated to the post of Secretary of State. Jointly with Henry Adams he built a house overlooking the White House and at the same time achieved the ultimate distinction of membership in that most exclusive fellowship: Adams's "Five of Hearts."

All very impressive but, in a curious way, all was anticlimax—just as every President whom Hay served after Lincoln was anti-climax.

Perhaps because he was young enough to be Lincoln's son, Hay's relations with the President he privately called "The Ancient One" and "The Tycoon" were more informal and even more intimate than those of Nicolay who was seven years his senior, and busy falling in love and getting married. Lincoln hated to read the flood of letters from Congressmen; he recognized Nicolay's precedence over Hay by assigning to him responsibility for answering all their mail, but left to Hay the less delicate task of responding to the flood of miscellaneous letters that poured in. (How interesting that Lincoln managed with two secretaries while current Presidents need hundreds!)

Night after night, long after the household had gone to sleep, the "Ancient One" would stray into Hay's bedroom, clad only in a long white nightgown and carpet-slippers, talking—mostly to himself—about men and issues that troubled him. It was, to be sure, mainly the men who troubled him—the issues were clear enough. He talked about Secretary of Treasury Chase who insisted on resigning, again and again, until the President finally let him have his way. He talked, too, about General McClellan, who could whip an army into shape but was reluctant to do anything with it, and who thought that *he* ought to be President and often acted as if he were. One of the earliest entries in Hay's notebook tells the otherwise incredible story of Lincoln and Secretary of State Seward calling on the General only to find that he was off to a wedding. Lincoln and Seward sat down to wait; finally McClellan came in and went up to his bedroom. After an hour passed, he sent down word that he had retired for the night. No wonder Senator Wade accused McClellan of having his theology all wrong, of thinking that there was a fourth member of the Trinity!

It is stories like this, with their stamp of authenticity, that give value and intimacy to Hay's diary. They bring home to us what Lincoln had to tolerate not only from a Chase and a McClellan but from Horace Greeley as well—Greeley who was ready to "let the erring sisters go in peace" and whom Lincoln thought insane. Ben Butler was another trouble-maker. It was Butler who earned the title "Beast Butler" in New Orleans and who took for granted that if only he were in command of the Union armies the war would soon be over. Butler's hubris prompted Lincoln to borrow an Illinois neighbor's recollection of his brother as "the damnedest scoundrel that ever lived but, in the infinite mercy of Providence, also the damnedest fool." Surrounded by some of the worst scoundrels and fools, Lincoln

FOREWORD

could still give his "utmost trust" to men in whom he could put his faith, like Ulysses Grant.

Not the least fascinating pages of these notebooks are those devoted to the election of 1864. Lincoln himself thought it probable that he would not be re-elected; the auspices were not favorable, not even on the military front, although Sherman's capture of Atlanta had a profound psychological effect. Even to the very day of election, there was a deep anxiety amongst his followers. The feeling of relief they experienced emerges from Hay's hour-by-hour account as the results came in over the wires. In the end, Lincoln swept the country; poor, vain McClellan carried only one free state, New Jersey. Through it all the President appeared calm and confident—if not of victory, then of the ultimate triumph of justice and virtue. Hay captures this well in one of his more moving tributes:

> What a man it is! Occupied all day with matters of vast moment. Deeply anxious about the fate of the greatest army in the world, with his own fame and future hanging in the events of the passing hour. Yet he has such a wealth of simple bonhomie and good fellowship that he gets out of bed and perambulates the house in his shift to find us that we may share with him [some little anecdote].

—HENRY STEELE COMMAGER
Amherst, Massachusetts
May 1988

INTRODUCTION

Six months before he was twenty-three years of age, John Hay arrived in Washington from Springfield, Illinois, with the Lincoln suite. On March 4, 1861, with the Lincoln family, he moved into the Executive Mansion as it was then usually called. Technically, on the government pay-roll, he was a clerk in the Interior Department assigned to duty in the office of the President of the United States. Actually he began his service as assistant to John G. Nicolay, only six years his senior, who, in turn, was Private Secretary to President Lincoln. Later he was "one of the President's secretaries" and eventually, although probably without warrant in law, he ventured to exercise the franking privilege, writing his name in place of the stamp in the upper right hand corner of the envelope. For four years of the American Civil War Hay and Nicolay worked together in the White House, and for much of the period slept together in the northeast corner room on the second floor, adjacent to the Executive Offices across the hall. Rarely has it been the fortune of two such young men to be placed in such intimate relations with great events and with great men.

In March, 1865, John Hay was appointed Secretary of Legation in Paris where he was associated first with John Bigelow with whom he formed a lasting and profitable friendship and then briefly with John A. Dix, who followed Bigelow as American minister. Hay remained in Paris about a year and a half. In June, 1867, he was appointed Chargé d'Affaires in Vienna following the indignant resignation of John Lothrop Motley as Minister. Upon the appointment of Motley's successor he resigned and returned to the United States. In June, 1869, he went to Madrid as Secretary of Legation to serve a little more than a year as the first assistant to General Daniel E. Sickles, the newly appointed American Minister. Thus, not only by frequent return to Washington, but also at his various posts in Europe which, as he wrote from Paris, suffered an *"inondation Générale"* of American generals after the Civil

v

War, Hay kept in touch with the early years of the Reconstruction —the entire administration of Andrew Johnson, and the first year or more of Grant's. First Lincoln, then to an almost equal degree Seward, and later many others, made John Hay the recipient of their confidences and their reminiscences and with him shared the current gossip. The latter, whether true or false, indicated the changing atmosphere of the extraordinary decade which began with the Civil War in America and ended with the Franco-Prussian War in Europe: it was peculiarly a war decade.

Six weeks after entering upon his official duties with President Lincoln John Hay began to keep a journal in a seven-by-eight-inch note-book. Never a methodical person, Hay began it on page twenty-three, probably intending to go back later and fill in for the precious weeks he had neglected. The notes were made intermittently and spasmodically from April 18, 1861 onward. There are four of these books, and three smaller ones which could be slipped into a pocket for use away from the desk. There is also an old-fashioned letterpress copy-book half full of copies from Madrid in 1869 and 1870 where Hay was vainly helping General Sickles to negotiate for the separation of Cuba from Spain, and perhaps for its acquisition by the United States. In addition there are preserved from this period some, though probably only a small proportion, of Hay's original letters. These letters are, most of them, to Nicolay when one or the other was absent from Washington, to Nicolay when the latter was Consul General in Paris, 1865–69, and to members of Hay's family.

Not long after John Hay's death in 1905, Mrs. Hay invited those with whom her husband was known to have been in frequent correspondence to return to her the original letters. From these, and from a diary kept from January, 1904, to Mr. Hay's death the following year, Mrs. Hay made a selection and printed for private distribution in three volumes in 1908 an edition of about two hundred copies, under the title, "Letters and Extracts from the Diary of John Hay." In the initiation of this labor of love she had the assistance of Henry Adams, but for some reason, perhaps because the latter could not reconcile his historical sense with Mrs. Hay's not very objective and quite feminine editing, the three volumes were at length printed without Mr. Adams's continued help. Mrs. Hay deleted all proper names except for the initial letters so that Abraham Lincoln became A——— L——— and Washington W————. While this device did not always achieve the obscurity which Mrs. Hay quite properly might have desired when so many of her husband's correspondents were still her neighbors and friends or still in public life, it did suffuse the printed pages with baffling uncertainties about incidents and people long since belonging mainly to history. Furthermore the selections were sometimes of more interest to a wife than to readers who later turned eagerly to these books for important historical information which the pages carried as on photographic plates only half developed. And yet the privately printed volumes are important because some of the original letters, with the passage of time, have disappeared. These volumes may now be treated as a source but to be used cautiously and where possible always to be checked against originals. Some letters from Mrs. Hay's collection have been used.

There are also included in the following pages a few letters to Mr. or to Mrs. John Bigelow, the originals of which are in the possession of their granddaughter, Mrs. J. Francis Clark, who generously permitted the editor to make copies.

The letters and diaries not otherwise indicated are in the John Hay Papers in the possession of the Hay family to which the editor is again deeply indebted for free access and much kindness.

John Hay was an exceptionally good letter-writer; at his best one of the best which America has produced. Throughout his extraordinary life he was so placed as to have things of the greatest interest to write about and his skill in writing, while slow in maturing, at times reached high levels. He was at his very best in personal letters to intimate friends and in journal entries where he was without self-consciousness and could indulge his gift of phrasing. To publish all of his good letters, good either for literary excellence or for the information they contain, would require more volumes than a distracted and brain-fagged modern world would read. Rigorous selection and pruning are demanded. In the following pages are collected whatever throws light on Abraham Lincoln,

on the American Civil War, and on the early politics of the Reconstruction. They may be read for information, for remarkable
vignettes of remarkable people, for a sense of the social and political atmosphere of war-time Washington—fundamentally not very
different from war-time Washington sixty years later—or they may
be read merely for amusement. This fresh, enthusiastic young ob-
server, who worked hard all day and then played hard far into the
night—he was then as always one of those men who "went everywhere," with discrimination—was in a position to draw intimate
portraitures not alone of Abraham Lincoln but as well of William H. Seward, Salmon P. Chase, George B. McClellan, Ulysses
S. Grant, Benjamin B. Butler and of many others. He had his
heroes and he had his hates; it is a terrible fate to be disliked or
distrusted by a young man with a pen like John Hay's.

The assertion that Hay was a good letter-writer must be qualified by adding that, especially in his early literary period, before
he had served his time as editorial writer on the *New York
Tribune,* he was as to punctuation, sometimes as to spelling, even
as to grammar, as thoughtless as a modern undergraduate. The
originals from which the following pages of text have been prepared were dashed off at odd moments, often late at night, with
never a thought that they would ever be considered important
enough to publish. Those to whom minutia are important—they
never were to Hay in this period—may find reason to reproach the
editor for having suffered the printer to set up these pages in disregard of some of the elementary rules of the language in which
they were written; only mere slips of the pen have been corrected.

Editing in these pages has been severely restrained. This material was one of the main sources of Nicolay's and Hay's "Abraham
Lincoln A History" (10 Vols. The Century Company, 1890). It
has usually been possible to clear up obscurities by resort to these
monumental volumes. For the general history of the period the
editor has followed mainly James Ford Rhodes. "The Dictionary
of American Biography" and the "Biographical Directory of the
American Congress 1774–1927," published as House Document
783, 69th Cong., 2 Ses., have also been used freely. To have gone
far beyond these standard reference works would have tempted

one to elaborations of footnotes which would be inappropriate to the material and of help to only a few. John Hay as a person and as a writer had a sparkle which should not be dulled by much foot-noting.

The editing of such material, to an extent far more than in ordinary literary composition, demands attention to small details.

No merely perfunctory acknowledgment is therefore made to those who have so enthusiastically and faithfully entered into the task of copying, verifying, and checking the text, and then have joined so completely in the editing that this book is as much theirs as the editor's: J. Myrtle D'Arcy and Kathleen O'Connell.

CONTENTS

xi

LINCOLN AND THE CIVIL WAR

in the Diaries and Letters of

JOHN HAY

In this volume the ordinary subject index is preceded by a list of names with brief biographical and occasional descriptive data needed either to identify the person or to explain the text. After each name is the page reference. Some bracketed comment is inserted into the text as an alternative to footnotes. References to "N. and H.," are to Nicolay's and Hay's "Abraham Lincoln A History" (Century Company, 1890); to "Complete Works" are to "Abraham Lincoln Complete Works" (Century, 1894) by Nicolay and Hay. By "John Hay" is indicated the editor's "John Hay From Poetry to Politics" (Dodd, Mead and Company, 1933), a biography in which three chapters are given to the period covered by these diaries and letters. Some letters used in the biography are omitted here to make a place for other material not before published. When not otherwise indicated the original source in the following pages is the Hay Papers.

CHAPTER I

April 18—May 12, 1861

DIARY

April 18, 1861. The White House is turned into barracks.[1] Jim Lane marshalled his Kansas Warriors today at Willard's and placed them at the disposal of Maj. Hunter, who turned them tonight into the East Room. It is a splendid company—worthy such an armory. Besides the western Jayhawkers it comprises some of the best *materiel* of the East. Senator Pomeroy and old Anthony Bleecker stood shoulder to shoulder in the ranks. Jim Lane walked proudly up and down the ranks with a new sword that the Major had given him. The Major has made me his aid, and I labored under some uncertainty as to whether I should speak to privates or not.

The President today received this despatch.

"We entreat you to take immediate measures to protect American Commerce in the Southern waters and we respectfully suggest the charter or purchase of steamers of which a number can be fitted from here without delay." Signed by Grinnell Minturn, & many others of the leading business men of the place. The President im-

[1] To sense the surcharged atmosphere in which the Hay diary opens one may recall the following facts:

The Confederate Constitutional Convention met in Montgomery, Alabama, Feb. 4, 1861, a full month before the inauguration of President Lincoln. General P. T. G. Beauregard opened fire on Fort Sumter April 12, and the Federal garrison, unable to defend itself, surrendered the next day. The effect of this initial Southern victory was to draw hesitating Virginia, and then North Carolina, Tennessee and Arkansas into the Confederacy. The current doubt about the loyalty of Maryland, Kentucky and Missouri is reflected in the first few pages of the diary. After the fall of Fort Sumter it was predicted freely in the South that the Confederate armies would be in Washington by the first of May. Of this the President himself appears to have been somewhat apprehensive. To meet the emergency, while improvising temporary measures of defense in Washington, the President, April 15, called for 75,000 militia to be supplied by the states. The first to appear was the 6th Massachusetts which, the day after the diary opens, encountered an angry mob while marching across Baltimore from one railroad station to the other.

mediately sent for the Cabinet. They came together and Seward answered the despatch in these words.

"Despatch to the President received and letters under consideration. W. H. Seward." [2]

All day the notes of preparation have been heard at the public buildings and the Armories. Everybody seems to be expecting a son or brother or "a young man" in the coming regiments.

Tonight Edward brought me a card from Mrs. Ann S. Stephens expressing a wish to see the President on matters concerning his personal safety. As the Ancient was in bed, I volunteered to receive the harrowing communication. Edward took me to his little room adjoining the Hall and I waited. Mrs. Stephens, who is neither young nor yet fair to any miraculous extent, came in leading a lady who was a little of both, whom she introduced as Mrs. Col. Lander. I was infinitely delighted at this chance interview with the Medea, the Julia, the Mona Lisa, of my stage-struck salad days. After many hesitating and bashful trials, Mrs. Lander told the impulse that brought them. Some young Virginian, long-haired, swaggering, chivalrous, of course, and indiscreet friend, had come into town in great anxiety for a new saddle, and meeting her had said that he and half a dozen others, including a daredevil guerilla from Richmond named Ficklin, would do a thing within forty-eight hours that would ring through the world. Connecting this central fact with a multiplicity of attendant details she concluded that the President was either to be assassinated or captured. She ended by renewing her protestations of earnest solicitude mingled with fears of the impropriety of the step. Lander has made her very womanly since he married her. Imagine Jean M. Davenport a blushing, hesitating wife.

They went away and I went to the bedside of the Chief *couché*. I told him the yarn; he quietly grinned.

Going to my room, I met the Capt. He was a little boozy and very eloquent. He dilated on the troubles of the time and bewailed the existence of a garrison in the White House "to give *éclat* to Jim Lane."

[2] The next day the President proclaimed a blockade of southern ports from South Carolina to Texas inclusive.

Hill Lamon came in about midnight saying that Cash Clay was drilling a splendid company at Willard's Hall and that the town was in a general tempest of enthusiastic excitement, which not being very new, I went to sleep.

Friday. April 19, 1861. Early this morning I consulted with Maj. Hunter as to measures proper to be taken in the matter of guarding the house. He told me that he would fulfill any demand I should make. The forenoon brought us news of the destruction of Gov^t property at Harper's Ferry.[3] It delighted the Major, regarding it as a deadly blow at the prosperity of the recusant Virginia.

I called to see Joe Jefferson & found him more of a gentleman than I had expected. A very intellectual face, thin and eager, with large, intense blue eyes, the lines firm, and the hair darker than I had thought. I then went to see Mrs. Lander and made her tell the story all over again "just by way of a slant." Miss Lander, the sculptor, was there. I liked Jean M. more and more. Coming up, I found the streets full of the bruit of the Baltimore mob & at the White House was a nervous gentleman who insisted on seeing the President to say that a mortar battery has been planted on the Virginia heights, commanding the town. He separated himself from the information and instantly retired. I had to do some very dexterous lying to calm the awakened fears of Mrs. Lincoln in regard to the assassination suspicion.

After tea came Partridge and Petherbridge from Baltimore. They came to announce that they had taken possession of the Pikesville Arsenal in the name of the Government—to represent the feeling of the Baltimore Conservatives in regard to the present embroglio there and to assure the President of the entire fidelity of the Governor and the State authorities. The President showed them Hick's and Brown's despatch. Which "Send no troops here. The authorities here are loyal to the Constitution. Our police force and local militia will be sufficient." Meaning, as they all seem to think, that they wanted no Washington troops to preserve order, but, as Seward insists, that no more troops must be sent through the city. Scott seemed

---

[3] When threatened by a raiding force from Virginia, the commanding officer at Harper's Ferry burned the arsenal and armory and retreated into Maryland.

to agree with Seward & his answer to a despatch of inquiry was, "Gov. Hicks has no authority to prevent troops from passing through Baltimore." Seward interpolated, "no right." Partridge and Petherbridge seemed both loyal and hopeful. They spoke of the danger of the North being roused to fury by the bloodshed of today and pouring in an avalanche over the border. The President most solemnly assured them that there was no danger. "Our people are easily influenced by reason. They have determined to prosecute this matter with energy but with the most temperate spirit. You are entirely safe from lawless invasion."

Wood came up to say that young Henry saw a steamer landing troops off Fort Washington. I told the President. Seward immediately drove to Scott's.

About midnight we made a tour of the house. Hunter and the Italian exile Vivaldi were quietly asleep on the floor of the East Room and a young and careless guard loafed around the furnace fires in the basement. Good looking and energetic young fellows, too good to be food for gunpowder,—if anything is.

Miss Dix called today, to offer her services in the Hospital branch. She makes the most munificent and generous offers.

April 20, 1861. Col. Washington called this morning but could not see the President. It would seem like a happy omen to have a General Washington living and fighting among us at this time.

The streets were full of the talk of Baltimore. It seems to be generally thought that a mere handful of men has raised this storm that now threatens the loyalty of a State.

I went up with Nicolay, Pangborn, and Whitely to see the Massachusetts troops quartered in the Capitol. The scene was very novel. The contrast was very painful between the grey-haired dignity that filled the Senate Chamber when I saw it last and the present throng of bright-looking Yankee boys, the most of them bearing the signs of New England rusticity in voice and manner, scattered over the desks, chairs and galleries, some loafing, many writing letters, slowly and with plough-hardened hands, or with rapid glancing clerkly fingers, while Grow stood patient by the desk and franked for everybody. The Hall of Representatives is as yet empty. Lying on a sofa

and looking upward, the magnificence of the barracks made me
envy the soldiery who should be quartered there. The wide-
spreading skylights overarching the vast hall like heaven blushed
and blazed with gold and the heraldic devices of the married States,
while all around it the eye was rested by the massive simple splendor
of the stalagmitic bronze reliefs. The Spirit of our institutions
seemed visibly present to inspire and nerve the acolyte, sleeping in
her temple beside his unfleshed sword.

This evening Speed Butler came from Illinois, bearing despatches
in relation to the garrisoning of St. Louis and Cairo and the state of
the Sub-Treasury at St. Louis. Scott listened with great satisfaction
to the plans proposed by the State Government & with his own hand
wrote an order which Cameron signed, commanding the Commander at the Arsenal to provide accommodations for the Illinois
troops, at the Arsenal or Jefferson Barracks, and to furnish to the
order of the Govr of Ills. ten thousand stand of arms.[4] Speed will
instantly return with these.

The town is full tonight of feverish rumours about a meditated
assault upon this town, and one, which seems to me more probable,
on Fort McHenry.[5] The garrison there is weak and inadequate and
in spite of the acknowledged bravery of Robinson and Hazard it
must fall if attacked. Ellsworth telegraphs that his regiment has
been raised, accepted, and that he wants them sent to Ft. Hamilton
for preliminary drill. Cameron authorized the answer that the
Commander there should have orders to that effect. Much is hoped
from the gallant Colonel's Blood-tubs. They would be worth their
weight in Virginia currency at Ft. McHenry tonight.

The Massachusetts men drilled tonight on the Avenue. They afford a happy contrast to the unlicked patriotism that has poured
ragged and unarmed out of Pennsylvania. They step together well
and look as if they meant business.

Jim Lane wrote a note to the President today offering to bring
any assignable number of Northern fighting men over the border at
the shortest possible notice. This the Tycoon quietly shelved. Gen.

[4] The department commander at St. Louis had been obstructing the recruiting
and arming of volunteers. Three Illinois regiments were sent down to assist in guarding the arsenal.
[5] At Baltimore.

Scott seems to think that four or five thousand men will be a sufficient garrison to hold this town against any force that may be brought from the Maryland or Virginia woods.

April 21, 1861. This morning came a penitent and suppliant crowd of conditional Secessionists from Baltimore, who having sowed the wind seem to have no particular desire to reap the whirlwind. They begged that no more Federal troops should be sent through Baltimore at present; that their mob was thoroughly unmanageable and that they would give the Government all possible assistance in transporting its troops safely across the State by any other route. The President, always inclined to give all men credit for fairness and sincerity, consented to this arrangement contrary to the advice of some of his most prominent counsellors. And afterwards said, that this was the last time he was going to interfere in matters of strictly military concernment. That he would leave them hereafter wholly to military men.

I spoke of the intended resignation of Col. Magruder. The Tycoon was astonished. Three days ago, Magruder had been in his room making the loudest protestations of undying devotion to the Union. This canker of secession has wonderfully demoralized the Army. Capt. Fry is the firmest and soundest man I meet. He seems to combine great honesty of purpose with accurate and industrious business habits and a lively and patriotic soldier spirit that is better than anything else today.

This morning we mounted the battlements of the Executive Mansion and the Ancient took a long look down the bay. It was a "water-haul."

Any amount of feverish rumors filled the evening. The despatch from Mead Addison in regard to 1,500 Mass. troops being seen off Annapolis seemed to please the Pres^t very much. Then there was a Fort Monroe rumour and a 7th Reg^t rumour and a R.I. rumour, all which tomorrow will sift.[6]

We passed the evening pleasantly at Ann's, where were the Eng-

---

[6] The 7th New York, arriving in Philadelphia by train, April 20, proceeded thence by chartered steamer to Annapolis which they reached April 22. The 8th Mass., under Gen. Benj. F. Butler, detoured around Baltimore by water from Perryville to Annapolis. They reached Washington on the 25th.

lish Legation, and returned to find Vivaldi and his borderers guarding the Imperial palace, pacing in belted and revolvered dignity up and down the wide portico, to give style and tone to the defensive guard, looking, as he said, like gentlemen in feature and dress. We went up and found a despatch stating that no troops had arrived at the Navy Yard. *Tant pis* we said and slept.

April 22, 1861. The President this morning recommended the appointment of Peck of Chicago to a lieutenancy and of Capt. Todd to the vacant Quartermastergeneralship. Chase and the Chief were talking together. Chase said, "All these failures are for want of a strong young head. Everything goes in confused disorder. Gen. Scott gives an order, Mr. Cameron gives another. Half of both are executed, neutralizing each other."

The whining traitors from Baltimore were here again this morning. The President I think has done with them. In conversation with Major Hunter last night, in reply to the Major's blunt assertion that the troops should have been brought through Baltimore if the town had to be leveled to the earth, he said, that that order commanding their return to Pa. was given at the earnest solicitation of the Maryland conservatives who avowed their powerlessness in Baltimore but their intention to protect the Federal troops elsewhere; granted them, as a special extension, as an exhaustion of the means of conciliation & kindness.[7] Hereafter, however, he would interfere with no war measures of the Army.

A young lady called today from Baltimore, sent by her father, H. Pollock, Esq., to convey to the Gov^t information as to the state of affairs in the plug-ugly city. She was very pretty and Southern in features and voice and wonderfully plucky and earnest in the enunciation of her devotion to the Stars and Stripes. She stated that the mails had been stopped at the Balto. P.O.—arms expected from Va. —Ft. McHenry to be attacked tonight—the scared Com^rs here thoroughly traitorous & other things. . . .

This afternoon the *Pocahontas* and the *Anacostia* came peacefully back from their cruise and folded their wings in the harbor.

---

[7] A thousand unarmed Pennsylvania troops were sent back across the Susquehanna River.

The *Pocahontas* has done her duty at Norfolk and is welcome to our bay, with its traitor-haunted shores. She reports no batteries at the White House Point and makes no record of any hostile demonstrations from the banks of Alexandria. The very fact of the *Pocahontas* coming so quietly in, is a good one.

A telegram intercepted on its way to Baltimore states that our Yankees and New Yorkers have landed at Annapolis. Weary and foot-sore but very welcome, they will probably greet us tomorrow. . . .

It is amusing to drop in some evening at Clay's Armory. The raw patriots lounge elegantly on the benches—drink coffee in the anteroom—change the boots of unconscious sleepers in the hall—scribble busily in editorial notebooks, while the sentries snore at the doors and the grizzled Captain talks politics on the raised platform and dreams of border battle and the hot noons of Monterey.

It was dramatic [8] to see Cassius Clay come into the President's reception room today. He wore, with a sublimely unconscious air, three pistols and an Arkansas toothpick and looked like an admirable vignette to 25-cents-worth of yellow-covered romance.

Housekeepers here are beginning to dread famine. Flour has made a sudden spring to $18.00 a bbl. and corn meal rejoices in the respectable atmosphere of $2.50 a bushel. Willard is preparing for war, furling all sails for the storm. The dinner-table is lorn of *cartes* and the tea-table reduced to the severe simplicity of pound-cake.

April 23, 1861. This morning Doug. Wallack came rushing into the office looking for Seward with what he called important news. He said that two ships at the Navy Yard were the *Pawnee* and the *Keystone.* They brought Marines and naval stores from Norfolk, which place they left after carrying out to the letter their instructions, to destroy what Government property they could not remove. The Premier cussed quietly because the *Baltic* had not come, told Wallack not to contradict the report that the *Baltic* had come—said the treason of Hicks [9] would not surprise him—that the Seventh could cut their way through three thousand rioters—that Baltimore

---

[8] At some later date Mr. Hay added the prefix "melo-."

[9] But a year later the President offered him a brig. generalship, which he declined.

delenda est—and other things, and strolled back into the audience chamber.

At dinner we sat opposite old Gen. Spinner who was fierce and jubilant. No frenzied poet ever predicted the ruin of a hostile house with more energy and fervor than he, issuing the rescript of destiny against Baltimore. "We've got 'em," he said. "It is *our* turn now. We keep steadily one week ahead of them, as Scott says. We have burned their hospital and poor-house, Harper's Ferry and the Norfolk Navy Yard. Now let them fight or starve." He was peculiarly disgusted with the impertinence of Delaware. "The contemptible little neighborhood, without population enough for a decent country village, gets upon her hind legs and talks about armed neutrality. The only good use for traitors is to hang them. They are worth more, dead, than alive." Thus the old liberty-loving Teuton raged.

A gaunt, tattered, uncombed and unshorn figure appeared at the door and marched solemnly up to the table. He wore a rough rusty overcoat, a torn shirt, and suspenderless breeches. His neck was innocent of collar, guiltless of necktie. His thin hair stood fretful—porcupine-quill-wise upon his crown. He sat down and gloomily charged upon his dinner. A couple of young exquisites were eating and chatting opposite him. They were guessing when the road would be open through Baltimore. "Thursday," growled the grim apparition, "or Baltimore will be laid in ashes." It was the ally of Montgomery, the King of the Jayhawkers, and the friend of John Brown of Ossawatomie.

It was Jim Lane.

Tonight there seemed to be reliable news at the State Department that the Seventh Regiment and the Mass. troops would start from Annapolis tonight and through the favoring moonlight march to the Junction, where the Government has possession of the Road. The hostile peasantry can harrass them fearfully on the way from fence corners and hillsides if they are ready and brave.

Cameron today informed Lord Lyons that he could not give a friend of his Lordship a safe passage to Baltimore as the Government only holds this end of the Road.

We got some three-days-old New York papers and it seemed like a glimpse of a better world to contrast the warm open enthusiasm of the Empire City with the cold distrust and grim earnestness that mark the countenance of the dwellers in Washington.

A large and disappointed throng gathered at the depot this morning hoping to get deliverance. But the hope was futile. They seem doomed to see the rising of the curtain.

April 24, 1861. On account of the stoppage of trains, on the Northern railroads, we have nothing this morning but a Southern mail. . . .

One Southern letter in a dozen differs from the rest in being comparatively decently written and expressed. But we have the same lamentable hebetude of conscience, the same lack of vividness of moral perception, the same logic that assumes as its major premise "All Southerners are honest, generous, and brave" and for its minor "All Northerners are faithless, tyrannical, and cowardly" & deduces from these all needful conclusions. The defense of the Capital is coercion. The succor of starving soldiers is trampling on the dearest rights of the South. The stoning to death of inoffensive strangers is a calm and earnest protest against lawless invasion. Slavery is the persecuted princess of faery. The longhaired whisky runners of the piney woods are her gentle and brave knights-errant. The vile, deformed, and malevolent North is wooed in the tenderest terms to forego his wicked spite and lay down his oppressive arms, vacate the throne he has usurped to dishonor, and kneel in penitent allegiance at the feet of the adored and restored goddess of the chain and thong.

Abe Lincoln is adjoured in the name of God to resign in favor of Jeff. Davis. The Northern Congress is requested with arctic coolness to recommend the Constitution of the C.S.A. to the people of the North, at the same time distinctly avowing that it is by no means probable that Northern States will be admitted into this holy congregation, on any terms.

The wounded soldiers from Massachusetts came up to the President's House today. He received them kindly and cordially. They came in, confused and flushed, they went out easy, proud and happy. A few kind words are very powerful if they go down. Coming up, they have less weight.

This has been a day of gloom and doubt. Everybody seems filled with a vague distrust and recklessness. The idea seemed to be reached by Lincoln; when chatting with the volunteers this morning he said, "I don't believe there is any North. The Seventh Regiment is a myth. R. Island is not known in our geography any longer. *You are the only Northern realities.*" Seward's messengers sent out by the dozen do not return. The Seventh & Butler's are probably still at Annapolis. A rumour this evening says the R.R. is in the hands of the Gov^t, and the 7th's sappers & miners are at work repairing it.

The *Pocahontas* went puffing down the river at sundown to meet the New York companies in the transport fleet that left there Sunday night. She looked busy and resolute.

April 25, 1861. At the request of the Tycoon, who imagined he had seen something significant steaming up the river, I went down to the Navy Yard. Saw Dahlgren who at once impressed me as a man of great coolness & power. The boat was the *Mt. Vernon* who reported everything right in the river.

About noon the 7th Regiment came. I went to the depot and saw Lefferts who communicated the intelligence of their peaceful passage, with which I straightway gladdened the heart of the Ancient. Cale Smith was with him as I returned. He was just reading a letter from Hamlin advising the immediate manufacture of rifled cannon from the Chicopee Works. Lincoln seemed to be in a pleasant, hopeful mood, and in the course of conversation partially foreshadowed his present plan. He said, "I intend at present, always leaving an opportunity for change of mind, to fill Fortress Monroe with men and stores, blockade the ports effectually, provide for the entire safety of the Capital, keep them quietly employed in this way, and then go down to Charleston and pay her the little debt we are owing her" [for the capture of Fort Sumter].

This morning a jolly whole-hearted Shaker from N. H. came in & filled the room with the freshness of his presence. He said they were late getting here, as their driver, who was a constable, had to stop to whip a nigger! It was a rich and novel idea to the broad-brimmed Northerner.

Gen. Butler has sent an imploring request to the President to be allowed to bag the whole nest of traitorous Maryland Legislators and bring them in triumph here. This the Tycoon, wishing to observe every comity even with a recusant state, forbade. Today we got a few letters and papers & felt not quite so forlorn.

* * * *

April 26, 1861. Massachusetts & Rhode Island troops in large numbers arrived today from Annapolis. Helme tells me that all through Maryland the slaves followed begging to be allowed to come with them as servants. One fellow who had bought himself said, "If I had known you gun men was acoming, I'd a saved my money."

I called on Sprague, the Governor of R.I., with Nicolay—a small, insignificant youth, who bought his place. But who is certainly all right now. He is very proud of his company, of its wealth and social standing.

Carl Schurz was here today. He spoke with wild enthusiasm of his desire to mingle in this war. He has great confidence in his military powers, and his capability of arousing the enthusiasm of the young. He contemplates the career of a great guerilla chief with ardent longing. He objects to the taking of Charleston & advises forays on the interior States.[10]

April 27, 1861. Jackson Grimshaw has come here from Illinois to urge upon the Government the absolute necessity from a military point of view for the Government to seize the Hannibal & St. Joe R.R. His views are very sound. He objects to the President conferring any important military trusts upon those who have been fighting in the interests of the slave power all their lives.

The President rec'd a letter from Wm. E. Channing advising abolition of slavery by martial law as the surest way to conquer rebellious States & preserve the border ones. The Seventh Regiment Band played gloriously on the shaven lawn at the south front of the Executive Mansion. The scene was very beautiful. Through the luxuriant grounds the gaily dressed crowd idly strolled, sol-

[10] Added to the text subsequently: "That seems scarcely possible but it must be true."

diers loafed in the promenades, the martial music filled the sweet
air with vague suggestions of heroism, & Carl Schurz and the
President talked war.

April 28, 1861. All this blessed Sunday, free from war's alarms, we
have lounged *sans souci.* Sprague & his staff called on the President,
and the Cabinet dropped in and gave a last word as to the new
proclamation blockading Va. Yesterday the President sent an order
to Gen[1] Scott authorizing and directing him to suspend the writ
of habeas corpus on all necessary occasions along the lines of military occupation leading to this city from Philadelphia &c.

April 29, 1861. Going into Nicolay's room this morning, Carl
Schurz and Jim Lane were sitting. Jim was at the window filling
his soul with gall by steady telescopic contemplation of a Secession
flag impudently flaunting over a roof in Alexandria. "Let me tell
you," said he to the eloquent Teuton, "we have got to whip these
scoundrels like hell, Cairl Schurz. They did a good thing stoning
our men at Baltimore & shooting away the flag at Sumter. It has
set the great North a howling for blood and they'll have it."
"I heard," said Schurz, "you preached a sermon to yr. men yesterday."
"No sir, this is no time for preaching. When I went to Mexico,
there were four preachers in my rigiment. In less than a week I
issued orders for them all to stop preaching and go to playing
cards. In a month or so they was the biggest devils & best fighters
I had."
An hour afterward Carl Schurz told me he was going home to
arm his clansmen for the wars. He has obtained three months leave
of absence from his diplomatic duties & permission to raise a
cavalry regiment.[11] I doubt the propriety of the movement. He will
make a wonderful land pirate, bold, quick, brilliant and reckless.
He will be hard to control and difficult to direct. Still, we shall
see. He is a wonderful man.
The R.I. troops passed in review today. They look wonderfully

11 Schurz had been named U. S. Minister to Spain.

well in their simple coarse uniforms relieved only by the fierce coloring in blankets.

April 30, 1861. I went up to the Interior Department to see the Rhodian heroes. I saw Goddard, Hoppin, De Wolf, Sackett, Pearce and others of the whilom loungers of Westminster, all dressed in the coarse blue flannel and all doing duty, the severest duty, without a murmur, and without any apparent consciousness that there was anything at all remarkable about it. Scattered through the rubbish and camp-litter of Company C's quarters there was enough of breeding and honor to retone the society of the Gulf and wealth enough to purchase the entire state of Florida, and take the poor beggarly Montgomery loan.[12] When men like these leave their horses, their women and their wine, harden their hands, eat crackers for dinner, wear a shirt for a week and never black their shoes,—all for a principle—it is hard to set any bounds to the possibilities of such an army. The good blood of the North must now be mingled with that of the South in battle and the first fight will determine which is the redder.

Horatio J. Perry was this morning appointed Secretary of Legation at Madrid *ad interim* to give Carl Schurz the benefit of his three months' leave. Perry is living at the capital city of Spain at present, is married to the poet Carolina Coronado & is certainly the best man for the place. I wish his appointment were permanent instead of temporary.

Three Indians of the Pottawatomies called today upon their Great Father. The Spokesman's English was very exceptional, the other two were mute. One was a magnificent broad-chested, bare-armed giant with a barbaric regal adornment of bear's claws. The second a quiet Uncas-looking fellow. The Spokesman was dressed in a wonderful style of shabby genteel. The Tycoon amused them immensely by airing the two or three Indian words he knew. I was amused by his awkward efforts to make himself understood by speaking bad English, e.g., "Where live now? When go back Iowa?"

---

[12] $15,000,000 at 8%, authorized by Confederate Provisional Congress, Feb. 28, 1861, at Montgomery.

Frederick Hassaurek & I dined together. He seemed stung by the inaction which his lameness besides his foreign duties imposes upon him. He evidently chafes with generous emulation of the coming glories of Schurz in the field. He is a delicate-souled and thoughtful genius, but has not the vigor and animal arrogance that help Schurz to bully his way through life. Hassaurek will probably indulge his bent for literature in the high solitude of Quito. He intimated a course of articles in the *Atlantic* and an ultimate book.

Coming home from the theater I met Blair,[13] Schurz and Fox coming out of the audience chamber. Going in, I saw the great map of Virginia, newly hung, and fronted by conscious-looking chairs. The air is full of ghastly promises for Maryland & Virginia. Destiny is even now casting over them the gloom of her shadowing wings.

Meanwhile the North is growing impatient. Correspondents talk impertinently, and the "little villain" of the N.Y. *Times,* advises the immediate resignation of the Cabinet, & warns the President that he will be superseded.

Van Wyck is here occasionally. I never saw him so jolly as when he came up Sunday morning with Capt Viele. He had manned a gun all the way up river & was flushed with the honor. He had artistically inked his shot pouch to the following effect:

> "We will go through to Washington
> Or sleep in the Potomac."

On the reverse,

> "What our fathers died to establish
> We will maintain."

May 1, 1861. Yesterday I read a letter from prominent Unionists of western Virginia, asking help from the Government in resisting the coercion of the Eastern & rebellious portion of the State. Their plan is to endeavor to remove the State Government from Richmond west of the mountains, or failing in that, to cut themselves

---

[13] Presumably Montgomery Blair, Postmaster General, although it might have been his father, F. P. Blair, or his brother, F. P. Blair, Jr. of St. Louis.

off from the eastern district, or rather, by remaining in the Union, let the eastern portion cut itself off. The letter was signed by G. W. Caldwell. Nicolay answered it cautiously today, leaving the door open for future negotiations. This morning some of the same men called upon the President. Loyalty will be safer in western Virginia than rebellion will be on the eastern slopes of the Blue Ridge.

There were a half-dozen good-looking members of the Seventh Regiment called upon the Commander in Chief of the Armies & Navies this afternoon. He was very frank & cordial with them. He spoke amusedly of the *Times'* proposition of deposing him and said that the Government had three things to do: defend Washington, blockade the ports, and retake Government property. All possible despatch was to be used in these matters & it wd. be well if the people would cordially assist in these matters before clamoring for additional work. The proclamation calling out the troops is only two weeks old. No people on earth could have done what we have in that time.

Montgomery Blair came in with the intelligence that our office holders had been quietly installed at Baltimore under the floating of the constellated banner and that the Police Board had removed the restriction on the sale of flour. He thought the outbreak at the Massachusetts passage was the work of secession officials who were unwilling to lose their lease of plunder. He thoroughly believed in the loyalty of Maryland. The President seemed to think that if quiet was kept in Baltimore a little longer Maryland might be considered the first of the redeemed.

The little Jew who has so singularly attached himself to Seward who is named in the directory Herrmann but whom the Premier has rechristened Flibbertygibbet, came in with advices that Ellsworth's regiment was at Annapolis in good order and well-conditioned. Also that the R.I. Artillery was now on its way hither by water.

Ellsworth's whereabouts pleased the Tycoon as it enabled him to correct a funk of Scott's that the Firemen were cutting their way through Baltimore. They will find the subtle [undecipherable] of Wilson's command a thousand times worse than Ellsworth in insubordination & rowdyism. I think the best use for them will be to detail them at once to the retaking of Sumter. They will probably all perish & provide themselves with a numerous escort of palmetto rebels to the warm regions down below.

May 2, 1861. Tonight Ellsworth & his stalwart troup arrived. He was dressed like his men, red cap, red shirt, grey breeches, grey jacket. In his belt, a sword, a very heavy revolver, and what was still more significant of the measures necessary with the turbulent spirits under his command, an enormously large and bloodthirsty-looking bowie knife, more than a foot long in the blade and with body enough to go through a man's head from crown to chin as you would split an apple. His hair was cut short. His face thin from constant labor and excitement. His voice had assumed that tone of hoarse strength that I recognized at the end of the triumphant trip last year. He seemed contented and at ease about his regiment. He indulged in a little mild blasphemy when he found that no suitable quarters had been provided but was mollified by the proffer of the 69th's rooms & the Capitol.

I went up. It was a jolly, gay set of blackguards. They had reduced their hair to a war footing. There was not a pound of capillary integument in the house. Their noses were concave, their mouths vulgar but good humored, the eyes small crafty and fur-tive.

They were in a pretty complete state of don't care a damn, modified by an affectionate and respectful deference to the Colonel. He thought only of his men. We went, after making all possible provisions for their suppers, to hammocks. The Zouave could not enjoy his tea, as he thought it unbecoming an officer to eat before his men.

He spoke with honest exultation of the fruitless attempt made to stop him the morning of embarkation.

May 3, 1861. This morning in the President's mail I came across some warlike documents. One from Fernandy Wood offering his services in a military capacity which was very cool but not so arctic as the cheekiness of Govr. Harris of Tenn. who demanded an immediate explanation of the seizing of the *Hillman* at Cairo (which the Tycoon glanced at & quietly observed, "He be d—d.") A New Jersey General White offers his division for an unlimited time.

May 4, 1861. The Maryland Disunionists, that branch of them represented by Bob McLane, called today upon the President. Their roaring was exquisitely modulated. It had lost the ferocious timbre of the April days. They roared as gently as twere any nightingale. The only point they particularly desired to press was that there was no particular necessity at present existing for the armed occupation of Maryland. That it would irritate and inflame. Still they admitted that the right of the Government to occupy the city and State was undeniable; that the people were on the side of the Union, a majority unconditionally, and a majority of the minority favorably inclined; while nearly all were for avoiding any conflict with the Federal authorities. They also implored the President not to act in any spirit of revenge for the murdered soldiery. The President coolly replied that he never acted from any such impulse & as to their other views he should take them into consideration and should decline giving them any answer at present.

Gen¹ Scott gave orders to Gen¹ Butler to occupy the Relay House as soon as practicable and Butler instantly replied that he should hold divine service with his command there tomorrow, Sunday.

May 5. Which he did.

May 6, 1861. Maj. Sparks of Baltimore, who seems alarmingly tricky, came noisily in with a yarn that the decessionists, who are hovering ten thousand strong around Harper's Ferry, are removing gun-barrels, gun-stocks, and machinery away from there—that there are batteries scattered among the rocks which thoroughly command the situation—that they can only be fought successfully from the Maryland side—that Ben McCullough [14] is there & had

---

[14] Ben McCullough, the Texas Ranger, Confederate Brigadier-General, came up from Texas in 1861 but never east of the Mississippi River. He was killed in Missouri in 1862.

recently sent a budget of information to the Legislature at Frederick—that Butler was snug at the Relay, unconscious until Sparks told him that the enemy were rigging up a battery on the opposite heights which would rake his camp, and other items to the like sensational purpose. I gave them to Howard who straightway sent them *Tribune*-wards.

The President came into Nicolay's room this afternoon. He had just written a letter to Hamlin, requesting him to write him a daily letter in regard to the number of troops arriving, departing, or expected, each day. He said it seemed there was no certain knowledge on these subjects at the War Department, that even Genl. Scott was usually in the dark in respect to them.

* * * *

May 7, 1861. Ellsworth came in this m.

I went in to give the President some little items of Illinois news, saying among other things that Singleton was behaving very badly. He replied with emphasis that Singleton was a miracle of meanness, calmly looking out of the window looking at the smoke of two strange steamers puffing up the way, resting the end of the telescope on his toes sublime.

I spoke of the proposition of Browning to subjugate the South, establish a black republic in lieu of the exterminated whites, and extend a protectorate over them, while they raised our cotton. He said, "Some of our Northerners seem bewildered and dazzled by the excitement of the hour. Doolittle seems inclined to think that this war is to result in the entire abolition of slavery. Old Col. Hamilton, a venerable and most respectable gentleman, impressed upon me most earnestly the propriety of enlisting the slaves in our Army."

I told him his daily correspondence was thickly interspersed by such suggestions.

"For my part," he said, "I consider the central idea pervading this struggle is the necessity that is upon us, of proving that popular government is not an absurdity. We must settle this question now, whether in a free government the minority have the right to break up the government whenever they choose. If we fail it will go far to prove the incapability of the people to govern themselves. There may be one consideration used in stay of such final judgment, but that is not for us to use in advance.

"That is, that there exists in our case, an instance of so vast and farreaching a disturbing element, which the history of no other free nation will probably ever present. That, however, is not for us to say at present. Taking the government as we found it we will see if the majority can preserve it."

He is engaged in constant thought upon his Message: it will be an exhaustive review of the questions of the hour & of the future.

In the afternoon we went up to see Ellsworth's Zouave Firemen. They are the largest, sturdiest, and physically the most magnificent men I ever saw collected together. They played over the sward like kittens, lithe and agile in their strength.

Ellsworth has been intensely disgusted at the wild yarns afloat about them which are, for the most part, utterly untrue. A few graceless rascals have been caught in various lapses. These are in irons. One horrible story which has been terrifying all the maiden antiques of the city for several days, has the element of horror pretty well eliminated today, by the injured fair, who proves a most yielding seducee, offering to settle the matter for 25 dollars. Other yarns are due to the restless brains of the press-gang.

The youthful Colonel formed his men in a hollow square, and made a great speech at them. There was more commonsense, dramatic power, tact, energy, & that eloquence that naturally flowers into deeds in *le petit* Colonel's fifteen-minute harangue than in all the speeches that stripped the plumes from our unfortunate ensign in the spread-eagle days of the Congress that has flitted. He spoke to them as men. Made them proud in their good name; spoke bitterly & witheringly of the disgrace of the recreant; contrasted with cutting emphasis which his men delighted in, the enlistment of the dandy regiment for thirty days, with *theirs* for the war; spoke solemnly & impressively of the disgrace of expulsion; roused them to wild enthusiasm by announcing that he had heard of one officer who treated his men with less consideration than himself and that, if on inquiry the rumour proved true, he would strip him & send him home in irons. The men yelled with delight, clapped their hands, & shouted "Bully for you." He closed with wonderful tact and dramatic spirit by saying, "Now laddies, if anyone of you wants to go home, he had better sneak around the back alleys, crawl over fences, and get out of sight before we see him," which got them again. He must have run with this crowd sometime in his varied career. He knows them and handles them so perfectly.

May 8, 1861. Eames called this morning & brought to my notice a singular omission in Jeff. Davis' manifesto—his ignoring all mention of the right of revolution and confining his defense of his position to the reserved constitutional right of a State to secede. By this means he estops his claim upon the recognition of the world. For even those governments that acknowledge the necessity of recognizing all governments, which by virtue of revolution have a *de facto* existence, would most naturally say to a new government basing its claim to nationality on the constitution of the government vs. which it rebels, "We can entertain no such question of legal construction. The contest as stated by you between you and your government is a municipal one. We have no right to interfere or prejudge the decision of such a case of conflicting interpretation." Jeff. Davis seems to have been so anxious to satisfy the restless conscience of the Borderers, that he utterly overlooks the importance of conciliating the good opinion of the outside world. "There is a hole in your best coat, Master Davis."

May 9, 1861. There was a very fine matinée at the Navy Yard given by some musical members of the 12th New York. They sang well, the band played well, and the President listened well. After the programme, the President begged for the Marseillaise. The prime gentlemen gave the first verse and then generously repeated it, interpolating nonchalantly "Liberty or death" in place of "Abreuve nos sillions," which he had forgotten.

Then we went down to the *Pensacola* and observed the shooting of the great Dahlgren gun Plymouth. Two ricochet shots were sent through the target and one plumper. The splendid course of the 11 inch shell flying through 1300 yds of air, the lighting, the quick rebound, & flight through the target with wild skips, throwing up a 30 ft. column of spray at every jump, the decreasing leaps and the steady roll into the waves were scenes as novel and pleasant to me as to all the rest of the party. The Pres^t was delighted. Capt Gillis was bored at Dahlgren for laughing at the bad firing from the *Pocahontas*.

This morning Ellsworth's Zouaves covered themselves with glory as with a blanket in saving Willard's Hotel and quenching a most ugly looking fire. They are utterly unapproachable in anything they attempt. Their respectful demeanor to their chief and his anxious solicitude for their comfort & safety are absolutely touching to behold.

May 10, 1861. Carl Schurz loafed into my room this morning & we spoke of the slaves & their ominous discontent. He agreed with me that the Commandants at Pickens & Monroe were unnecessarily squeamish in imprisoning & returning to their masters the fugitives who came to their gates begging to be employed. Their owners are in a state of open rebellion against the Government & nothing would bring them to their senses more readily than a gentle reminder that they are dependent upon the good-will of the Government for the security of their lives and property. The action would be entirely just and eminently practicable. Schurz says that thousands of Democrats are declaring that now is the time to remove the cause of all our woes. What we could not have done in many lifetimes the madness and folly of the South has accomplished for us. Slavery offers itself more vulnerable to our attack than at any point in any century and the wild malignity of the South is excusing us before God & the World.

So we talked in the morning.

But tonight I saw a letter from Mrs. Whitman stating that Thomas Earl, T. W. Higginson, the essayist of Boston, and young John Brown were "going to free the slaves." What we were dreaming of came over my mind with horrible distinctness and I shrunk from the apparition. This is not the time nor are these the men to do it. They should wait till the Government gives some kind of sanction to the work. Otherwise the horrors of the brutal massacre will move the pity of the magnanimous North, and in the suppression of the insurrection the warring sections may fuse and compromise.

May 11, 1861. I told Helme to come & see me, and I impressed as strongly as possible upon his mind the importance of the view just taken—that the administration could do nothing but hang the insurrectionists, and that any such rash outbreak would terribly weaken the hands of the government. He said he would write Brown & Higginson.

This afternoon the Marine Band played on the South Lawn and Carl Schurz sat with Lincoln on the balcony. After the President had kissed some thousand children and retired, Carl went into the library and developed a new accomplishment. He played with great skill & feeling, sitting in the dusk twilight at the piano, until the President came by & took him down to tea. Schurz is a wonderful man. An orator, a soldier, a philosopher, an exiled patriot, a skilled musician. He has every quality of romance and of dramatic picturesqueness.

May 12, 1861. We spent this afternoon at Camp Lincoln, the habitation of Ellsworth's "pet lambs." They seemed very comfortable and happy. Ellsworth was playing ball with them as we approached looking fine and blouzy in his red shirt. We went to his tent. Col. Pritchard (here from St. Louis to gain indemnity for his losses on the *C. E. Hillman*) was jubilant over the capture of Frost's Brigade. They seemed to think it would prove the *coup de grâce* to secession in Missouri. Frank Blair writes today that St. Louis is getting too quiet. He wants his regiment sent to Charleston.

Wm. P. Thomasson was here today trying to gain authority for the Kentucky Unionists to raise troops in the State for service in the State.[15] Col. Rousseau says that they can be more easily raised and controlled in this way than in any other.[16]

[15] Gov. Magoffin had declined to furnish state militia. The tentative policy in Kentucky was to maintain neutrality.

[16] There is a lapse in the diary after May 12. For the convenience of the reader there are recalled the following facts: May 24, the Federal forces crossed the Potomac and occupied Arlington Heights. Congress met July 4 and adjourned Aug. 6. Responsive to popular demand that the Federal Government force a battle in Virginia, but contrary to the opinion of Gen. Scott, on July 16 McDowell advanced 27 miles from Washington. Gen. Beauregard fell back and prepared for the battle of Bull Run, which, July 21, was a great disaster for the Federal Government.

CHAPTER II

August 22—November 13, 1861

DIARY

August 22, 1861. A long hiatus. The nights have been too busy for jottings.

Today Dudley & Hunt, the Ky. Com^rs, called on the President begging for permission of neutrality. He told them that professed Unionists gave him more trouble than rebels. They put their case strongly, but gained no commitment from him. It is a deep scheme of Magoffin's to put the responsibility of the first blow upon the Gov^t. The President cannot consent to what they ask, for neutrality won't continue long—we want to go through the State —and the North will not permit the disarming of the Unionists. On his refusal Davis of course will assent to all demands & place the Gov^t wrong before the people.

We went over to Seward's, found him comfortably slippered & after talking about consular nuisances went over to McClellan's. Everything seems going right. Discipline is perfecting. The Dry Tortugas have squelched mutiny. The drills & reviews keep the men alive. Hunter is soon to go to Illinois as they need a head. At first he wanted to take McDowell but Scott objected. Regiments are constantly coming in, and [going] down for them. McClellan is growing jolly.[1] Seward is in a better humor than I have lately seen him.

[1] McClellan, after notable success in Western Virginia, was called to Washington after McDowell's failure at Bull Run and, July 27, assumed command of the Washington troops.

TO J. G. NICOLAY

WASHINGTON. *Aug. 24. 1861*

DEAR GEORGE

Yours of the 22 received this morning. I don't wish to hurry you, but write simply to say that Dr. Pope's prediction has been realized. I am flat on my back with bilious fever. I had a gay old delirium yesterday, but am some better today. Dr. thinks I will be around in a day or two. Bob Lincoln came this morning bringing positive orders from his mother for me to join her at New York for an extension of her trip. I don't know where. Of course I can't go—as things look. There is no necessity whatever for you to return just now. There is no business in the office and Stoddard is here all the time. He can do as well as either of us. As soon as I get able, I shall leave. The air here is stifling. You had better stay as long as you like for there is nothing but idleness here. As soon as I get on my pins I shall shab. It will be a sort of breach of etiquette but, as Joe Gargery feelingly observes, "Manners is manners, but your 'elth's your 'elth."

Don't come till you get ready.

JOHN HAY

DIARY

August 28, 1861. I went West, and passed several days in St. Louis. Saw very much of Frémont and his wife. He was quiet, earnest, industrious, imperious. She very much like him, though talking more and louder. I wrote articles in the *World* and *Journal* for Frémont. Coming to New York I found Thur. Weed had blabbed it to the President.[2]

October 10, 1861. Tonight I went over to McClellan's quarters with the Tycoon and Seward. Lander was with us, part of the way. Lander was gasconading a little. He said he would like a good place to die in with a corporal's guard, to set the nation right in the face of the world after the cowardly shame of Bull Run. The President, as Lander walked off, said, "If he really wanted a job

[2] First reference to Hay's journalistic writing from the White House. See "John Hay" p. 71.

like that I could give it to him. Let him take his squad and go down behind Manassas and break up their railroad." Seward said he disbelieved in personal courage as a civilized institution. He had always acted on the opposite principle, admitting that you are scared and assuming that the enemy is. If this matter had been managed on his basis it would have been arranged satisfactorily and honorably before now.

We came to McClellan's quarters and met in the telegraph office a long and awkward youth who spoke in a high-pitched and rapid tone to Seward, "We are just in from a ride of all day." Seward introduced him to me as Captain Orleans. He went upstairs to call McClellan and the President said quietly, "One doesn't like to make a messenger of the King of France, as that youth, the Count of Paris, would be if his family had kept the throne."

McClellan came hurriedly in and began to talk with the President. They discussed the events of today and yesterday. McClellan was much pleased at the conduct of his men—no rowdyism or plundering today. He was merely today finishing yesterday's work. The rest of the week will be used in the same way. Says the Tycoon, "We have gained a day on our sea expedition. The vessels will leave on the 14th it is thought instead of the 15th." [3]

As we left, McClellan said, "I think we shall have our arrangements made for a strong reconnaissance about Monday to feel the strength of the enemy. I intend to be careful, and do as well as possible. Don't let them hurry me, is all I ask." "You shall have your own way in the matter, I assure you," said the Tycoon, and went home.

October 12, 1861. Tonight the President went to Seward's, I with him. At the door a telegram was handed him—from McClellan, stating that the enemy was before him in force and would probably attack in the morning. "If they attack," he added, "I shall beat them." [4] We went to Seward's and talked of many things. Seward spoke of Lander's restlessness & griefs at inaction, his offered resig-

---

[3] During the summer of 1861 the plan was matured for a joint naval and military expedition to capture Port Royal, South Carolina, as a base to facilitate the blockade and for military operations in South Carolina. The fleet actually did not sail from Fort Monroe until Oct. 29. N. & H. V, 16.

[4] The attack did not materialize.

nation, and resolve to go West and begin again—that watching the Potomac was not congenial, and other such. Seward told him to be of good cheer. Gen[1]. Scott was already fixing his orders for exactly the work he wanted to do.

Col. Scott came in with despatches from McCl., one ordering Hooker's Bladensburg Brigade in—one countermanding & one re-affirming. Scott then went out to order transportation for 6000.

G. V. Fox came in and began to talk about the great expedition that is fitting at Annapolis.[5] He wants when they have sailed to have 14,000 more men detached from the Army of the Potomac to be held in readiness awaiting the result of the expedition. If it causes a retreat of the rebels, then this additional force can be easily spared. The fleet will probably sail on Thursday and will have some work to do at Fernandina, Pensacola, Mobile. Gen[1] Scott told Fox that 3500 men would be enough to take Mobile, assisted by their ships. Fox himself seemed very confident that the expedition would succeed. His only nervousness was in relation to submarine batteries which modern science has rendered very destructive and entirely feasible.

Seward spoke also of Motley's despatch which seemed to contain a most cheering account of the real sentiment of honest sympathy existing in the best class of English Society towards us.[6] Motley's letter embraced free and cordial conversations with Earl Russell, Earl Grey, Cobden, Mr. Layard, Prince Albert, and the Queen.

There was much talk of Daniel Webster in which the financial sansouciism of the great man was strikingly prominent. Seward said he would not live, nor Clay, a tithe as long as J. Q. Adams. The President disagreed with him, and thought Webster will be read forever.

October 17, 1861. At Seward's tonight we met Capt. Schultz who showed very bad taste by alluding to the Chicago Convention and Seward. The Pres[t] told a good yarn.

[5] to capture Mathias Point on the Potomac and thus prevent the blockade of the river. N. & H. IV, 452.

[6] Motley was living in London, at work on the second volume of "The United Netherlands." He was also conducting some propaganda on behalf of the Union cause and a month later secured the appointment as Minister to Austria.

One day in Springfield shortly after some of the lower counties had held meetings and passed resolutions eulogistic of Trumbull, John Wentworth, sitting near Lincoln at breakfast one morning, said, "Lincoln, have you seen them resolutions?" "I have seen what I suppose you refer to."

"Them Trumbull fellers are going to trick you again." [7]

"I don't see any trickery about it, and if there was, there is no way to help the matter."

"I tell you what, Lincoln," said John with a look of unutterable sagacity, "You must do like Seward does—get a feller to run you."

It was vastly amusing to both the Tycoon and Secretary.

The Sec. State talked about intercepted correspondence and the double dealing and lying of our young English friends, Fergusson and Bourke.

Going to McClellan's with Banks they talked about the campaign. McC. thought the enemy were massing at Manassas. He said he was not such a fool as to buck against that place in the spot designated by the foe. While there, the President received a despatch from Sherman at Annapolis asking for the 79th N. Y., the Highlanders. The President was vexed at this and at Sherman's intimation that the fleet would not sail before Sunday. McC. was also bored by the request but Seward strongly seconded it. McC. said he would sleep on it.

We came away, the Tycoon still vexed at Sherman. At Seward's door, he turned suddenly and said, "I think I will telegraph to Sherman that I will not break up McClellan's command and that I haven't much hope of his expedition anyway." [8]

"No," said Seward, "You won't say discouraging things to a man going off with his life in his hand. Send them some hopeful and cheering despatch."

The Tycoon came home and this morning telegraphed Sherman, "I will not break up McC's army without his consent. I do

[7] Wentworth possibly may have spoken that way but he was the grandson of a Harvard graduate and he was an alumnus of Dartmouth. Perhaps the story was retouched a bit.

[8] Gen. Thomas W. Sherman was in command of the army; Capt., later Admiral, DuPont of the naval force. Contrary to the President's expectation the expedition was successful. Port Royal, S. Car., fell Nov. 7. It is twenty miles from Savannah and thirty miles from Charleston.

not think I will come to Annapolis." This was all. I think his petulance very unaccountable.

October 22, 1861. This has been a heavy day. Last night Col. Baker was killed at Leesburg at the head of his Brigade.[9] McClellan & the Pres^t talked sadly over it. McClellan said, "There is many a good fellow that wears the shoulder-straps going under the sod before this thing is over. There is no loss too great to be repaired. If I should get knocked on the head, Mr. President, you will put another man immediately into my shoes." "I want you to take care of yourself," said the President.

McClellan seemed very hopeful and confident—thought he had the enemy, if in force or not—we left him making arrangements for the morrow. [Added to the diary at some later date: During this evening's conversation it became painfully evident that he had *no plan,* nor the slightest idea of what Stone was about.]

Tonight we went over again. M^c was at Poolesville. Telegraphs that loss is heavy and the troops behaved well. All right in that quarter.

At Seward's tonight the President talked about secession, compromise, and other such. He spoke of a committee of Southern pseudo-Unionists coming to him before Inauguration for guarantees &c. He promised to evacuate Sumter if they would break up their convention, without any row or nonsense. They demurred. Subsequently he renewed proposition to Summers,[10] but without any result. The President was most anxious to prevent bloodshed.

I never heard secession made more absurd than by the conversation of tonight. Seward, Chase, Kennedy & Bp. McIlvaine.

Today Dep. Marshal came & asked what he should do with process to be served on Porter in contempt business. I took him over to Seward & Seward said:

"The President instructs you that the habeas corpus is suspended in this city at present and forbids you to serve any process upon any officer here." Turning to me, "That is what the Pres^t

9 Battle of Ball's Bluff.

10 George W. Summers of Virginia, who was one of the delegates to the "Peace Conference," February, 1861, at which former President Tyler presided.

says, is it not, Mr. Hay?" "Precisely his words," I replied and the thing was done.

October 26, 1861. This evening the Jacobin club, represented by Trumbull, Chandler and Wade, came up to worry the administration into a battle. The wild howl of the summer is to be renewed. The President stood up for McClellan's deliberateness. We then went over to the General's Headquarters. We found Col. Key there. He was talking also about the grand necessity of an immediate battle to clean out the enemy, at once. He seemed to think we were ruined if we did not fight. The President asked what McC. thot about it. Key answered, "The General is troubled in his mind. I think he is much embarrassed by the radical difference between his views and those of General Scott."

Here McC. came in—Key went out—the President began to talk about his wonderful new repeating battery of rifled gun, shooting 50 balls a minute. The President is delighted with it and has ordered ten and asks McC. to go down and see it, and if proper, detail a corp of men to work it. He further told the General that Reverdy Johnson wants the Maryland Vol's in Maryld to vote in November.[11] All right.

They then talked about the Jacobins. McC. said that Wade preferred an unsuccessful battle to delay. He said a defeat could be easily repaired, by the swarming recruits. McClellan answered that he would rather have a few recruits before a victory than a good many after a defeat.

The President deprecated this new manifestation of senseless popular impatience but at the same time said it was a reality and should be taken into the account. "At the same time, General, you must not fight till you are ready."

"I have everything at stake," said the General. "If I fail, I will not see you again or anybody."

"I have a notion to go out with you and stand or fall with the battle."

The President has written a letter to St. Louis giving plan of

[11] Reverdy Johnson was then a candidate for Senator from Maryland, a position to which he was elected, evidently with the aid of the army vote.

campaign as suggestion [to] the officer in command, probably Hunter. It is to halt the pursuit of Price, go back in two columns to Rolla and Sedalia, and there observe, taking the surplus for active operation in the South. The plan, though entirely original with the Tycoon, seemed a good one both to Scott and McC. and will probably be followed.

October 27, 1861. We went over to Seward's tonight and found Chandler and Wade there. They had been talking to Seward to get up a battle saying that one must be fought, saying that defeat was no worse than delay, & a great deal more trash. Morton & Speed then began to growl about their guns. Seward and the President soon dried that up. Wilson came in, a strong, healthy, hearty Senator, soldier and man. He was bitter on the Jacobins, saying the safety of the country demanded that the General should have his time. Going up to McClellan's, we discussed the Leesburg [Ball's Bluff] business. McC. saying that Stone's report would be in tomorrow, everyone forebore comment.

Yesterday the Pres^t received two despatches from St. Louis—one from Lamon deprecating the removal of Frémont and one from Washburne who seems at last thoroughly frightened about the Missouri matter, saying there is a promise of anarchy and revolution in case of Frémont's deposition.[12] "Forewarned, forearmed," he says.

Today we got a despatch from Kelley announcing a victory at Romney and tonight one from Frémont announcing a brilliant charge of Zagonyi and the body guard at Springfield, from which we learn that they have been rapidly advancing of late. The President was pleased therewith.[13]

[*Undated.*] The night of the 1st November we went over to McClellan's. The General was there and read us his general order in regard to Scott's resignation & his own assumption of command. The President thanked him for it and said it greatly relieved him. He added, "I should be perfectly satisfied if I thought that this vast in-

---

[12] Frémont, after an arrogant and intolerable brief career as commander of the Dept. of the West in St. Louis was superseded, Nov. 2, by Gen. David Hunter.
[13] Gen. Scott resigned Oct. 31, 1861 and was succeeded by Gen. McClellan.

crease of responsibility would not embarrass you." "It is a great relief, Sir. I feel as if several tons were taken from my shoulders today.
I am now in contact with you, and the Secretary. I am not embarrassed by intervention." "Well," says the Tycoon, "draw on me for
all the sense I have, and all the information. In addition to your
present command, the supreme command of the Army will entail
a vast labor upon you." "I can do it all," McC. said quietly.

Going to Seward's, he talked long and earnestly about the matter. He had been giving a grave and fatherly lecture to McC. which
was taken in good part; advising him to enlarge the sphere of his
thoughts and feel the weight of the occasion.

Then we went up and talked a little while to the Orleans
princes. De Joinville is deaf and says little.[14] The boys talk very
well and fluently.

November 7. I talked tonight with the President about the opening of the cotton trade by our seaside excursionists. I represented
the interest felt by Northern spinners who want it still blockaded.
He doubted their statement that they had a large supply on hand
whose price would be reduced by opening the trade and seemed
to think that we equally with France and England would gain by
it. He said it was an object to show the world we were fair in this
matter favoring outsiders as much as ourselves. That it was by no
means sure that they would bring their cotton to the port after
we opened it. But it would be well to show Europe that it was
secession that distressed them and not we. That the chief difficulty
was in discovering how far the planters who bring us their cotton
can be trusted with the money they receive for it.

I went in strong for the opening of the ports, I don't know why,
using all the arguments I could think of, and rather gained the
idea that he also slanted in that direction.

November 8. Here is a letter just recd. It displays a wild and absurd miracle of cheek.

[14] Count de Joinville accompanied the Count of Paris and his brother while they
were in the United States.

"My dear Sir:

"Genl Wool has resigned. General Frémont must. General Scott has retired.

"I have an ambition and I trust a laudable one to be Major General of the United States Army.

"Has anybody done more to deserve it? No one will do more. May I rely upon you as you may have confidence in me, to take this matter into consideration?

"I will not disgrace the position. I may fail in its duties.

"Truly yours,
"BENJ. F. BUTLER [15]

"The President.

"P.S. I have made the same suggestion to other of my friends."

November 11. Tonight Bleaker's Germans had a torchlight procession in honor of McC. promotion. I never saw such a scene of strange and wild magnificence as this night-march was. Afterwards we went over to McC[s] and talked about the Southern flurry. The President thought this a good time to feel them. McC. said, "I have not been unmindful of that. We will feel them tomorrow." The Tycoon and the General were both very jolly over the news.

November 13. I wish here to record what I consider a portent of evil to come. The President, Governor Seward, and I, went over to McClellan's house tonight. The servant at the door said the General was at the wedding of Col. Wheaton at General Buell's, and would soon return. We went in, and after we had waited about an hour, McC. came in and without paying any particular attention to the porter, who told him the President was waiting to see him, went up stairs, passing the door of the room where the President and Secretary of State were seated. They waited about half-an-hour, and sent once more a servant to tell the General they were there, and the answer coolly came that the General had gone to bed.

[15] This signature was inserted at a later date. Butler had been made a major general of volunteers in May, 1861. Apparently he was seeking the position made vacant by Scott's retirement. The latter, although general-in-chief, held the rank of major general while Butler was only a brevet major general.

I merely record this unparalleled insolence of epaulettes without comment. It is the first indication I have yet seen of the threatened supremacy of the military authorities.

Coming home I spoke to the President about the matter but he seemed not to have noticed it, specially, saying it was better at this time not to be making points of etiquette & personal dignity.

CHAPTER III

January 27—April 16, 1862

DIARY

1862. On the 27th day of January, the President issued his General War Order No. One to those whose direction it was to be.[1] He wrote it without any consultation and read it to the Cabinet, not for their sanction but for their information. From that time he influenced actively the operations of the Campaign. He stopped going to McClellan's and sent for the General to come to him. Everything grew busy and animated after this order. It was not fully carried out in its details. Some of the Corps anticipated; others delayed action. Fort Henry and Ft. Donelson showed that Halleck was doing his share.[2] The Army of the Potomac still was sluggish. His next order was issued after a consultation with all the Generals of the Potomac Army in which, as Stanton told me next morning, "We saw ten Generals afraid to fight." The fighting Generals were McDowell, Sumner, Heintzelman & Keyes, and Banks. These were placed next day at the head of the Army Corps.

So things began to look vigorous. Sunday morning, the 9th of March, the news of the *Merrimac's* frolic came here. Stanton was fearfully stampeded. He said they would capture our fleet, take Ft. Monroe, be in Washington before night. The Tycoon thought it was a great bore, but blew less than Stanton. As the day went on the news grew better. And at four o'clock the telegraph was com-

---

[1] Gen. Order No. One was not very specific, merely setting Feb. 22 as the date for "a general movement of all the land and naval forces of the U. S." It reflected the growing irritation both of the President and of the people at the inactivity of the forces which had little or nothing to show since the fall of Sumter and the defeats at Bull Run and Ball's Bluff.

[2] Gen. Hunter at St. Louis was succeeded, after a brief interval, by Gen. Henry W. Halleck, but it was Grant who, with Halleck's reluctant approval, took Fort Henry on the Tennessee River, Feb. 5, and Fort Donelson on the 8th.

pleted and we heard of the splendid performance of the *Monitor*.[3] That evening also we heard of the evacuation of the Potomac batteries, the luckiest of all possible chances, as the most appalling thing about the *Merrimac's* damages was the fact that they would impede the enterprise of taking those batteries. This was McDowell's explanation to me when I told him of it.

At evening came the news of Manassas being evacuated; [4] this came through contrabands.[5] McClellan started instantly over the river. The next day the news were confirmed, and the next night Manassas was occupied. People said a great deal about it and thought a great deal more.

On the evening of the 11th of March the President requested me to call together the heads of the departments of War, State & Treasury. Seward came first. The President read to him General Order No. 3. He approved it thoroughly. He agreed with the President when he, the Prest, said that though the duty of relieving Gen. McClellan was a most painful one, he yet thought he was doing Gen. McC. a very great kindness in permitting him to retain command of the Army of the Potomac, and giving him an opportunity to retrieve his errors.[6] Seward spoke very bitterly of the imbecility which had characterized the General's operations on the upper Potomac. The Secretary of State urged that the War Order go out in the name of Stanton. He said it would strengthen the hands of the Secretary and he needed public confidence. While he was urging this Stanton came in and at once insisted that it go

[3] In Hampton Roads, March 8, the Confederate ironclad *Merrimac* attacked the blockading fleet and nearly destroyed it, thus breaking the blockade and also presenting a threat to all northern ports since it was immediately assumed that the wooden ships were defenceless against this new type of vessel. The next day the *Monitor* fought its historic duel with the *Merrimac* and restored Northern confidence.

[4] Notwithstanding Gen. War Order No. One, and a more specific one to McClellan to advance on Manassas Junction "on or before the 22nd of February next," no such move was made. However, on Mar. 8 the Confederate forces evacuated.

[5] The use of the word "contraband" to describe negroes who escaped to the Union lines was first used in the *N. Y. Tribune*, May 27, 1861, in a despatch from Fort Munroe, but whether credit for the coinage belongs to Ben Butler, then in command of the fort, is not clear. N. & H. IV, 388.

[6] In "Complete Works" II, 137 this is captioned Special War Order No. 3. Major-Gen. McClellan, while retaining command of the Army of the Potomac, is "relieved from the command of the other military departments." Halleck is placed in command of a newly created Department of the Mississippi. Frémont is given command of a newly formed Mountain Dept.

in the President's name. He said that a row had grown up between him and McC.'s friends and he feared it would be thought to spring from personal feeling. The President decided to take the responsibility.

Blair was not consulted. The Pres^t knew that he would object to the disposition of Frémont and preferred to have no words about it. Blair and the Pres^t continued on very good terms in spite of the publication of Blair's letter to Frémont. Blair came to explain it to the Pres^t but he told him that he was too busy to quarrel with him. If he, B., didn't show him the letter he would probably never see it. Chase had previously forgiven him in a quietly careless sort of way & he retained his old status in Cabinet councils.

Schuyler Colfax told me the other day that he had seen a letter from F. P. Blair, Sr., asking Frémont's influence to make Frank Blair a Major Genl. of Missouri Militia: and the original manuscripts of the proposals for clothing contracts that Frémont had refused to Frank Blair on McKinstry's representation of their unfairness. So there is one point in that Frémont business settled.

TO J. G. NICOLAY

Monday. March 31st. [*1862*]

Little Mac sails today for down river. He was in last night to see Tycoon. He was much more pleasant and social in manner than formerly. He seems to be anxious for the good opinion of everyone.

Nothing new as yet in any direction. Miss Mary Hamilton is at Eames. A first class woman every way.

What did you do with the safe key? I cannot find it anywhere.

*   *   *   *

TO J. G. NICOLAY

Monday night. March 31, 1862

Still nothing new in politics or war.

Mrs. Eames gives a little party next Wednesday night. Don't you wish you were here?

That's all.

The "enemy" is still planning [a] campaign in quiet. She is rapidly being reinforced from Springfield. A dozen Todds of the Edwards Breed in the house.

TO J. G. NICOLAY

Thursday morning. [April 3, 1862]

Gen. McC. is in danger. Not in front but in rear. The President is making up his mind to give him a peremptory order to march. It is disgraceful to think how the little squad at Yorktown keeps him at bay.[7]

TO J. G. NICOLAY

Thursday morning. [April 3.] 1862

I am engaged in a horse-trade. John lately discovered what he considered a splendid match for our off-horse, in the possession of Major Beckwith. I have got him now trying him, a splendid fellow really, and I think I can bamboozle our friend Beckwith into a trade somehow.

I wish you would write me immediately to tell me what you have done & what remains to be done in the case of Reinmüller, the deserter. Carl Schurz has become much interested in him and bothers me horribly to do something. I want to know what you have done.

Mrs. Eames had a nice party last night.

W. H. Russell is hideously outraged because Stanton had him ordered off the ship on which he was going to Ft. Monroe. No news from Mc. yet.

---

[7] McClellan, Apr. 2, reached Fortress Monroe to begin his famous Peninsular campaign. He had 58,000 men; Magruder, the opposing general at Yorktown, which barred the way toward Richmond, had 11,000.

TO J. G. NICOLAY

Friday, April 4, 1862.

McClellan is at last in motion. He is now moving on Richmond. The secret is very well kept. Nobody out of the Cabinet knows it in town. Dug Wallack is in a great fidget about it. He knows something is in the wind but can't guess what. Madame has mounted me to pay her the Steward's salary. . . .

TO J. G. NICOLAY

EXECUTIVE MANSION
April 5, 1862

MY DEAR NICO.

The devil is abroad, having great wrath. His daughter, the Hellcat, sent Stockpole in to blackguard me about the feed of her horses. She thinks there is cheating round the board and with that candor so charming in the young does not hesitate to say so. I declined opening communications on the subject.

She is in "a state of mind" about the Steward's salary. There is no steward. Mrs. Watt has gone off and there is no *locum tenens*. She thinks she will blackguard your angelic representative into giving it to her "which I don't think she'll do it, Hallelujah!"

My horse trade has fallen through: the new horse, though fine looking, was vicious. So I took back the "near horse."

J.H.

TO J. G. NICOLAY

EXECUTIVE MANSION,
WASHINGTON, *April 9, 1862.*

Glorious news come borne on every wind but the South Wind. While Pope is crossing the turbid and broad torrent of the Mississippi in the blaze of the evening's fire and Grant is fighting the overwhelming legions of Beauregard at Pittsburgh, the little Napoleon sits trembling before the handful of men at Yorktown

afraid either to fight or run. Stanton feels devilish about it. He
would like to remove him if he thought it would do.[8]

Things go on here about as usual. There is no fun at all. The
Hell-cat is getting more Hell-cattical day by day.

Lamon has indicted Horace Greeley criminally for libel and
thinks of going to New York to bring him down to the jail here.
He would not be persuaded by his best friends.

We have made Van Alen a Brig. Gen. The Senate, however,
have not yet confirmed him. I am getting along pretty well. I only
work about 20 hours a day. I do all of your work & half of my
own now you are away.

Don't hurry yourself. We are getting on very well. I talk a little
French, too, now. I have taken a devil of a notion to the Gerolts.
I went to see them the other day. The children were less scared
than usual and they and Madame la Baronne talked long and
earnestly of the state of your hygiene and said, "it was good intentions you for to go to the West for small time."

The latest rumour in "our set" is that Mr. Hay and Miss Hooper
are *engagèd,* as Count Gurowski calls it. I wish I had that old
nuisance's neck in a slip noose. I'm afraid the Hoopers will hear
it and then my good times there will be up.

TO J. G. NICOLAY

EXECUTIVE MANSION
April 16, 1862

MY DEAR NICO.

There is nothing new. Yes there is. A Pretty Girl at Willard's.
Haight is going to introduce me tonight. Haight is a good egg.
He votes straight Republican every time. He and Odell both went
for Abolition in the Deestreck.

The President has appointed Berrett one of the Com[n] under the

8 Gen. Pope, April 7, captured Island No. 10. Grant, after a brilliant victory at
Fort Donelson in Tennessee, entered, April 6, the historic Battle of Shiloh in which
he was surprised at Pittsburg Landing by Beauregard with superior numbers. This
was, in fact, Grant's least distinguished battle.

Abolition Act. I am glad. It is a graceful compliment & a proper *amende* for the former injury.

McDougall got skinned alive by Wade yesterday. Mc. didn't mind it.[9] He was pretty drunk.

Forrest is playing at the New Theatre. That's all.[10]

J.H.

[9] April 16 the President signed a bill abolishing slavery in the District of Columbia with compensation for the owners. Senator J. A. McDougall of California opposed Lincoln's plan of emancipation. (Rhodes III, 632.) The skinning appears to have been done by Senator B. F. Wade of Ohio.

[10] Following this entry there is a lapse of more than three months in the Hay Papers. It was in this interval that Gen. Butler occupied New Orleans, May 1; McClellan's Peninsula Campaign was a failure. He could have broken through to Richmond but stopped to besiege Yorktown. Gen. Joseph T. Johnston evacuated Yorktown, May 3. McClellan reiterated his demand for reenforcements. Stonewall Jackson, by his feint in the Shenandoah Valley, alarmed the President who ordered McDowell to protect the Capital instead of reenforcing McClellan, who had reached the vicinity of Richmond, June 1. Gen. Robert E. Lee was placed in command of the Confederate army. June 25–July 1 occurred the Seven Days Battles after which McClellan began his mournful retreat to the James River. July 22, Lincoln read to Cabinet a proposed proclamation of emancipation, the publication of which was deferred because of McClellan's failure at Richmond.

CHAPTER IV

August 11—September 5, 1862

EXECUTIVE MANSION,
WASHINGTON, *August 11, 1862*

MY DEAR GEORGE

You will have seen by the papers that Pope has been running his head into a hornet's nest. He fought a desperate battle the other day—or rather Banks did—Pope coming up at the end of it.[1]

He stands now in good position eager for another fight and confident of licking the enemy.

The Tycoon has given orders that he shan't fight unless there is a first rate chance of cleaning them out. The Tycoon thinks a defeat then would be a greater nuisance than several victories would abate.

There is no further news. It is horribly hot all but me who have gone to shaking again. Your infernal South windows always give me the chills. Stone has broken them up however and doses me remorselessly to keep them away.

If in the wild woods you scrouge an Indian damsel, steal her moccasins while she sleeps and bring them to me. The Tycoon has just received a pair gorgeously quilled, from an Indian Agent who is accused of stealing. He put them on & grinned. Will he remember them on the day when Caleb [2] proposes another to fill the peculating donor's office? I fear not, my boy, I fear not.

Your ducks are all as usual. Nobody in town but Miss Seward and La Baronne de Gerolt.

God be with you.

1 Battle of Cedar Mountain, Aug. 9, where Banks attacked Stonewall Jackson and failed. Jackson had four times the larger force.
2 Caleb B. Smith, Secretary of the Interior, who had the supervision of the Indian Agents.

TO J. G. NICOLAY

EXECUTIVE MANSION,
WASHINGTON, *Aug 29. 1862.*

MY DEAR SIR

Where is your scalp? If anybody believes you don't wish you were at home, he can get a pretty lively bet out of me. I write this letter firing into the air. If it hits you, well. It will not hurt so much as a Yancton's rifle. If in God's good Providence your long locks adorn the lodge of an aboriginal warrior and the festive tom-tom is made of your stretched hide, I will not grudge the time thus spent, for auld lang syne. In fancy's eye I often behold you the centre and ornament of a wildwood circle delighting the un-tutored children of the forest with Tuscan melodies. . . .

Washington is not at the present speaking an alluring village. Everybody is out of town and nobody cares for nobody that is here. One exception *tres charmante,* which is French for devilish tidy. Miss Census Kennedy [3] is here with a pretty cousin from Baltimore [undecipherable]. Stoddard is quite spooney about her, while I am languidly appreciative.

Grover's Theatre reopens next Saturday and Dahlgren breathes again. Some pretty women are engaged to whom I am promised introductions. There is also a new Club House established in the city to which I have sometimes gone to satisfy the ragings of fam-ine. I think you will patronize it extensively when you come back. I ride on horseback mornings. I ride the off horse. He has grown so rampageous by being never driven (I have no time to drive) that no one else whom I can find can ride him. Stoddard, Boutwell & Leutze ride sometimes the near horse.

I am yours

JOHN HAY

DIARY

[*September 1,*] *1862.* Saturday morning, the 30th of August, I rode out into the country and turned in at the "Soldiers' Home." The

---

[3] Presumably the daughter of the Supt. of the Census, J. C. G. Kennedy.

President's horse was standing by the door and in a moment the President appeared and we rode into town together.

We talked about the state of things by Bull Run and Pope's prospect.[4] The President was very outspoken in regard to Mc-Clellan's present conduct. He said it really seemed to him that McC. wanted Pope defeated. He mentioned to me a despatch of McC.[5] in which he proposed, as one plan of action, to "leave Pope to get out of his own scrape, and devote ourselves to securing Washington." He spoke also of McC's dreadful cowardice in the matter of Chain Bridge, which he had ordered blown up the night before, but which order had been countermanded; and also of his incomprehensible interference with Franklin's corps which he recalled once, and then when they had been sent ahead by Halleck's order, begged permission to recall them again & only desisted after Halleck's sharp injunction to push them ahead till they whipped something or got whipped themselves. The President seemed to think him a little crazy. Envy, jealousy, and spite are probably a better explanation of his present conduct. He is constantly sending despatches to the President and Halleck asking what is his real position and command. He acts as chief alarmist and grand marplot of the Army.

The President, on my asking if Halleck had any prejudices, rejoined, "No! Halleck is wholly for the service. He does not care who succeeds or who fails so the service is benefited." [5]

Later in the day we were in Halleck's room. H. was at dinner & Stanton came in while we were waiting for him and carried us off to dinner. A pleasant little dinner and a pretty wife as white and cold and motionless as marble, whose rare smiles seemed to pain her. Stanton was loud about the McC. business. He was unqualifiedly severe upon McClellan. He said that after these battles there should be one Court Martial, if never any more. He said

4 August 30, the Second Battle of Bull Run. McClellan, then at Alexandria, was deprived of his command. The initial impression in Washington was that Pope had won, but the next day it became clear that the Federal forces had met another disastrous defeat and that Washington was again in actual danger. As Pope retreated toward Washington, McClellan again became the commanding officer.

5 Halleck, July 11, 1862, was made general-in-chief of "the whole land forces of United States." McClellan, as commander of the Army of the Potomac, was subordinate.

that nothing but foul play could lose us this battle & that it rested with McC. and his friends. Stanton seemed to believe very strongly in Pope. So did the President for that matter. We went back to the Headquarters and found General Halleck. He seemed quiet and somewhat confident. He said the greatest battle of the century was now being fought. He said he had sent every man that could go, to the field. At the War Department we found that Mr Stanton had sent a vast army of Volunteer Nurses out to the field, probably utterly useless, over which he gave Gen^1 Wadsworth command.

Everything seemed to be going well and hilarious on Saturday & we went to bed expecting glad tidings at sunrise. But about eight o'clock the President came to my room as I was dressing and, calling me out, said, "Well, John, we are whipped again, I am afraid. The enemy reinforced on Pope and drove back his left wing and he has retired to Centreville where he says he will be able to hold his men. I don't like that expression. I don't like to hear him admit that his men need 'holding.'"

After a while, however, things began to look better and people's spirits rose as the heavens cleared. The President was in a singularly defiant tone of mind. He often repeated, "We must hurt this enemy before it gets away." And this morning, Monday, he said to me when I made a remark in regard to the bad look of things, "No, Mr. Hay, we must whip these people now. Pope must fight them. If they are too strong for him, he can gradually retire to these fortifications. If this be not so, if we are really whipped and to be whipped, we may as well stop fighting."

It is due in great measure to his indomitable will, that Army movements have been characterized by such energy and celerity for the last few days. There is one man who seems thoroughly to reflect and satisfy him in everything he undertakes. This is Haupt, the railroad man at Alexandria. He has, as Chase says, a Major General's head on his shoulders. The President is particularly struck with the business-like character of his despatch, telling in the fewest words the information most sought for, which contrasted so strongly with the weak, whiney, vague, and incorrect despatches of the whilom General-in-Chief. If heads or shoulder-straps could be exchanged, it would be a good thing, in either case, here. A good railroader would be spoiled but the General gained would compensate. The corps of Haupt starting from Alexandria have acted as pioneer advance guard, *voltigeur,* and every other light-infantry arm of the service.

September 5, 1862. This morning I walked with the President over to the War Department to ascertain the truth of the report that Jackson had crossed the Potomac. We went to the telegraph office and found it true. On the way over the President said, "Mc-Clellan is working like a beaver. He seems to be aroused to doing something, by the sort of snubbing he got last week.[6] I am of the opinion that this public feeling against him will make it expedient to take important command from him. The Cabinet yesterday were unanimous against him. They were all ready to denounce me for it, except Blair. He has acted badly in this matter, but we must use what tools we have. There is no man in the Army who can man these fortifications and lick these troops of ours into shape half as well as he." I spoke of the general feeling against McClellan as evinced by the Pres[ts] mail. He rejoined, "Unquestionably he has acted badly toward Pope! He wanted him to fail. That is unpardonable, but he is too useful just now to sacrifice." At another time he said, "If he can't fight himself, he excels in making others ready to fight."

Going to breakfast, I sat down by Banks. He received the news I gave him of the enemy's crossing the river with a little elevation of the eyebrows—nothing more. Old Genl Spinner sat down and began to gird at the *Nat. In[tl]* for its alarm at the project of the New York Defense Committee for the raising of 50,000 filibusters under Frémont and Mitchell. I condemned it. He defended it. I said he would soon have our country divided as Italy is between V.I. & Garibaldi. He said, "There is no question which is right?" I said, "No! Victor Immanuel is right." He replied that I was a worse conservative than he had thot me.

Banks said that the war was steadily verging to one point and

---

[6] After Pope's defeat at Bull Run the Army of Virginia was combined with the Army of the Potomac with McClellan again in command.

that no efforts of misguided friends or malignant enemies could prevent it. He said there was no real difference of opinion among loyal people. It was only their expressions that differed and caused quarreling. Therefore he was opposed to proclamations & especially to resolutions, that they would accomplish nothing.

*   *   *   *

Banks went away and S. said, "I hope to see him at the head of the Army some day." I said I had little hope of it, as the right man was rarely seen in the right place in a Republic. He instanced Jackson as evidence to the contrary. I disagreed with him, thinking Jackson was a brawling and violent old loafer with no good quality but bravery.

Major Wightman has been here. He is a fussy little Democrat with strong anti-abolition prejudices. The African sits heavily on his mind. He thinks this is a Wight-man's war.

Carl Schurz says his division is terribly thin but what is left of them is Iron and Steel. I proposed they should adopt as their motto, "I run and Steal."

CHAPTER V

September 5—November 15, 1862

DIARY

[*September 5, 1862*] Today, going into the Executive Mansion, I met Governor Seward coming out. I turned back and walked home with him. He said our foreign affairs are very much confused. He acknowledged himself a little saddened. Walking on, he said, "Mr. Hay, what is the use of growing old? You learn something of men and things but never until too late to use it. I have only just now found out what military jealousy is. I have been wishing for some months to go home to my people but could not while our armies were scattered and in danger. The other day I went down to Alexandria and found General McClellan's army landing. I considered our armies united virtually and thought them invincible. I went home and the first news I received was that each had been attacked and each in effect beaten. It never had occurred to me that any jealousy could prevent these generals from acting for their common fame and the welfare of the country."

I said it never should have seemed possible to me that one American general should write of another to the President, suggesting that "Pope be allowed to get out of his own scrape his own way."

He answered, "I don't see why you should have expected it. You are not old. I should have known it." He said this gloomily and sadly.[1]

---

[1] Following up their success at Bull Run, the Confederate troops under Jackson crossed the Potomac above Washington Sept. 4 and occupied Frederick, Md. A few days later Lee ordered Jackson back to Virginia to capture Harper's Ferry while he, with Longstreet, proceeded toward Hagerstown (Rhodes IV, 143). McClellan came up from Washington and Sept. 15 fought Lee at Antietam. Sept 19, Lee recrossed the Potomac. The Union victory created a favorable condition for the Emancipation Proclamation.

[*September 26, 1862.*] The President wrote the Proclamation on Sunday morning carefully. He called the Cabinet together on Monday [Sept. 22], made a little talk to them (see (a)) and read the momentous document. Mr. Blair and Mr. Bates made objections, otherwise the Cabinet was unanimous.[2] The next day Mr. Blair, who had promised to file his objections, sent a note stating that as his objections were only to the time of the act, he would not file them, lest they should be subject to misconstruction.

I told the President of the serenade that was coming and asked if he would make any remarks. He said, "No," but he did say half a dozen words, & said them with great grace and dignity. I spoke to him about the editorials in the leading papers. He said he had studied the matter so long that he knew more about it than they did.

At Governor Chase's there was some talking after the serenade. Chase and Clay made speeches and the crowd was in a glorious humor. After the crowd went away to force Mr. Bates to say something, a few old fogies staid at the Governor's and drank wine. Chase spoke earnestly of the Proclamation. He said, "This was a most wonderful history of an insanity of a class that the world had ever seen. If the slaveholders had staid in the Union they might have kept the life in their institution for many years to come. That what no party and no public feeling in the North could ever have hoped to touch they had madly placed in the very path of destruction." They all seemed to feel a sort of new and exhilarated life; they breathed freer; the Pres^ts Proc^n had freed them as well as the slaves. They gleefully and merrily called each other and themselves abolitionists, and seemed to enjoy the novel sensation of appropriating that horrible name.

Last night, September 25, the President and I were riding to Soldiers Home; he said he had heard of an officer who had said they did not mean to gain any decisive victory but to keep things

---

[2] Nicolay and Hay subsequently, VI, Chap. 7, corrected this statement. Seward proposed verbal alterations; Chase was somewhat reluctant; Blair yielded, having asked leave to file objections; Bates had approved the preliminary draft, read to the Cabinet July 22. The vote in the Cabinet Sept. 22 appears to have been unanimous. There is in the diary nothing to explain "(see (a))."

running on so that they, the Army, might manage things to suit themselves. He said he should have the matter examined and if any such language had been used, his head should go off.

I talked a great deal about the McClellan conspiracy but he would make no answer to anything. He merely said that McC. was doing nothing to make himself either respected or feared.

TO J. G. NICOLAY

WARSAW, ILLINOIS
October 28, 1862

MY DEAR NICO:

McGregor's on his native heath, and having quietly a good time. I sit by the wood-fire all day and talk with my mother and at night I do a little unobtrusive sparking. I am perfectly idle, and you, who always insist on being busy even when you ought to be pleasuring, can have no adequate conception of the enjoyment of the genuine *dolce far niente.* Just keep the Army still for a week or so and I will bless you with my latest breath.

I shall stay here a few days and try to put beef on my bones and then return by way of Springfield and Cincinnati.

I spent only one day in Springfield. But it paid.

*   *   *   *

Please send me as soon as you receive this, five or ten dollars worth of postal currency. There is none at all here and it is almost impossible to get a dollar changed. Send it care of Milton Hay, Springfield.

And believe me

Very truly yours

JOHN HAY

[P.S.] You cannot imagine the earnestness of denunciation which fills the West in regard to McClellan. *I have not heard one single man defend him.* If he should be sent West to command our troops his presence would demoralize the Army. His continuance in command in the East begins to shake the confidence of some of our best friends in the Government.

Things look badly around here politically. The inaction of the Army & the ill success of our arms have a bad effect, and worse than that, all our energetic and working Republicans are in the Army. The captains of tens & captains of hundreds who, you know, do our best work, are all in the field, and we have gained no strength from democratic accessions, as, in almost every case, as soon as a Democrat has his eyes opened, he enlists. This State is in great danger.

I have been astonished to hear so little objection to the proclamation. Republicans all like it and every Democrat who does not swear by Vallandigham comes up to it.

But everything depends on the Army of the Potomac.

Thank God that Buell is finished finally! [3]

TO J. G. NICOLAY

ca. November 15, 1862

Hell is to pay about Watt's affairs. I think the Tycoon begins to suspect him. I wish he could be struck with lightning. He has got William and Carroll turned off, and has his eye peeled for a pop at me, because I won't let Madame have our stationery fund. They have gone to New York together.

The "near horse," John says, has seen his best days. He is getting stiff. When you get back, you can trade him.

[3] Buell, after a succession of failures in East Tennessee, was peremptorily removed by order of the President, Oct. 24.

CHAPTER VI

March—May 10, 1863

[The following random notes are in the front of the 1863 diary:]

The President said the Army dwindled on the march like a shovelfull of fleas pitched from one place to another.

July 18, 1863. Captain Cutts was in trouble about looking through keyholes & over transoms at a lady undressing. The T[ycoon] said he should be elevated to the peerage for it with the title of Count Peeper.

I am growing thin as a shad (yea, worse—as thin as a shadder.)

I:—"The Richmond papers are trying to be jolly over Morgan's expedition; they call it a success."
Gen¹ Spinner:—"They remind me of a little fellow whom I saw once badly whipped by a bigger man, who was on top of him & jamming his head on the floor. The little cuss, still full of conceit & pluck, kept saying, 'Now, damn you, will you behave yourself?' "

Ben Wade says, "I prayed with earnestness for the life of Taney to be prolonged through Buchanan's Administration, and by G— I'm a little afraid I've overdone the matter."

Wade says Chase is a good man, but his theology is unsound. He thinks there is a fourth person in the Trinity.

Cartter says, "Millard Fillmore got a reputation for conservatism & wisdom by never swearing in company, always wearing a clean shirt, and never uttering a sentiment that the asses around him did not at once recognize as an old acquaintance."

Capt. LeRoy told the other day an incident of the invasion of Pa. A meek looking soldier (MacVeagh) was detailed as his clerk. He gave him some work, went to dinner, came back & found him a major, appointed in his absence & ranking him.

Lamon says General Mansfield is a good enough old man but he never had an idea till the next day.

The Presidential aspirations of Mr. Chase are said to have been compared by the President to a horsefly on the neck of a plow-horse—which kept him lively about his work.

TO J. G. NICOLAY

[March, 1863.]

For two weeks send my letters to Hilton Head. After that, keep them for me here.

If I should get knocked over, Gus will come down and take care of matters.

TO MRS. CHARLES HAY

WASHINGTON, March 19, 1863

My DEAR MOTHER

I started for Port Royal a week ago, but finding myself a little sick when I arrived at New York, I thought it would be more prudent to return to Washington and make repairs before setting out.

I am now getting quite well again and will soon make a fresh start to visit Charlie. I have a great deal to talk to him about and cannot of course write many things that I want to say. We hear rumours here of disaster to the colored troops.[1] I am in hopes they

---

[1] Gen. Hunter, Commander of the Dept. of the South, to whom Hay was going, as early as April, 1862, had received authorization to organize colored troops. The experiment had been a doubtful success.

may turn out to be untrue. I shall take a careful and deliberate survey of matters in the Department and can then understandingly advise Charlie for his own good.

I saw a good deal of Augustus in N.Y. and became acquainted with our cousin C. G. Thompson. He is a very agreeable old gentleman and a fine artist.

Always affectionately

J.H.

DIARY

Saturday, April 4, 1863. Left New York at noon—got into rough weather in the course of the afternoon—made an enormous dinner with a light and defiant heart—cast it up with great heaviness of spirit—solitary agony—weariness of living—disgust for the sea—enthusiastic promises of future land residence—cold-blooded preparations made by the steward—distant echoes of troubled diaphragms—sleep.

Tuesday. April 7. Too far to hear the sound of bombardment. The last dinner.

Abreast of the forts. *Golden Gate* comes alongside. Cunningham & Capt Carbin [?]—General on board—Who? News from the North. The ball opens today in Charleston Harbor. The attack on F^t Sumter begins at 3 o'clock. Going ashore. Hilton Head. Search for transportation. Smith, Skinner & Hawley. Come aboard again. Vogdes asserts himself. The sunset scene. The wild tropical splendor of the dying day. The weird-like mist that hangs over the woods. The gathering shadows of the water & the lights glimmering up one by one from the black bulks of the fleet.

A splendid harbor going to waste. A great country aroused & filling it with hostile power. The *Wabash*. Early night. A great city with its scattered lights. Moonrise. The liquid distances and sleeping ships make a city in the sea.

On board the propeller, *Christian Commission.*

TO J. G. NICOLAY

STONE RIVER, SOUTH CAROLINA
Wednesday, April 8, 1863

MY DEAR NICO:

I arrived here tonight at the General's Headquarters & was very pleasantly received by both him and Halpine. They are both in fine health and spirits. Halpine is looking better than I ever saw him before.[2] They asked after you. On the way down I had for *compagnons du voyage* Generals Vogdes and Gordon; Gordon on sick leave and Vogdes to report for duty.

I hear nothing but encouraging accounts of the fight of yesterday in Charleston Harbor. Gen. Seymour, Chief of Staff, says we are sure to whip them, much surer than we were before the attack. The monitors behaved splendidly. The *Keokuk* was sunk and the *Patapsco* somewhat damaged but as a whole they encountered the furious and concentrated fire of the enemy in a style for which even our own officers had scarcely dared to hope. The attack will soon be resumed with greater confidence and greater certainty of what they are able to do than before. An expedition is on foot for the Army from which they hope important results. The force of the enemy is much larger than ours, but not so well posted, and as they are entirely ignorant of our plans they are forced to scatter and distribute their strength so as greatly to diminish its efficiency. Our troops are in good order and fine spirits apparently. I think highly of Seymour, from the way he talks—like a firm, quick, and cool headed man. On the whole, things look well, if not very brilliant.

The General says he is going to announce me tomorrow as a Volunteer Aide, without rank. I am glad of it, as the thing stands. If I had not been published as having accepted, hesitated and re-

---

[2] Halpine, of whom Hay saw a good deal, deserves more than passing notice. He was an Irish journalist who had been private secretary to P. T. Barnum. Under the name of Miles O'Reilly he wrote humorous sketches for the *New York Tribune*. After the war he entered New York politics, becoming Registrar of the County and City on an anti-Tammany ticket. We are accustomed to think of government propaganda as having been developed during the World War. From the Hay diary it would appear that throughout the Civil War it was not uncommon to place journalists in important military and political positions whence they could write for the papers with a view to directing public opinion.

jected such an appointment I would not now have it. But I want my abolition record clearly defined and that will do it better than anything else, in my own mind and the minds of the few dozen people who know me.[3]

Vogdes & I came up here alone as the rest could not get transportation. Littlefield is still at Hilton Head but the General is glad to receive him & will put him in position immediately. He directs me to say to you this, and to convey his kindest remembrances. I wish you could be down here. You would enjoy it beyond measure. The air is like June at noon & like May at morning and evening. The scenery is tropical. The sunsets unlike anything I ever saw before. They are not gorgeous like ours but singularly quiet and solemn. The sun goes down over the pines through a sky like ashes-of-roses and hangs for an instant on the horizon like a bubble of blood. Then there is twilight, such as you dream about.

*   *   *   *

April 9. Alas for the pleasant prognostications of the military men! The Gen[l] this morning rec[d] the despatches which you will see before this, confessing that the attack has been a failure! I do not as yet know all the results of this bitter disappointment.[4] Charleston is not to be ours as yet, and another instance is added to the many, of the President having clearer perceptions of military possibilities than any man in the Cabinet or the field. He thought it would fail.

Yours, etc.

[P.S.] Write to me care Gen. Hunter. I have seen Admiral Dupont. Rodgers, Fleet Captain, & Preston, Flag Lieutenant, desired to be remembered to you.

DIARY

Thursday, April 9. Arriving on board the *Ironsides* I was met by an orderly and conducted to the Admiral in the after-cabin. Cap-

---

[3] "John Hay," p. 42.
[4] The naval attack with monitors, iron-clads and armored gunboats on Charleston, S. C., under the direction of Admiral Dupont resulted in what has been considered the worst naval defeat of the war. The Admiral was removed.

tain Rodgers presented me & I gave him, the Admr¹, my despatches which he at once sat down to read. Rodgers said, "Mr Hay, you come to us at an unhappy time. Though unfortunate in view of the lively hopes that have been raised, as the issue is, we think that we may be grateful that what is an unsuccess, is not a disaster. The matter has been fairly tried. The monitor fleet has been given into the hands of officers in whom the Depᵗ & the country had confidence. Admiral Dupont has spared no possible effort and the only issue of it all is that we have reason to congratulate ourselves that with a loss of one vessel and the injury of many others we are still safely beyond the range of the enemy & the coast is still ours. The country must either follow its preconceived idea of the invincibility of the ironclads and condemn us for too hasty a retreat, or take the deliberate and unanimous verdict of the Naval officers and justify us. [What follows in the diary is repeated in Hay's report to the President. *post,* pp. 59–60.]

TO J. G. NICOLAY

[STONE RIVER, S.C., *April 10, 1863*]

I have written some particulars of my interview with Admiral Dupont which I thought the President should know. Please give it to him, reading it yourself if you care to. I went up into the Harbor yesterday. Everything was quiet. The grey-coated rascals were on both sides, waiting for another attack. A crowd of them were crawling cautiously over the bluff to look at the wreck of the *Keokuk* which has sunk near the shore. They are very busy throwing up new batteries on Morris Island, and did not fire on us though we were in easy range.

*   *   *   *

TO PRESIDENT LINCOLN

STONE RIVER, S.C., *April 10, 1863*

MY DEAR SIR

I went yesterday morning to Charleston Harbor to deliver to Admiral Dupont the despatches with which the Navy Department had charged me. I found the Admiral on board the *Ironsides* which with the rest of the monitor fleet was lying inside the Bar at the point where they had anchored after the engagement of Tuesday. I delivered my despatches and while he was reading them, I had some conversation with Capt Rodgers, Fleet Captain of the S.A.B. Squadron. He said that although the attack had been unsuccessful & the failure would of course produce a most unhappy effect upon the country, which had so far trusted implicitly in the invincibility of the monitors, all the officers of the Navy, without exception, united in the belief that what they had attempted was impossible, and that we had reason for congratulation that what is merely a failure had not been converted into a terrible disaster. "The matter has now been fairly tried. With favoring circumstances, with good officers, with good management, the experiment has completely failed. We sailed into the Harbor not sanguine of victory. We fought only about 40 minutes, and the unanimous conclusion of the officers of the Navy is that an hour of that fire would have destroyed us. We had reached and touched the obstructions. To have remained there long enough to remove them would have ensured the destruction of some of the vessels. If the others had gone by the Fort, they would still have been the target of the encircling batteries. There was no sufficient land force to have taken possession of the city. There was no means of supplying them with ammunition and provision, for no wooden ship could live ten minutes in that fire. The only issue would have been the capture of the surviving & the raising of the sunken vessels. This would have lost us the command of the coast, and irremediable disaster. So the Admiral took the responsibility of avoiding the greater evil, by saving the fleet and abandoning an enterprise which we think has been fairly proved impossible."

The Admiral who had been listening and assenting to the latter portion of what Rodgers had been saying, added, "And as if we were to have a visible sign that an Almighty hand was over us for our good, the orders you have given me show how vast was the importance of my preserving this fleet, whose power and prestige are still great and valuable, for the work which I agree with the President in thinking most momentous, the opening & the control of the

Mississippi River. After a fight of 40 minutes we had lost the use of 7 guns. I might have pushed some of the vessels past Fort Sumter, but in that case we ran the enormous risk of giving them to the enemy & thus losing the control of the coast. I could not answer for that to my conscience."

The perfect approval of their own consciences, which these officers evidently felt, did not prevent their feeling the deepest grief and sorrow for the unhappy result of the enterprise. Their whole conversation was as solemn as a scene of death. At one time I spoke of the estimation in which they were held by the Government and the country, which in my opinion rendered it impossible that blame should be attached to them, and their eyes suddenly filled with tears. A first repulse is a terrible thing to brave and conscientious men, accustomed only to victory.

I was several times struck by the identity of opinion and sentiment between Admiral Dupont and yourself. You had repeatedly uttered, during my last week in Washington, predictions which have become history.

When I left the Harbor, they were preparing the torpedo raft for the destruction of the sunken *Keokuk*.

I have taken the liberty of writing thus at length, as I thought you should know the sentiments of these experienced officers in regard to this unfortunate matter. I hope, however the news may be received, that due honor may be given to those who fought with such bravery and discretion, the losing fight.

Yours very respectfully

JOHN HAY

TO J. G. NICOLAY

HILTON HEAD, S.C., *April 16, 1863*

The General and the Admiral this morning received the orders from Washington, directing the continuance of operations against Charleston. The contrast was very great in the manner in which they received them. The General was absolutely delighted. He said he felt more encouraged, and was in better heart and hope than before. at this indication of the earnestness of the Government to finish this business here. He said, however, that the Admiral seemed in very low spirits about it. He talked despondingly about it, adhering to the same impression of the desperate character of the enterprise as I reported to the President after my first interview with him. Perhaps, having so strongly expressed his belief that the enterprise was impracticable, he feels that he is rebuked by an opposite opinion from Washington.

General Hunter, however, is in the best feather about the matter. He believed before we came back, that with the help of the gunboats we could take Morris Island and from that point reduce Fort Sumter, and he is well-pleased to have another chance at it. Whether the intention of the Government be to reduce Charleston now, with adequate men and means, or by powerful demonstration to retain a large force of the enemy here, he is equally anxious to go to work again.

I write this entirely confidentially for you and for the President to know the ideas prevalent here.

Gen. Seymour has been with you before this & has given to the Government the fullest information relative to military matters here. His arrival, I suppose, will only confirm the resolution already taken. Admiral Dupont's despatches by the *Flambeau,* of course, put a darker shade on the matter than anything Seymour will say, as he was strongly in favor of staying there & fighting it out.

Charlie has been quite sick since I got here with pneumonia. I am occupied nearly all the time taking care of him. I hope he will be well in a day or two that I may move with the new expedition. I am getting browned by equitation, and can digest an enormous quantity of beef and sleep.

Write to me when you have nothing else to do & be good enough to remember that I have a pretty extensive handle to my name.

*   *   *   *

TO J. G. NICOLAY

HILTON HEAD, S.C., *April 23, 1863*

In yours of the 15th received last night you say "there was verbal indication of much wrath at the report that Dupont intended to withdraw his fleet and abandon his position." I was surprised at this. If you have received my different letters you will see why. He would have obeyed orders, had he done so. You say we have gained *points d'appui* for future work. The Navy say not. They say they cannot lie off Morris Island to cover the landing of our troops (or rather the crossing from Folley Island, the only practical route) without imminent danger of being driven ashore & wrecked by the first northeasterly breeze that comes. It is not for me to say what is or what is not possible. My old ideas have been horridly shattered when I have seen two men, each of whom I had formerly considered an oracle on every subject connected with ships, accusing each other of ignorance and *charlatanerie*. I do not think Dupont is either a fool or a coward. I think there is a great deal of truth in his statement that while the fight in Charleston Harbor demonstrated the great defensive properties of the monitors it also proved that they could not be relied upon for aggressive operations.

With an adequate force I think Hunter could dislodge the enemy from Morris Island & from that point make a hole in Fort Sumter, but even then, little has been done. The General is sanguine. He wants a fight. I hope he may have one before I return.

Today I start to Florida. Charlie has been very sick since I arrived & I have been with him most of the time. We will be gone only a few days and will see Fernandina, St. Augustine [undecipherable]. I take the liberty of making a note or two on several letters you sent me and respectfully referring them to you.

DIARY

[Fernandina.] *April 24.* We got away from Fort Pulaski at 5 o'clock this morning. We skirted along within sight of land, among porpoises & pelicans which were equally inaccessible till 3 P.M. when we entered the harbor of Fernandina. . . . The female portion of the party resolve to start for St Augustine in the morning.

April 25. Went to Fort Clinch with Cap^tn Sears in charge of the work. When we got there the sea was too high to land. Beached the boat & we were carried to shore in the arms of negroes. The

mazeppa-ride. The Fort. The sandhills commanding it. The sea.
The alligators. The songs of the boatmen.

> The bully boats a-coming
> Oh ho, Oh ho
> Don't you hear the oars a humming
> Hang, boys, hang.
> We'll all hang together
> We will hang one another, &c., &c.

Perfect time harmonizing with the click of the oars by the falsetting
of the voices. . . .

April 26, Sunday. The buzzards & the kingfisher. The thriving
darkey & the robbed contraband. Fishing on the pier.
With Col. Gardiner to the Dunginess estate. The landing. Foot-
prints & the trace of horses' hoofs on the moist sand. Evidently made
since the last tide, proves the presence of strangers on the Island.
Deployed skirmishers who devoted themselves to blackberries on
the way to the house. The house was ruinous. The upper rooms being somewhat furnished while the lower ones never were. The
garden a magnificent one. Bamboo, banana, fig & pomegranate,
with commoner vegetation, century plant, &c.

Behind the house a road runs for 2 or 3 miles through a wonderful forest of moss-draped live-oak.

The view from the top of the house was beautiful in extreme.
The most superb estate I ever saw. I was lost in wonder at the luxuriance of nature & the evident shiftlessness & idleness that had
characterized the owners.

Seth H. advocated tearing off the moss & selling it for the stuffing
of mattresses, . . .

Inscription on the walls by Yankee soldiers.

Came home having seen no rebels. Saw a turtle.

*   *   *   *

April 27. With Read, spectacled Comd^t, went to the colored
schools. Miss Harris & Miss Smith in charge of the A-b-c-d-arians.
Their singing & exercises.

Miss Foote & Miss Merrick in charge of the high school. Light mulatto girls & white children. All together. Singing—

> Say, my brother ain't you ready?
> Get ready to go home,
> For I hear de word of promise
> At de breaking of the day.
> I'll take de wings of de morning
> And fly away to Jesus.
> I'll take de wings of de morning
> And sound de Jubilee.

[ST. AUGUSTINE.] *April 28.* Waked up, the ship in motion. Arrived off the bar at 1. Shark in sight. After a few minutes saw the little skiff of Capo, the pilot. Came on board. A grave old fellow of some sixty years. His quiet ignoring the impertinent ribaldry of the purser. Crossing the bar.

* * * *

[HILTON HEAD.] *May 1.* Ran up to the lightship, turned & went to Fort Pulaski. Got away & met quite a stiff breeze. Got to Hilton Head about noon. . . .

May 8. We rode to Stewart's plantation. Coming back met Preston.

The *Arago* arrives with accounts up to Sunday, the 3ᵈ of May, of Hookers operations in Virginia.[5] Unsatisfactory. Skinner gives an account of the rebel pickets near Folley Island shouting, "Joe Hooker's licked." Hermit crabs.

May 9. Rode out with Charlie to Elliotts. Did nothing else specially all day except read Charleston papers of 4 & 7 giving accounts of the fights on the Rappahannock.

---

[5] Gen. Hooker ordered Gen. Sedgwick to attack Fredericksburg, May 3, and then to advance upon Lee's rear. Sedgwick carried out his orders but Hooker, incapacitated during part of the day, failed to carry out his plan and two days later the Army of the Potomac, beaten again, in the famous Chancellorsville campaign, retreated across the Rappahannock.

May 10, Sunday. Eugene, an intelligent contraband—his story. The condition of the rebels in Georgia. The secret understanding among the negroes. More w^d come but they are afraid of being caught & sent back, and not until lately were they sure of their reception. The rebels more afraid of Rosecrans than anything else. . . .

CHAPTER VII

July 11—August, 1863

DIARY

[WASHINGTON.] *Saturday, the 11th of July, 1863.*[1] The President seemed in a specially good humor today, as he had pretty good evidence that the enemy were still on the north side of the Potomac and Meade had announced his intention of attacking them in the morning. The Pres[t] seemed very happy in the prospect of a brilliant success. He had been rather impatient with Gen Meade's slow movements since Gettysburg, but concluded today that Meade would yet show sufficient activity to inflict the *coup de grace* upon the flying rebels.

Sunday, 12th July. Rained all the afternoon. Have not yet heard of Meade's expected attack.

Monday, 13th. The President begins to grow anxious and impatient about Meade's silence. I thought and told him there was nothing to prevent the enemy from getting away by the Falling Waters, if they were not vigorously attacked. Eckert says Kelly is up on their rear. Nothing can save them if Meade does his duty. I doubt him. He is an engineer.

14th July. This morning the Pres[t] seemed depressed by Meade's despatches of last night. They were so cautiously & almost timidly worded—talking about reconnoitering to find the enemy's weak

[1] The battle of Gettysburg began July 2. While it is regrettable that Hay did not resume his diary after his return from South Carolina and Florida until July 11, in the entries for the following few days there are, here and there, notes of conversations with the President and others which record contemporaneous opinions about the battle and especially Gen. Meade's failure to follow the retreating confederate army.

place and other such. He said he feared he would do nothing. About noon came the despatch stating that our worst fears were true. The enemy had gotten away unhurt. The Prest was deeply grieved. "We had them within our grasp," he said. "We had only to stretch forth our hands & they were ours. And nothing I could say or do could make the Army move."

Several days ago he sent a despatch to Meade which must have cut like a scourge, but Meade returned so reasonable and earnest a reply that the Prest concluded he knew best what he was doing & was reconciled to the apparent inaction which he hoped was merely apparent.

Every day he has watched the progress of the Army with agonizing impatience, hope struggling with fear. He has never been easy in his own mind about Gen. Meade since Meade's General Order in which he called on his troops to drive the invader from our soil. The Prest says, "This is a dreadful reminiscence of McClellan. The same spirit that moved McC. to claim a great victory because Pa. & Md. were safe. The hearts of 10 million people sunk within them when McClellan raised that shout last fall. Will our Generals never get that idea out of their heads? The whole country is our soil."

* * * *

15th July. R.T.L. says the Tycoon is grieved silently but deeply about the escape of Lee. He said, "If I had gone up there, I could have whipped them myself." I know he had that idea.

16 July. Nicolay leaves today for the Rocky Mountains. . . .

This evening at tea was talking with Lt Col. Alexander & Judge Whiting. We agreed in ascribing vast importance to the crushing of Lee at Williamsport. I thought that in the present aspect of affairs, with Bragg deserting the lines of Corinth, Grant & Banks victorious & North Carolina mutinous, if Meade had destroyed Lee, the Rebellion would have been restricted to S.C. & Georgia.

Genl Wadsworth came in. He said in answer to Alexander's question, "Why did Lee escape?" "Because nobody stopped him," rather gruffly.

Wadsworth says that at a Council of War of Corps Commanders

held on Sunday, the 12ᵗʰ, he was present, on account of the sickness of his Corps Commander, he, Wadsworth, being temporarily in command of Corps. On the question of fight or no fight, the weight of authority was against fighting. French, Sedgwick, Slocum strenuously opposed a fight. Meade was in favor of it, so was Warren, who did most of the talking on that side, & Pleasanton was very eager for it, as also was Wadsworth himself. The non-fighters thought, or seemed to think, that if we did not attack, the enemy would, & even Meade, though he was in for action, had no idea that the enemy intended to get away at once. Howard had little to say on the subject.

Meade was in favor of attacking in three columns of 20,000 men each. Wadsworth was in favor of doing as Stonewall Jackson did at Chancellorsville, double up their left & drive them down on Williamsport. I do not question that either plan would have succeeded. Wadsworth said to Hunter, who sat beside him, "General, there are a good many officers of the regular Army who have not yet entirely lost the West Point [idea] of Southern superiority. That sometimes accounts for an otherwise unaccountable slowness of attack."

In the course of the evening Hunter told me that he thought a failure of Gillmore was among probabilities by the enemy reinforcing by means of their causeway & gobbling him up. The danger of a blow which would drive away the ironclads must also be considered.[2]

July 18, 1863. Today we spent 6 hours deciding on Court Martials, the President, Judge Holt, & I. I was amused at the eagerness with which the President caught at any fact which would justify him in saving the life of a condemned soldier. He was only merciless in cases where meanness or cruelty were shown.

Cases of cowardice he was specially averse to punishing with death. He said it would frighten the poor devils too terribly, to shoot them. On the case of a soldier who had once deserted & reinlisted he indorsed, "Let him fight instead of shooting him."

One fellow who had deserted & escaped after conviction into Mex-

[2] Gen. Gillmore and Admiral Dahlgren were cooperating in an attack on Charleston Harbor early in July. After some preliminary successes the attack on Fort Wagner, July 18, failed. A negro regiment, under Col. Robert G. Shaw, led the advance.

ico, he sentenced, saying, "We will condemn him as they used to sell hogs in Indiana, as they run."

* * * *

19 July, Sunday, 1863. Spent this morning at St. Aloysius. A dry priest declaimed against science & human reason & after demolishing both, glorified the dogma of Immaculate Conception. The Tycoon was in very good humour. Early in the morning he scribbled this doggerel & gave it to me.[3] In the afternoon, he & I were talking about the position at Williamsport the other day. He said, "Our Army held the war in the hollow of their hand & they would not close it." Again he said, "We had gone through all the labor of tilling & planting an enormous crop & when it was ripe we did not harvest it." "Still," he added, "I am very grateful to Meade for the great service he did at Gettysburg."

They say now that McClernand has a little show of probability of his claim that Vicksburg was taken by his plans; that at the time he moved on New Carthage Grant was preparing to go to digging again. Our State officers at Springfield are trying to keep out of the mess between McClernand & Grant. Butler & Dubois are here.

I was talking a few days ago with Mr. Chase and he told me that he considered the subject of reconstruction one that should now be employing the best meditations of the statesmen of the country, especially the Government. He thought that before any rebellious State were admitted to its former rights under the Constitution, we should insist upon it as a necessary condition precedent that the people of the State should in convention remodel their existing laws on the basis of emancipation, taking as an accomplished fact the emancipation of the slaves by the Proclamation of the President. He thinks that a Union on other terms, besides being a stultification of ourselves & our acts, would be a delusion and a snare & would never enjoy a lasting or honorable peace.

Blair was talking the other day about his Concord speech & Wendell Phillips's backguardly reply. He began because I had avowed myself no colonizationist.

He said that some time since, in conversation with Henry Wilson,

---

[3] Doggerel not in the diary.

he had referred to the discussions rapidly rising & growing among loyal people, & had said that he thought Mr. Lincoln the best name for the nomination to unite the scattered elements; that Wilson agreed with him, and afterward went back on him. He says Seward & Chase are both scheming for the succession. Stanton would cut the President's throat if he could, &c.

Wilson was here the other day & says Phillips lied when he reported a conversation with the President in his 4th July speech at Framingham. I knew that he did, but I was a little surprised to hear Wilson admit it. He would not do it at Framingham.

July 21, 1863. A fine day for the wedding of Carlota Wilhelmina Maria von Gerolt and John Ward of the Bengal Civil Service. Adjourned from the Church to the Legation. Rather dull for the first hour as people were fearful of coming too early; afterwards quite festive. I never saw three so pretty sisters together before. Madame was *triste* but the Baron walked in rose-colored clouds. Stanton was there, which was strange rather. Seward of course was there officially. The diplomatic body, the deadest of all possible dead-wood was there in plenary council.

I dined in the evening with Wise. I heard Dr. Pyne say that Lee was within an ace of going with the North, that he said his whole life was bound up in the Union, that he cherished the profoundest contempt for this whole business of secession, that if he had a thousand negroes he would hold them all as nothing in comparison with the benefits conferred by the Union, and that (Oh! most lame & impotent conclusion!) he must go with his State. He hoped most earnestly that she would not secede, but in case she did, &c., &c. That infernal heresy of State sovereignty was in the minds of many good men "the little speck within the garnered fruit, that rotting inward slowly ruined all."

The Prest recd today a letter fr. Gen. Howard in which he expressed his entire confidence in Gen. Meade & said that fr. his standpoint Meade's whole action was justifiable.

The Prest answered him stating his deep mortification at the escape of Lee, rendered deeper by the high hopes excited by the brilliant conduct of our Army at Gettysburg; referred to his own long cherished & often expressed conviction that if the enemy ever crossed the Potomac he might have been destroyed; said that Meade & his army had expended the skill & toil & blood up to the ripe harvest & then allowed it to go to waste. He then said that after the lapse of several days, he now felt profoundly grateful to Meade & his army for what they had done, without indulging in any criticisms for what they had not done, & that Gen. Meade had his full confidence as a brave & skillful officer & a true man.[4]

July 23, 1863. Today I gave the President a letter from Govr. Gamble in which he alternately whined and growled through many pages over the President's letter to Schofield.[5] The Tycoon told me to put it away. He wrote an answer to Gamble telling him he had not read the letter & would not as he wished to keep his temper and avoid irritants and that he meant no discourtesy by his Schofield letter.

July 25, 1863. Halpine has been here. He tells me that Seymour [Gov. of N.Y.] is in a terrible state of nervous excitement; that there is absolute danger of the loss of his wits. He is tormented both by the terrible reminiscence of the riots & by the constant assertions of the Press that he is concerned in a conspiracy of which the outbreak was a mismanaged portion.[6] He shudders even now at the dreadful picture which his imagination conjures up of the possible results of that miserable business. The mob, he said, aimed to destroy the great necessities of New York; light, water, & communication. In the former two they almost succeeded. The Haarlem Bridge was at their mercy, but a rain came up & wet them & somebody had neg-

---

[4] In a letter written to Meade by Lincoln, but never sent, he said: "I do not believe you appreciate the magnitude of the misfortune involved in Lee's escape. . . . As it is, the war will be prolonged indefinitely." N. and II., VII, 280.

[5] Lincoln's very difficult political problem in Missouri was to carry along two Union factions, one of which under Gov. Gamble had favored gradual emancipation, and the other, the Radicals, who were for extreme measures. Gen. Schofield, after an interval in which he had been subordinate to a civilian general, had been reappointed to full command in May, 1863. He became, in a way, the personal as well as the military representative of the President.

[6] The New York City draft riots began July 11, 1863.

lected to supply the conflagrating party with kindling wood which alone prevented them. The Jersey City ferry boats hauled off & were saved. The Governor's mind is tortured with visions of an isolated city without light or water, given over to a howling mob, whose accomplices in every kitchen in the city held the lives & property of the whole population at their mercy.

Halpine was also talking about Gillmore. He says that his appointment is part of a programme arranged by the friends of Butler, to get as far as possible the "soldier influence for the Pres^t." Greeley was first fooled over and his influence got Gillmore a hearing at Washington. When he went South he took with him Turner and Strong, two special adherents of Butler.

He says that Butler's party is growing enormously. All the fanatics —all the corruptionists—a vast stock-jobbing interest headed by Col. Butler who has brought his stolen two millions to N.Y. & says he is willing to spend it all for this great object.

Hunter wrote a letter to Greeley on learning of his share in the appointment of Gillmore, congratulating him on his enlisting & receiving bounty in the "On to Charleston" movement, & hoping it would be as successful as the "On to Rich^d" in which he (G.) & other men bled.

I rode out to Soldiers' Home with the Tycoon tonight. Bob was down the river with Seward. I could not go as Chas. was here. Had a talk on philology for which the T. has a little indulged inclination. Rode home in the dark amid a party of drunken gamblers & harlots returning in the twilight from [erased].

July 29, 1863. The President today wrote a letter to General Halleck, stating that as he inferred from one of Gen. Meade's despatches that M. thought the Gov^t were pressing him to an engagement with Lee, that the impression was erroneous, that he was opposed to it unless that were in harmony with Halleck's & Meade's views; that if it were imprudent to attack them at Williamsport it was certainly more so now when Meade has no more than $\frac{2}{3}$ of his then force; that he was in favor at Williamsport [7] of Meade's crossing and harass-

---

[7] Williamsport, on the Potomac above Harper's Ferry and near Hagerstown, is where Lee recrossed the river.

ing the enemy. This had been done and now he was rather in favor of delay than immediate attack & desired Gen. Halleck to so communicate to Meade unless he saw good reasons to the contrary.

July 31. Carl Schurz was in my room today: he spoke very highly of Meade. He says the rebels are deserting as much as they can in the face of their severe discipline.

The President today received a letter from General Meade in answer to one he had written. Meade says that if Hooker is willing to serve under him he will be glad to have the benefit of his services. Hooker chafes in inaction. Fighting Joe has not finished his history yet by a great deal.

The President today wrote a letter to Steve Hurlbut—who is talking about resigning,—urging him to reconsider his intention and remain in the service if he can without too serious detriment to his own private interests.

He further urges him to see Sebastian, if he can, and ascertain if S. really intends to present himself next session for admission into the Senate. That he (the Pres¹) stands by the Proclamation, considers it valid in law & to be sustained by the Courts, and that if Sebastian will come next winter prepared, basing himself on that, to try to bring in his State with a system of apprenticeship—not like the Missouri System, which is faulty in *postponing* the benefits of freedom to the slave, instead of giving him an immediate vested interest therein—he (L.) will be glad to see him and Sebastian will be doing the greatest possible good that one man can do.[8]

I had considerable talk with the President this evening on this subject. It deeply interests him now. He considers it the greatest question ever presented to practical statesmanship. While the rest are grinding their little private organs for their own glorification the old man is working with the strength of a giant and the purity of an angel to do this great work.

The President a day or two ago gave General Halleck directions

8 From this time on until the 1864 Convention there are many references like this indicating the extent to which Lincoln was depending on the military occupation in the Southern states to supply both members of Congress and convention delegates who would support the President's policies. W. K. Sebastian, Senator from Arkansas, had been expelled from the Senate. July 11, 1861.

to prepare an order for the protection of our black soldiers. Gen. Halleck brought him today a draft of it. He said he was troubled to know how to retaliate in kind for selling into slavery and concluded to make it imprisonment at hard labor. That will be rare. To see the swaggering lords of lash, lazy & lousy, long-haired & languid (a hell of an alliteration) in zebra garb and zouave scarcity of *chevelure* breaking stone or digging the first ditch instead of dying in the last.

August 1, 1863. Forney dedicated his new printing office today with a blow-out at the Chronicle Buildings on 9th Street. The President went up with me. Gen. Thomas was there. As the President shook hands with him & said Good-bye (Thomas being about to start for the West) he said, "General, you are going about a most important work. There is a draft down there which can be enforced." "I will enforce it," Thomas replied. A few moments afterward at the lunch at Forney's quarters he used the Tycoon's expression as his own & was cheered for it. I regard his attitude as most significant. He is a man accustomed through long lifetime to watch with eager interest the intentions of power and the course of events; till he has acquired an instinct of expediency which answers to him the place of sagacity & principle. He is a straw which shows whither the wind is blowing. The tendency of the country is to universal freedom, when men like Thomas make abolition speeches at public dinners.

*   *   *   *

August 3. Dined with Wise. He and Aulick say the whole British Embassy here are actively secesh: aided and abetted Lawrence to go South, and then assisted him out of jail when he was caught.

August 6. This was the day of thanksgiving appointed by the President. We went to Dr. Sunderland's but he was away, so went to Gurley's. G. came out pretty strongly in prayer and sermon, more decidedly than ever before. The President said after church, that he supposed his faith in ultimate success must be decidedly strengthened or he would not have talked so.

The Tycoon says there is no foundation for the rumor of war with England.

Two good things on Hale.[9] Got four votes out of a whole convention, against the Adm[n]. Found himself cut out of a job by a statute of Congress passed by himself. He then wanted the Secretary to construe it liberally.

The President has rec[d] an enormous letter from Seymour about draft, and intends to enforce the draft with such arrangements as will take from the present enrollment its present look of unfairness. He says he is willing and anxious to have the matter before the courts.

Matters from Louisiana look very well. Banks in a letter to Boutwell says the State will do anything we want her to. In reference to that the President has written Banks this letter, a very careful & I think admirable one.[10]

Cuthbert Bullitt, collector at New Orleans, is in hot water because he is not of the chair dynasty devotees.

TO J. G. NICOLAY

EXECUTIVE MANSION,
WASHINGTON, *August 7, 1863.*

The draft fell pretty heavily in our end of town. William Johnson (cullud) was taken while polishing the Executive boots and rasping the Imperial Abolition whisker. Henry Stoddard is a conscript bold. You remember that good-natured shiny-faced darkey who used to be my special favorite a year ago at Willard's. He is gone, *en haut de la spout.* And the gorgeous headwaiter, G. Washington. A clerk in the War Department named Ramsey committed suicide on hearing he was drafted. Our friend Henry A. Blood was snatched from his jealous desk. And Bob Lamon is on the [torn off]. Bob [Lincoln] and his mother have gone to the white mountains. (I don't take any special stock in the matter & write the locality in small letters.) Bob

9 Senator Hale was chairman of Com. on Naval Affairs. An investigation late in 1863 disclosed that he accepted a fee from a man accused of fraud and appeared in his behalf before the Secretary of War. In 1864 he was defeated for reelection.
10 Printed in "Complete Works," II, 380. Policy on emancipation in Louisiana.

was so shattered by the wedding of the idol of all of us, the bright particular *Teutonne,* that he rushed madly off to sympathize with nature in her sternest aspects. They will be gone some time. The newspapers say the Tycoon will join them after a while. If so, he does not know it. He may possibly go for a few days to Cape May where Hill Lamon is now staying, though that is not certain.

This town is as dismal now as a defaced tombstone. Everybody has gone. I am getting apathetic & write blackguardly articles for the *Chronicle* from which West extracts the dirt & fun & publishes the dreary remains. The Tycoon is in fine whack. I have rarely seen him more serene & busy. He is managing this war, the draft, foreign relations, and planning a reconstruction of the Union, all at once. I never knew with what tyrannous authority he rules the Cabinet, till now. The most important things he decides & there is no cavil. I am growing more and more firmly convinced that the good of the country absolutely demands that he should be kept where he is till this thing is over. There is no man in the country, so wise, so gentle and so firm. I believe the hand of God placed him where he is.

They are working against him like beavers though; Hale & that crowd, but don't seem to make anything by it. I believe the people know what they want and unless politics have gained in power & lost in principle they will have it.

I am getting on very comfortably. Howe is a very good fellow. I hate to give orders to a man who was a Senator in Massachusetts while I was in jackets & button-cinctured trousers. Still he is better than Stod. as he is never stuffy and always on hand.

I will wind up with a little gossip. Mrs. Davenport told it to Wise & Wise told me. Mrs. Davenport *loquitur.* "Have you heard the dreadful story about Miss Carroll of Baltimore? Raped by a negro! What are we coming to?"

Wise. "How did she appear to like it?"

Mrs. D. "You have heard about Mrs. Emory's maid? Gone to Philadelphia to be *confined!*"

Wise. "Who has gotten her that way; not Mrs. Emory, I hope."

Mrs. D. "No! you naughty fellow. Lord Lyons' valet."

That's all I know of high life that would interest you. Take care of yourself & write when you have nothing better to do.

August 9, 1863. This being Sunday & a fine day, I went down with the President to have his picture taken at Gardner's. He was in very good spirits. He thinks that the rebel power is at last beginning to disintegrate, that they will break to pieces if we only stand firm now. Referring to the controversy between two factions in Richmond, one of whom believes still in foreign intervention, Northern treason & other chimeras, and the other, the Administration party, trusts to nothing but the army, he said, "Davis is right. His army is his only hope, not only against us, but against his own people. If that were crushed the people would be ready to swing back to their old bearings."

He is very anxious that Texas should be occupied and firmly held in view of French possibilities. He thinks it just now more important than Mobile. He would prefer that Grant should not throw his army into the Mobile business before the Texas matter is safe. He wrote in that sense, I believe, to Grant today.

He wrote also to Rosecrans, in answer to Rosecrans' letter to him, which is one of the worst specimens of epistolary literature I have ever come across. Rosecrans' letter deprecated any dissatisfaction with his apparent slowness & gave his reasons for it: the extreme length of his lines; the scarcity of cavalry; the terrible mud of the roads; their narrowness, which prevents trains from passing each other readily, &c.

The President in his answer disclaimed all unkindness or any diminution of confidence and regard. He said that when Grant invested Vicksburg he was very anxious on account of Johnston and when he heard that Bragg had sent reinforcements to J. he thought that that was Rosecrans' time to attack Bragg, & says with all kindness, he still thinks so. As time wore on he became convinced that Rosecrans should either attack the enemy or stand on the defensive and send reinforcements to Grant. He gave that order to Halleck to send to R[osecrans]. H. said he had already done it in substance.

After Vicksburg [July 3] fell his anxiety was relieved. He could not agree with Rosecrans in thinking that his best time for attacking Bragg would be after rather than before fall of Vicksburg.

Now, however, he was relieved of anxiety and would trust to R.

himself. He was very anxious that E. Tennessee should be relieved. But the question was, if we could take the country, could we hold it? In conclusion he begged Rosecrans to believe that he was not blaming him, or watching him with an evil eye.

August 10, 1863. Today the answer of the Pres^t to Seymour was printed: everybody seems to consider it as a sockdolager to the Govr. Poor Seymour! A weak timid vacillating man, afraid to do either right or wrong. If he were under good influences, he would do yeoman's service for his country. Now, he is wearing himself into lunacy by trying to serve the plans of his owners and his own good impulses at once.

The President today wrote a letter to the East Tennesseeans, who recently presented him a most touching petition, which, circulated by stealth among the mountains of that suffering but loyal district, has obtained thousands of signatures. He answered that he had not seen them because he knew what they would say—the same true and painful story he had heard so often from Maynard & Johnson & Clements—that he was not indifferent to their sufferings, as they might know by the efforts he had made to build a railroad specially for their relief—that he could do no more than he had been doing if his own family & home were in Knoxville—that they were too much distressed to argue and he would not argue with them. The reason of the long and agonizing delay could not be plainly seen by those who were mad and blinded by their sufferings. The impossibility so far, of supplying a great army in East Tennessee & the facility with which a small army could be concentrated upon and destroyed, were the main ones. He added that even now Stanton, Halleck, Rosecrans & Burnside were trying to do something which might result in their relief.

Seymour writes a coppery little letter in which he says the shameless frauds, &c., &c.

August 11, 1863. Seymour sends another ponderous document accusing the draft of partisanship.

President read today Drake's letter and gave the substance of Gamble's, each accusing him of outrageous partisanship with the other.

Fred Douglass in company with Sen. Pomeroy visited the President yesterday. Frederick intends to go South and help the recruiting among his people.

August 13, 1863. Rode today with the President and the Secretary of State to the Capitol. Saw the statuary of the East Pediment. The Pres^t objected to Power's statue of the Woodchopper, as he did not make a sufficiently clean cut.[11]

Coming home the President told Seward of what Frank Blair said about an interview he had had with Poindexter in the West. Poindexter said, "We are gone up, there is no further use of talking." "How about yr. institution?" Frank asked. "Gone to the devil."

Seward said, "Slavery is dead: the only trouble is that the fools who support it from the outside do not recognize this, and will not till the thing is over. In our Masonic warfare, we made a great fight. The masons were beaten: they knew & felt it, and retired from the fight.[12] But the Jack Masons, as they were called, kept up their dismal howls of sympathy for the Masons long after *they* had given up the fight & forgotten all about it. So now, though slavery is dead, the Democratic party insists on devoting itself to guarding the corpse."

Brady has recently written a letter in which he says he is sorry to say that Seymour is at present actuated by no higher ambition than to carry an election.

Seward says, "He is silly and short sighted. One fundamental principle of politics is to be always on the side of your country in a war. It kills any party to oppose a war. When Mr. Buchanan got up his Mormon War, our people, Wade & Fessenden & the Tribune

[11] The original Capitol, without dome or wings, was in process of extensive rebuilding at the outbreak of the Civil War. The work was completed in 1863.

[12] Probably a reference to the Morgan-Miller episode in New York state in 1826–27 which rapidly produced an anti-Masonic movement on a nation-wide scale. The anti-Masons twice nominated candidates for the Presidency.

led off furiously against it.[13] I supported it to the immense disgust of enemies and friends. If you want to sicken your opponents with their own war, go in for it till they give it up."

Pres[t] says, "Butterfield of Illinois was asked at the beginning of the Mexican War if he were not opposed to it; he said, 'No. I opposed one war. That was enough for me. I am now perpetually in favor of war, pestilence and famine.' "

There is to be a diplomatic excursion to the North. Seward asked me to go. It will be a very hefty affair.

I saw Forney this morning. He says he thinks they will elect Curtin, though a bad choice for Gov[r]. He would not have been nominated had it not been for Cameron's foolish attack upon him.

Conness has been here, the guest of Chase. James is made collector at San Franc[o] in place of Low. I rather intimated to the Pres[t] that this was Chase's game and he replied good-humoredly, "I suppose C. thinks it is to his advantage. Let him have him."

August 14, 1863. Meade was in town today. In one thing he evinces want of candor or failure of memory. The President, July 27, asked him if he would like to have Hooker with him. He replied by return mail that "he would be very glad to have the benefit of his services." The President showed the letter to Hooker who was pleased with the prospect of fight and then wrote asking Meade if he would wish Hooker to come at once or could he as well wait till the 1st of September. In case there should be a battle Hooker would like to come at once. Meade answers that as to the probabilities of a battle, we at Washington can tell as well as he, as the Army is now lying inactive, waiting reinforcements from the draft or orders to advance. What the enemy may please to do we don't know. As to Hooker, he says he never entertained or expressed any desire for him, that his part in the matter was simply one of acquiescence. This of course very much embarrasses the President. He must rely entirely on Hooker's generosity and magnanimity to

---

[13] In his first annual message, 1857, Pres. Buchanan asked for five regiments to reassert federal authority in Utah where the Mormons refused to acquiesce in the displacement of Brigham Young as territorial governor. Most of the Republicans opposed the measure on the ground that the President might use them against the Free State party in Kansas.

get out of the snarl, as Meade evidently does not want him with the Army of the Potomac.

The preparations for the draft still continue in New York. Dix is getting ready rather slowly. Fry goes to N.Y. tonight, armed with various powers. He carries a paper to be used in certain contingencies calling the militia of the State into the service of the general Government, and calling upon rioters to disperse K.L.D. Dix has already authority to declare martial law when it appears necessary. The devil of treason is pretty well muzzled there. We must tear out its fangs if it takes off the muzzle. Seymour is half lunatic, half demagogue. He is a delicate soul, without courage or honesty, fallen on evil times. His reason, never the most robust, is giving way under its overwork. If old Gen. Sandford is entirely sound, we may manage it without trouble. The Gov^t was never intended by the Constitution to be left helpless to the attacks of discontented State officers. I thank God for the riot if as one of its results we set a great authoritative precedent of the absolute supremacy of the National power, military and civil, over the State. Every nail that enters the coffin of that dead-and-gone humbug of State's Rights is a promise of future & enduring peace & power.

August 19, 1863. This morning a letter came from Steve Hurlbut formally withdrawing his resignation and another, a splendid letter, full of the old arrogant and incisive energy of the man, saying that he thinks the rebellion is falling to pieces by disintegration in the West. He sends also a sketch of a letter he intends to write to the Mississippi planters, telling them to get themselves out of their miserable scrape by accepting the events of the war, including emancipation, as accomplished facts, and forming a plan of gradually lightening apprenticeship in accordance with them, and offering themselves back to the Union. He thinks the horrors of rebellion have so broken their spirits that they will do whatever seems best for peace and the old security.

He says if East Tennessee were only redeemed, Tennessee would vote herself free and loyal in a few months, and send an earnestly loyal delegation to Congress from every district.

The whole letter is very like the old Hurlbut we used to know in

Illinois, the reliant, arrogant, brilliant leader in a political war.

This evening and yesterday evening an hour was spent by the President in shooting with Spencer's new repeating rifle. A wonderful gun, loading with absolutely contemptible simplicity and ease with seven balls & firing the whole readily & deliberately in less than half a minute. The President made some pretty good shots. Spencer, the inventor, a quiet little Yankee who sold himself in relentless slavery to his idea for six weary years before it was perfect, did some splendid shooting. My shooting was the most lamentably bad. My eyes are gradually failing. I can scarcely see the target two inches wide at thirty yards.

An irrepressible patriot came up and talked about his son John who, when lying on his belly on a hilltop at Gettysburg, feeling the shot fly over him, like to lost his breath—felt himself puffing up like a toad—thought he would bust. Another, seeing the gun recoil slightly, said it wouldn't do; too much powder; a good piece of audience should not rekyle; if it did at all, it should rekyle a little forrid.

22nd August, 1863. The President today said John Logan was acting so splendidly now, that he absolved him in his own mind for all the wrong he ever did & all the will do hereafter.

I said I thought Quantrell would murder Lane if he caught him. He replied that if he did, Lane's friends w^d hunt Quantrell to his death.[14]

23d. Last night we went to the Observatory with Mrs. Long. They were very kind and attentive. The Prest took a look at the moon & Arcturus. I went with him to the Soldiers' Home & he read Shakespeare to me, the end of Henry VI and the beginning of Richard III, till my heavy eyelids caught his considerate notice & he sent me to bed. This morning we ate an egg and came in very early. He went to the library to write a letter to Conkling & I went to pack my trunk for the North.

[*Undated.*] Spent a day in New York. Dined with Andrews. He says Raymond came back from Washington full of admiration for

[14] This entry was on the day after the massacre at Lawrence, Kansas.

the President, saying he had more clearly than anybody the issues of this matter in his mind. This explains those remarkably sensible articles which have appeared recently in the *Times*.

Staid about a week at Long Branch. Fine air, disgusting bathing, pretty women and everything lovely. No politics, no war, nothing to remind me while there that there was such a thing as government, or a soul to save. Count Gurowski was an undertone of nuisance— that was all.

Went to Providence to attend commencement.[15] I was charmed and surprised to find with what affectionate and hearty confidence Mr. Lincoln was there regarded. The refined and scholarly people of that ancient city seem utterly free from that lurking treason which so deforms some towns of more pretense. At the commencement dinner especially I heard nothing but the most emphatic expression of advanced and liberal Republicanism.

[15] The fifth anniversary of Hay's graduation from Brown University.

CHAPTER VIII

September 9—September 30, 1863

September 9, 1863. Dined with Wise. Met Hooker, Butterfield & Fox. Hooker was in a fine flow. Before dinner we talked about Halleck and his connection with Hooker's resignation.[1] He says he was forced to ask to be relieved by repeated acts which proved that he was not to be allowed to manage his army as he thought best, but that it was to be maneuvered from Washington. He instanced Maryland Heights whose garrison he was forbidden to touch, yet which was ordered to be evacuated by the very mail which brought *his* (H.'s) relief. And other such many.

At dinner he spoke of our Army. He says: "It was the finest on the planet. He would like to see it fighting with foreigners. It gave him an electric feeling to be with it. It was far superior to the Southern army in everything but one. It had more valor, more strength, more endurance, more spirit. The rebels are only superior in vigor of attack. The reason of this is that in the first place our army came down here capable of everything but ignorant of everything. It fell into evil hands—the hands of a baby who knew something of drill, little of organization, and nothing of the *morale* of the army. It was fashioned by the congenial spirit of this man into a mass of languid inertness destitute of either dash or cohesion. The Prince de Joinville, by far the finest mind I have ever met with in the army, was struck by this singular and, as he said, inexplicable contrast between the character of American soldiers as integers and in mass. The one active, independent, alert, enterprising: the

---

[1] Halleck deeply resented Hooker's habit of communicating directly with Lincoln, N. and H., VII, 210 ff. This became sharply marked in June, 1863, when the Confederate forces had invaded Pennsylvania and were moving toward Harrisburg. Hooker, in command of the army of the Potomac below Harper's Ferry, resigned June 27, only a week before the Battle of Gettysburg.

other indolent, easy, wasteful, and slothful. It is not in the least singular. You find a ready explanation in the character of its original general. Stoneman is an instance of the cankerous influence of that staff. I sent him out to destroy the bridges behind Lee. He rode 150 miles and came back without seeing the bridges he should have destroyed. He took with him 11,000 men, he returned with 4,500. His purposeless ride had all the result of a defeat. He claimed to have brought in an enormous train of negroes and other cattle. He brought thirty contrabands and not a man or a mule. He is a brave good man but he is spoiled by McClellan and the piles.

"After the battle of Malvern and after the battle of Fair Oaks we could have marched into Richmond without serious resistance.[2] Yet the constitutional apathy of this man prevented."

Says Butterfield: "On the night of the battle of Malvern I saw the red lights of Meyer, signal officer, blazing near me and I went to him to gain information. Told me he had just received a despatch from Gen. McClellan asking where was General F. J. Porter, he wanted news. I volunteered a despatch. 'We have won a glorious victory and if we push on and seize our advantage Richmond is ours.' The day of Gaines' Mills I had taken my position, when Porter ordered me out of it into a hollow where I was compelled to assume a strictly defensive position. I once or twice terribly repulsed the enemy but my orders peremptorily forbade pursuit. I had to keep up the spirit of the men by starting the rumors that McClellan was in Richmond. I am sure I thought he would be there that day. In the night, going to Gen. McClellan's Headquarters, he asked me what about our Corps. I told him that with a few strong divisions we could attack and drive the enemy. He said he hadn't a man for us."

Fox said that the night before the evacuation of Yorktown he stayed in McClellan's tent. McC. said he expected to bag 18,000 of them. "You won't bag one," replied Tucker. And he didn't.

Hooker says: "Marcy sometimes sent important orders which McClellan never saw. On one occasion when I had advanced my pickets very near Richmond, I received an order through Heintzelman, 'Let Gen¹ Hooker return from his brilliant reconaissance, we

2 Peninsular campaign. Battle of Malvern Hill, June 30, 1862.

cannot afford to lose his division.' I did not see how my division could be lost as in that country there was no cutting me off. I started back, however, & soon met McClellan himself who asked me what it meant, my withdrawal. I showed him his own order. He said he had never seen it, and I ordered my men back. I returned over the swamp and held my position for weeks afterwards."

Hooker and Butterfield both agree as to the terrible defeat the rebels suffered at Malvern and the inefficiency which suffered them to escape without injury. They say there was a corps, fresh and unharmed, which might have pursued the rebels and entered Richmond in triumph (Franklin's).

Wise and H. talked about California, hydraulic mining, &c. Hooker asked me very anxiously about our relations with France. He seems very eager to raise an army on the Pacific Coast for a fight with a foreign nation. His eye brightened as he talked of it.

Hooker drank very little, not more than the rest who were all abstemious, yet what little he drank made his cheek hot and red & his eye brighter. I can easily see how the stories of his drunkenness have grown, if so little affects him as I have seen. He was looking very well tonight. A tall and statuesque form—grand fighting head and grizzled russet hair—red florid cheeks and bright blue eyes, forming a fine contrast with Butterfield who sat opposite, a small stout compact man with a closely chiselled Greek face and heavy black mustache like Eugene Beauharnais in the picture I have seen. Both very handsome and very different.

September 10, 1863. A despatch came yesterday morning from Rosecrans written in a most querulous and discouraged tone, saying to Halleck that his orders warning Rosecrans agst a junction of Johnston & Bragg were too late: the junction could not be prevented: he must fight both: Gen Burnside's movement was independent of his: he knew nothing and expected nothing from him: the gravest apprehensions were justifiable: they were the legitimate consequences of Halleck's orders: all that could now be done was for Burnside to close in on his (R.'s) left and throw forward his right to threaten the enemy while he (R.) caught the enemy in his grip & either strangled him or perished in the attempt.

The President read it with a quiet smile. He said he did not believe the story of Johnston's junction. Johnston was watching Mobile. Rosecrans was a little excited. In the afternoon a despatch in better tone came from Rosecrans. He intimated that the prospect was the enemy would leave Chattanooga without a fight. This morning the despatches confirmed the last view, justified, as usual, the President's instinct, and proved that Rosecrans was a little stampeded.

Frank Blair was in my office today. I congratulated him on his new position of leader of the Copperheads in the next Congress & asked what arrangement he would make with Fer[ndo] Wood.[3] He said he would drive him out of the party.

George Opdyke called to say that though the President had treated him very cavalierly when he last visited him he wanted to thank him for his recent admirable letter to the Springfield Convention.

I dined tonight at Wormley's with Hooker, Butterfield, Fox, Wise, and Col. Rush of Philad[a]. Early in the dinner we began to talk about England and the retribution to come for her insults and injuries when this war is over. Everybody had something to say. Fox said, "When the time comes, a publication will be made of insults and wrongs on every sea—of ports closed to us and opened to the enemy, of flags dipped to them and insultingly immovable to us, of courtesies ostentatiously shown them and brutally denied us—that will make the blood of every American boil in his brain-pan. We shall have men enough when this thing is over."

"We will be the greatest military power on earth," said Hooker, "greatest in numbers, in capability, in dash, in spirit, in intelligence of the soldiery. These fine fellows who have gotten a taste of campaigning in the last three years will not go back to plowing,

<hr/>

[3] Frank P. Blair, Jr., having been elected Representative from Missouri in 1860, resigned, July, '62, to become Colonel in the Union Army. Returned to Congress to serve from March, '63 to June, '64. Unsuccessful candidate for Vice-President on Democratic ticket in 1864.

and spinning and trading, and hewing wood and drawing water. They are spoiled for that and shaped for better work. If they can find no war to their hand, they will filibuster."

"Pleasant fields in Canada," suggested one, "very like Normandy!"

"A Prince of the blood Royal will not save them in that day, however much Davey McGee may put faith in him."

"In the patriot War," said Hooker, "when I was in command on our border there, the picked troops came over & deserted in squads. They had to place native recruits at last in all exposed places. They can never keep an English army together on our soil. They will desert and colonize." [4]

"We will make no fight on Canada," said Fox, "that will fall of itself. But we will cast our eyes at Bermuda, at Nassau, at the islands that infest our coast, nurseries of treason & piracy against us, by whose aid England has been at war with us & we at peace with her. We have found it is not good for these possessions to lie so near for our discomfort. We will come together again, the rebel leaders dispersed & exiled, the army scattered, the people weary and reconciled & only waiting for an outside quarrel to bind them closer together. We will turn to these islands and we will say, 'Get out of this! Go you to your own place,' and it will be the worse for them if they hesitate to go."

Wise: "As our war draws near its close the British Legation sometimes speak of the horrors of war. 'How very distressing it is, to be sure.' 'Nothing of the kind. We are getting the hang of the game and rather like it.' Which occasions vague uneasiness."

Hooker says our war has developed no great cavalry officer. Stoneman has good points but does not fulfill his early promise. Pleasanton is splendid, enterprising and brave, but full of mannerisms and weaknesses. Buford is far superior to any others in all the qualities of a great rider. But none of them approach the ideal.

Speaking of Lee, he expressed himself slightingly of Lee's abilities. He says he was never much respected in the Army. In Mexico he was surpassed by all his lieutenants. In the cavalry he was held

[4] The uprising, 1837, in lower Canada and along the border to Detroit was sometimes called the "Patriot War."

in no esteem. He was regarded very highly by Gen¹ Scott. He was a
courtier and readily recommended himself by his insinuating manner to the General whose petulant and arrogant temper has driven
of late years all officers of spirit and self-respect away from him.
"Look at all his staff officers—sleek and comfortable and respectable and obsequious: Townsend, Cullum, Hamilton Wright, &c."

"The strength of the rebel Army rests on the broad shoulders of
Longstreet. He is the brain of Lee as Stonewall Jackson was his
right arm. Before every battle he has been advised with. After
every battle Lee may be found in *his* tent. He is a weak man and
little of a soldier. He naturally rests on Longstreet who is a soldier
born."

*   *   *   *

Fox was more than usually funny tonight. After dinner he said
how delightful are the usages of society on the coasts of Africa.
There when you dine with a native prince, the etiquette is to
appear naked; free from the contingencies of bursting buttons.

He says one of his brother officers once made a present to a native
King of a cocked hat, a green velvet waistcoat, and a skillet. On
dining with him the next day, the grateful host appeared in the
cocked hat with the flaps drawn down like elephants ears over his
chaps, the green velvet waistcoat pulled to bursting over his stomach, the tense hide bulging out below like the swell of a Corin-
thian pediment, the second button left open to display his um-
bilical development, [two lines effaced] the skillet being moored
around his loins by cowhide thongs.

September 11, 1863. Today the President wrote a leter to Andrew
Johnson telling him now is the time to reorganize the loyal government of Tennessee. But it must be so done that the friends and not
the enemies of the Union should be in the ascendant. That the
toil of liberating Tennessee would be purposeless and futile if the
struggle ended by putting Gov. Johnson & Gov. Harris up.⁵
This must not be. Exclude from the Gov⁵ those who cannot be

⁵ Harris, the regularly elected governor, was southern in sympathies; Andrew
Johnson, Senator from Tennessee, had been by Lincoln appointed military governor.

trusted for the Union and you will be recognized by the Government here as the Republican gov^t guaranteed to the States and protected from invasion or internal tumult.

In connection with the question of time, the President cannot tell who will be the next occupant of his place or what he will do. Present action is therefore important.

He has heard that Johnson has lately declared for emancipation in Tennessee and says God bless him. Incorporate emancipation in the new state Gov^t constitution and there will be no such word as fail in the case.

Arming negroes he thinks will be advantageous in every way.

TO J. G. NICOLAY.

EXECUTIVE MANSION,
WASHINGTON, *September 11, 1863.*

A week or so ago I got frightened at

"The brow so haggard the chin so peaked
Fronting me silent in the glass"

and sending for Stoddard (who had been giving the northern watering places for the last two months a model of high breeding and unquestionable deportment), I left for a few days at Long Branch and two or three more at Providence. I was at the commencement at Brown University and made a small chunk of a talk. I only staid a little over a week and came back feeling heartier.

*   *   *   *

Washington is as dull here as an obsolete almanac. The weather is not so bad as it was. The nights are growing cool. But there is nobody here except us old stagers who can't get away. We have some comfortable dinners and some quiet little orgies on whiskey & cheese in my room. And the time slides away.

We are quietly jolly over the magnificent news from all round the board. Rosecrans won a great and bloodless victory at Chattanooga which he had no business to win.[6] The day that the enemy ran he sent a mutinous message to Halleck complaining of the very things that have secured us the victories, and foreshadowing only danger and defeat. You may talk as you please of the Abolition Cabal directing affairs from Washington: some well-meaning newspapers advise the President to keep his fingers out of the military pie: and all that sort of thing. The truth is, if he did, the pie would be a sorry mess. The old man sits here and wields like a backwoods Jupiter the bolts of war and the machinery of government with a hand equally steady & equally firm.

His last letter is a great thing. Some hideously bad rhetoric— some indecorums that are infamous—yet the whole letter takes its solid place in history, as a great utterance of a great man. The whole Cabinet could not have tinkered up a letter which could have been compared with it. He can snake a sophism out of its hole, better than all the trained logicians of all schools.

I do not know whether the nation is worthy of him for another term. I know the people want him. There is no mistaking that fact. But politicians are strong yet & he is not their "kind of a cat." I hope God won't see fit to scourge us for our sins by any one of the two or three most prominent candidates on the ground.

I hope you are getting well and hearty. Next winter will be the most exciting and laborious of all our lives. It will be worth any other ten.

DIARY

September 17, 1863. I went to Philadelphia to assist at the wedding of Becky Stewart to a fine young fellow named Grant.

I met at the Union League Rooms Geo. H. Baker, & at her father's house Mrs. LeRoy. One of the most lovable of men & most lovely of women. The loyalty of a truly patriotic Philadelphian is of that magnificent and uncompromising character such as is not seen elsewhere. It is carried into every incident of life.

Past the evening partly in Wayne MacVeagh's room (Chairman State Central Committee), partly in General Butler's. MacVeagh does not seem entirely rosy about the result in Pennsylvania. He

[6] occupied by Rosecrans, Sept. 9.

wanted everybody to beg Butler to make more speeches & specially wanted Cameron to come out strong for Curtin which he has not yet done. He thought the chief dangers were the solid Irish vote, the chill and discouragement of the draft, the proclamation of habeas corpus & such.

Butler talked of the folly of the Irish casting their votes as a solidarity—as having a tendency to rouse against them the bitter prejudices of race and religion & overwhelming them.

[*September 27, 1863.*] Sunday morning, the 20th of September the President showed me Rosecrans' despatch of the day before, detailing the first day's fighting, & promising a complete victory on the next day. The Pres^t was a little uneasy over the promise, and very uneasy that Burnside was not within supporting distance.

The next morning he came into my bedroom before I was up, & sitting down on my bed, said, "Well, Rosecrans has been whipped, as I feared.^{7} I have feared it for several days. I believe I feel trouble in the air before it comes. Rosecrans says we have met with a serious disaster—extent not ascertained. Burnside, instead of obeying the orders which were given him on the 14th & going to Rosecrans, has gone up on a foolish affair to Jonesboro to capture a party of guerillas who are there."

Day by day the news brightened up. Thomas held his own magnificently & virtually whipped the enemy opposed to him. The scattered divisions came together—the enemy halted—Rosecrans established himself again at Chattanooga. The stampede seemed to be over.

On Wednesday night, the 23^d, coming home I found on my table some interesting despatches from the rebel papers which I thought the President would like to read. They contained pretty full accounts of rebel losses in the late battles: among other things chronicling the death of B. Hardin Helm, Mrs. L.'s brother-in-law, who spent some time with the family here and was made a paymaster by the President. I took them over to the War Depart-

---

^{7} Rosecrans, in command of the Army of the Cumberland in East Tennessee, was entering the famous Battle of Chickamauga.

ment to give them to an orderly to carry to the President. I found there the Sec. of War who was just starting to the Soldiers' Home to request the President to come to the Department to attend a council to be held there that night, rendered expedient, as he said, by recent despatches from Chattanooga.

While I was in the room they were endeavoring to decipher an intricate message from Rosecrans giving reasons for the failure of the battle. The Sec^y says, "I know the reasons well enough. Rosecrans ran away from his fighting men and did not stop for 13 miles." A moment after he broke in, "No, they need not shuffle it off on McCook. He is not much of a soldier. I never was in favor of him for a Major Gen¹. But he is not accountable for this business. He & Crittenden both made pretty good time away from the fight to Chattanooga, but Rosecrans beat them both."

I went out to the Soldiers' Home, through a splendid moonlight & found the Tycoon abed. I delivered my message to him as he robed himself & he was considerably disturbed. I assured him as far as I could that it meant nothing serious, but he thought otherwise, as it was the first time Stanton had ever sent for him. When we got in, however, we found a despatch from Rosecrans stating that he could hold Chattanooga against double his number; could not be taken until after a great battle; his stampede evidently over.

They came together to discuss the practicability of reinforcing Rosecrans from Meade. Present: A. Lincoln, Halleck, Stanton, Seward, Chase, Watson, & Hardie, and for awhile McCallum. It was resolved to do it. The 11th and 12th Corps were selected for the purpose, Hooker to be placed in command of both. Finished the evening with a supper by Stanton at one o'clock, where few ate.

Tonight (Sep. 27) I rode out to the Soldiers' Home with Hooker. The President, who had been spending the evening at the War Dep^t arranging some plan by which Burnside may be allowed to continue his occupation and protection of East Tennessee, went out at nine o'clock & Hooker who wanted to take leave went out afterwards, picking me up on the street. He does not specially approve of the campaign down there. He thinks we might force them to fight at disadvantage, instead of allowing them to continually choose the battleground. Does not think much can be made by lengthening Rosecrans' line indefinitely into Georgia. Atlanta is a good thing on account of its railroads & storehouses & factories. But a long line weakens an army by constant details, while the enemy, falling back gradually, keeps his army intact till the itinerary equalizes the opposing forces.

Hooker goes in the morning. I hope they will give him a fair show. Slocum's hostility is very regrettable. Hooker is a fine fellow. The President says, "Whenever trouble arises I can always rely on Hooker's magnanimity." The President this morning asked him to write to him. I told him if he did not wish to write to the Tycoon he might write to me. I wish to God I was able to go with him. But Nicolay is in the mountains getting beef on his bones and I am a prisoner here. With Rosecrans, Sherman, Burnside & Hooker, they will have a magnificent army there in a few days & some great fighting if Bragg does not run. Deserters say R. P. Hill is coming. I don't believe that.

Sep. 28, 1863. The Missouri Radicals are here, staying at Willard's. They are making up their case with a great deal of care and have not yet waited upon the President. Hawkins Taylor is very anxious for the President to meet them on a friendly basis. He says he has been in Missouri the past season & knows the state of affairs; that these people are really the President's friends; that the Conservatives are only waiting a favorable opportunity to pronounce against him; that these Radicals will certainly carry the State in the next election; and that, to use their own expression, "It is for the President to decide whether he will ride in their wagon or not." I had previously been a good deal impressed with the fact that the Blairs were not the safest guides about Missouri matters, and that the surest reliance could be placed on men who were passionately devoted to the principle which the Republican party represents and upholds. The "Mo. Rep^n" devoted to the interest of the Conservatives in Missouri and of the Copperheads in Illinois, seems to me a significant indication of the ultimate tendencies of those people. In that sense I have spoken to the

President several times & have urged others to speak to him. He gets the greater part of his information from the Blairs & the Bates people who do not seem to me entirely impartial. Noble fellows they are, though; I have no sympathy with the Radical abuse of them. They stood by freedom in a dark hour and cannot be excommunicated by any eleventh hour converts. Hawkins Taylor had a talk with him yesterday morning & came out very much disheartened. He thinks there is no hope of an agreement. I dined yesterday with Cartter & Fisher at Lamon's. Cartter was very much exercised about the matter. He thinks the most momentous political issues depend upon the manner in which the Prest receives this delegation. He talked as usual in his coarse, arrogant, and brilliant way about the matter. He says Chase is about giving up his Presidential aspirations. Stanton has none & is for Lincoln. That every one is beginning to recognize that he is to save us if we are saved in the next election & he therefore hopes to have the TransMississippi states right when the time comes. I told him that I had said so much as already to appear partizan and advised him to speak for himself; to which he seemed disinclined.

29 *September, 1863*. I had a little talk with the Prest today about the Missourians. He says that they come, he supposes, to demand principally the removal of Schofield—and if they can show that Schofield has done anything wrong & has interfered to their disadvantage with State politics, or has so acted as to damage the cause of the Union and good order, their case is made. But on the contrary he (A.L.) thinks that it will be found that Schofield is a firm, competent, energetic & eminently fair man, and that he has incurred their illwill by refusing to take sides with them in their local politics; that he (A.L.) does not think it in the province of a military commander to interfere with the local politics or to influence elections actively in one way or another.

I told him the impression derived from talking with people from there was that there were two great parties in Missouri, the secession-sympathizing Democrats & the Radicals—that the Union Conservatives were too small to reckon—that the Radicals would carry the State and it would be well not to alienate them if it could be avoided, especially as their principles were in fact ours and their objects substantially the same as ours. He seemed fully to recognize this and other things in the same strain.

He suddenly said, "These people will come here claiming to be my best friends, but let me show you a letter from Joe Hay." He showed me one from Uncle Joe, saying that Drake had recently in a speech at LaGrange denounced him for a tyrannical interference with the Convention through his agent Schofield, referring of course to the letter he wrote Schofield in reply to S.'s telegram earnestly soliciting from him some statement of his views, in June, in favor of gradual emancipation and promising that the power of the general Government would not be used against the slaveowners for the time being, provided they adopted an ordinance of emancipation—stating at the same time that he hoped the time of consummation would be short and a provision be made against sales into permanent slavery in the meantime. He said after rereading his own letter, "I believe that to be right & I will stand by it." [8]

He said, "John, I think I understand this matter perfectly and I cannot do anything contrary to my convictions, to please these men, earnest and powerful as they may be."

Today came to the Executive Mansion an assembly of cold-water men & cold-water women to make a temperance speech at the Tycoon & receive a response. They filed into the East Room looking blue & thin in the keen autumnal air; Cooper, my coachman, who was about half tight, gazing at them with an air of complacent contempt and mild wonder. Three blue-skinned damsels did Love, Purity, & Fidelity in Red, White & Blue gowns. A few invalid soldiers stumped along in the dismal procession. They made a long speech at the Tycoon in which they called Intemperance the cause of our defeats. He could not see it, as the rebels drink more & worse whisky than we do. They filed off drearily to a collation of cold water & green apples, & then home to mulligrubs.

[8] Text in "Complete Works," II, 357.

September 30, 1863. The Missourians spent rather more than two hours with the President this morning. They discharged their speech at him which Drake read as pompously as if it were full of matter instead of wind, and then had a desultory talk for a great while. The President never appeared to better advantage in the world. Though he knows how immense is the danger to himself from the unreasoning anger of that committee, he never cringed to them for an instant. He stood where he thought he was right and crushed them with his candid logic. I was with those people all the while till today. They trifled with a great cause unpardonably. The personal character of the men, too, ill sustained their attitude. They are gone and I suppose have virtually failed.

CHAPTER IX

October 1—November 7, 1863

DIARY

4th October, 1863.[1] Went to the Episcopal Church this morning, A.L.[2] & I. In the evening had a talk with Brough.[3] He says they are going to carry the State by not less than 25,000 on the home vote and vastly greater on the soldiers. The canvass is one of singular energy and vigor. The Vallandighams are giving it up now however. They are spending no money and importing no men. I told him I thought they were diverting men and money into Pennsylvania. He said it was probable. He said he had been this morning doing the personal electioneering business among the Dutch [Germans] around here. Our people had given them up, but they were coming right of themselves. They would say to him, "Johnny, if you ain't elected it won't be de fault of Shenkenheimer's brewery," &c.

He was very anxious about Pennsylvania and seemed much gratified by the cheering news from Forney and especially Cameron. He was not personally friendly with Cameron, but thought him one of the most sagacious of men.

He says Prof. McCoy, after a good deal of indirect boring, came at him flatfooted this evening urging the absolute necessity of uniting on Gen. Butler as our Presidential candidate. He snubbed McC. severely saying, "One war at a time."

He says that when he heard he was nominated he sent a despatch to Tod[4] asking him to assure the President that the change of nominee argued no blame of either State or national

1 Hay was evidently on a trip westward. The diary discloses no certain clue to the place where this entry was made, but Cincinnati is plausible.
2 Hay's brother, Augustus Leonard Hay.
3 Brough was nominated on the Union ticket for the governorship of Ohio.
4 then governor.

administration and that there should be no difference in the attitude of Ohio towards the general Government. He says he was nominated against his earnest protest. He was in favor of Tod.

Governor Dennison [5] came in late this evening. He spoke also of the earnestness and passion of this canvass—gave illustrations of it. He said that the people at large were beginning to appreciate the importance of this struggle as the forerunner of the Presidential contest: that he had conversed much with leading men in different localities and he found a widespread and constantly increasing concurrence of sentiment in favor of the reelection of Mr. Lincoln. He requested me to say as much to him: that throughout the West so far as he knew the feeling was quietly assuming the same aspect; in New York it seemed to be the same.

WARSAW, ILL. *October 8th*. My birthday and my sister Mary was married today and started off to Cairo with her husband.[6]

SPRINGFIELD, *13th*. Saw Cullom & M. Hay. They are not so unfriendly to A.L. as I had been led to suppose. They were in a terrible miff about the appointment of Mark Delahay to the judgeship in Kansas. They had recommended Jack Grimshaw who is outraged at being beaten by Delahay. Still they seem as friendly as ever to the President in spite of what they call his faults. Judge Logan whom we had been led to give up is not at all copperish.

14th. Great rejoicing over the Ohio & Pennsylvania elections.[7]

NEW YORK, *October 17*. Saw Marston. He says if Chase would pay a little attention to his damned old paper mill in Washington instead of running around the country electioneering, the finances of the country would be better off.

Denison says C. is working like a beaver—that he sent a special confidential agent to N.Y. the other day: came to Denison who would not talk with him, saying he was pledged to Lincoln. Says

5 Governor of Ohio, 1859–61.
6 Mary Pierce Hay married Captain A. C. Woolfolk.
7 Brough won decisively over Vallandigham; Curtin (Penn.) reelected governor.

there is a persistent fight between Opdyke and Barney, Chase being with Opdyke as he thinks O. is for him. Says Andrews & Barney are very inefficient though good men.

Says he is investigating a great and disgraceful fraud perpetrated by Henry B. Stanton. He has been clearing goods for the Southern ports and cancelling their bonds-against-running-blockade, for fees paid in hand. It is a most painful affair, as he has been one of the loudest and most uncompromising anti-slavery men. His wife has also been very prominent in the Woman's Loyal League. Stanton is the chief fugleman of Mr. Chase in the Custom House.

D. says the whole thing is one way in the State of N.Y. Evarts says it is so in Vermont.

October 18, Sunday. I arrived in Washington today after an absence of a little more than two weeks.

On presenting myself to the President this morning, I told him what Govr Dennison had told me. He rejoined by telling me that Gov. D. had been here and repeated what he had said to me.

I gave him my impression of the unmanly conduct of Mr. C. in trying to cut under in the way he is doing, instancing what Denison of N.Y. had related. He said it was very bad taste, but that he had determined to shut his eyes to all these performances: that Chase made a good secretary and that he would keep him where he is. "If he becomes Pres^t all right. I hope we may never have a worse man. I have all along clearly seen his plan of strengthening himself. Whenever he sees that an important matter is troubling me, if I am compelled to decide it in a way to give offense to a man of some influence he always ranges himself in opposition to me and persuades the victim that he has been hardly dealt by and that he (C.) would have arranged it very differently. It was so with Gen. Frémont—with Gen¹ Hunter when I annulled his hasty proclamation ⁸—with Gen. Butler when he was recalled from New Or-

⁸ May 9, 1862, Gen. Hunter, as Commander of the Dept. of the South at Hilton Head, declared martial law and emancipation of the slaves in Georgia, Florida and South Carolina.

leans—with these Missouri people when they called the other day. I am entirely indifferent as to his success or failure in these schemes, so long as he does his duty as the head of the Treasury Department."

He talked of the Missouri matter and read to me the letter he had written Drake for the Committee. As it will probably be published, I forbear synopsis.[9] It is a superb affair, perfectly just and frank, courteous but immovable. He will not be bullied even by his friends. He tried to reason with those infuriated people. The world will hear him if they do not. He read to me a letter which he has today written to Governor Gamble, who it seems, is anxious to have the Pres[t] espouse his side of the quarrel and to recognize him as the State Government and use the Federal authority to crush out the Radicals, who, he says, meditate revolution and civil war in Missouri. The President answering says he will be at all times ready to extend to Missouri the protection guaranteed by the Constitution against domestic violence, whenever he (the Pres[t]) shall see cause to suspect such violence as imminent. He does not so regard it at present. He thinks the instructions given to Gen[l] Schofield cover the case.

We got into this vein of talk through my telling him what Joe Gillespie says and what I myself observed, of the tendency of public opinion in the West, almost universally in favor of the Radicals as against the Conservatives in Missouri.

Talking of the military situation he says Lee probably came up the other day thinking our Army weaker than it is and, finding his mistake from the fight at Bristow, is holding off at present. Rosecrans is all right though somewhat bothered about his supplies.

Tonight as I came in from dinner the Tycoon said a despatch had just come in from Meade, in which he says that the enemy has disappeared from in front of him but that he does not know where he is—that he has probably gone in the direction of the Rappa

---

[9] The letter to C. D. Drake and others, Oct. 5, 1863, is in "Complete Works," II, 419-23. Lincoln declined to appoint Butler to replace Gen. Schofield as head of the Dept. of Missouri.

hannock.[10]

Kent says Count Gurowski has broken with the Tribune Bureau here. He drew a revolver in a furious rage on Hill one evening. Hill wrote him a note forbidding him the office—sent it to him by a messenger, who says Adam G. read it carefully & scribbled on the envelope, "I have no time to read this. I have resolved to have nothing more to do with you."

October 19. The President told me this morning that Rosecrans was to be removed from command of the Army at Chattanooga. Thomas is to take his original army and Grant to command the whole force, including Hooker's and Burnsides's reinforcements. He says Rosecrans has seemed to lose spirit and nerve since the battle of Chickamauga.[11] I told him that I believed Thomas would fail in attack, like Meade and others. The *vis inertiae* which prevents those fellows from running when attacked will prevent them from moving in the initiative.

Dining in company with T. J. Coffey today. He says Covode is still in a bewildered state trying to understand why he was beaten for the nomination for Governor [in Penn.] & why Bill Mann did not make a better use of the $1,000 dollars he gave him to buy delegates. Coffey claims a sort of proprietorship in Covode as he sent him to Congress first.

Coffey says A.L. will be renominated by acclamation.

October 20. Sickles came to my room this morning. He thinks Lee should have been attacked on his last advance. He says the Army of the Potomac has made the usual mistake of waiting for a perfectly sure thing.

He thinks Grant and Rosecrans have won their great successes by disregarding the warnings and the maxims of the books and plunging ahead. The enemy are not prepared for desperate enter-

10 For months after Gettysburg, Meade and Lee had been facing one another but without action. Oct. 16, Lincoln, through Halleck, had ordered Meade to become more active. N. & H., VIII, 242.

11 Battle of Chickamauga, Sept. 20. Rosecrans entered the battle, near Nashville, with the odds in his favor, but made a serious mistake which permitted Bragg to break the line and send the Union troops in disorderly retreat toward Nashville. Grant superseded Rosecrans in command of all military operations in the West.

prises on our part. They think we can and will proceed deliberately and upon ascertained chances: while hunger and destitution impel them into quick and unexpected dashes. So Chattanooga fell. They had not apprehended an attack there at that time. They argued that the length of the line, the broken character of the country, and such considerations would keep us quiet for the present. But Rosecrans dashing ahead spoiled their theory.

I spoke of a Western brigade plunging over an open field under the direct fire of an earthwork, crossing a slough, cutting through an abattis, and storming the work successfully, thus performing what had been called by good regular officers four impossibilities. Battles are won and campaigns frequently decided by the accomplishment of what seems impossible or absurd.

Andrews says French was very drunk the other day when Sickles went down to the Army & was complaining of political generals cutting in and taking all the credit away from men who had been in service thirty years.

I could not help thinking how much happier Sickles was today sitting curled up in a boyish attitude on my sofa or stumping around my room on his one leg, talking pleasantly the while, in the broad sunshine of fame and popular favor, than ever before. He has wiped out by his magnificent record all old stains and stands even in his youth sure of an honored and useful life. One leg is a cheap price to pay for so much of the praise of men and the approval of his own soul.

Dined with Wise and Fox. Wise announced his discovery of the authorship of Miles O'Reilly. Fox seemed a little annoyed. Wise enjoys the articles.

After everybody had gone, Wise spoke sadly about Dahlgren: said he had applied to come home & will probably come. If so, he will scarcely go back. Rowan will succeed him, "a fine fellow," Wise says, "with the coolness of a hero & the ferocity of a wolf. Dahlgren has been in wretched health, dyspeptic, distrait and overworked. His brain seems to be a little affected. He seems to have lost his continuity of thought. His despatches have lost coherence. The business of the fleet is in chaos. He confides nothing to his officers; sometimes even calls a council of war, & when they come tells them not to talk or he can't sleep. His delicate organization seems giving way under the strain of his position."

Dupont is acting badly, trying to cherish a grievance against the Navy, for which there is no reason as he was relieved at his own request.

I said it seemed as if the Lord was managing this thing so that no vast and overshadowing success of any soldier or sailor should occur, to endanger the new liberty of the people.

"And that nothing that walks on two legs shall hereafter be sold in this land," added Wise, which surprised me as I had not expected to see him yet enrolled among the grand army of the Abolitionists.

Today I induced the President to sign a letter I wrote to Col. Rowland approving his proposed National Rifle Corps. I think Rowland himself rather a humbug but his idea is a good one. [Added by Hay, March, 1878: "I was not old enough to know that a good idea is worthless in the hands of a 'humbug.' "]

Fox said today that he was always glad to hear of the rebels getting more arms—that he wanted their whole able-bodied population involved in this business—so that after we whip them they will be whipped finally.

October 21, 1863. Grow and Usher and the Virginians, Chandler and Borden, were in my room this morning and in the other end was Governor Parker of New Jersey and Provost Marshal General Fry. Grow and one of the Virginians began pitching into Seymour and Parker, calling them traitors so far as they were not cowards. It seemed likely that there would be a row. Parker was discreetly deaf.

Bobb came in this morning with a couple of very intelligent East Tennesseans. They talked in a very friendly way with the President; I never saw him more at ease than he is with those first rate patriots of the border. He is of them really. They stood up before a map of the Mountain Country and talked war for a good while. They were urging upon the President the importance of a raid through Georgia and North Carolina to cut the Weldon

line of railway which will at once isolate the Army of Virginia.
They were full of admiration for the President's way of doing
things, and especially for that farsighted military instinct which
caused him to recommend last year and urge ineffectually upon
Congress the building of a railroad from Louisville to Knoxville
and Chattanooga. [Hay added, presumably in March, 1878, "He
selected for this work Amasa Stone of Cleveland & appointed him
a Brigadier General for the purpose."] [12]
Dined with Rogers & Taylor at Wise. Spent evening at Chase's.
Pretty Katie spoke a little spitefully about Rosecrans' removal.
Her father's old game.

October 22, 1863. I spoke to the President today about Blair—his
Rockville speech, and the action of the Union League of Philadelphia leaving out his name in resolutions electing the Cabinet
honorary members of the League. He says Blair is anxious to run
Swann and beat Winter Davis. The President on the contrary says
that Davis is the nominee of the Union convention & as we have
recognized him as our candidate, it would be mean to do anything
against him now.
Things in Maryland are badly mixed. The unconditional
Union people are not entirely acting in concert. Thomas seems
acceptable to everyone. Crisswell is going to make a good run. But
Schenck is complicating the canvass with an embarrassing element, that of forcible negro enlistments. The President is in favor
of the voluntary enlistment of negroes with the consent of their
masters & on payment of the price. But Schenck's favorite way (or
rather Birney's whom Schenck approves) is to take a file of soldiers
into a neighborhood & carry off into the army all the able-bodied
darkies they can find without asking master or slave to consent.
Hence results like the case of White & Sothoron. "The fact is,"
the Tycoon observes, "Schenck is wider across the head in the
region of the ears, & loves fight for its own sake, better than I do."
Went to the theater with Miss Chase. Saw there at Chase's
Robert Dale Owen, who is about to go West. The play was "The

[12] Congress rejected the proposal and nomination. Opposition was rising against
the practice of appointing civilians to non-military positions with military titles.

Pearl of Savoy" and was exquisitely done. It made the statuesque Kate cry like a baby.

I dined with Wise. Winthrop, Chanler & some others present. States' rights were severely attacked and Chanler defended them rather lamely I thought, though I am prejudiced. I think that pestilent doctrine has been only fruitful of harm for the last half century and I thank God that this war has bruised its head forever.

October 23, 1863. Reverdy Johnson and Dr. Stone were talking this morning in my room. They both have relatives and affiliations in the South. They get letters of the general hopeless look of the rebel cause. They think if the President will withdraw his proclamation the South would at once come back to the Union as soon as they could arrange the necessary machinery. Stone said if he did so he would be elected Prest by acclamation; Reverdy said, "& if he did not, he was ruined." Blind and childish groping after a fact which has been buried. Puerile babble over a ghost of an institution which is as odorously defunct as was Lazarus.

Schenck & Piatt came in. Piatt defends flatly the forcible enlistment of negroes. Says it will be a most popular measure among the people of Maryland, & unpopular only among the slaveholders & rebel sympathizers. He says that this man Sothoron is a recruiting agent for the rebels & that he would have been in the jug if they had got him as they expected before the murder.

*   *   *   *

October 24, 1863. This morning the President said that Dana has continually been telegraphing of Rosecrans' anxiety for food, but Thomas now telegraphs that there is no trouble on that score. I asked what Dana thought about Rosecrans. He said he agreed that Rosecrans was for the present completely broken down. The President says he is "confused and stunned like a duck hit on the head" ever since Chickamauga.

I saw last night Charlie Dahlgren, the Admiral's son, who is just from the South. He says you can see the double line of piles in Charleston Harbor at low water and the buoys which designate the torpedoes. That there is but one channel left from Charleston which runs just under the guns of Fort Johnson. [Hay added subsequently the following: "Oct. 29. Smith says Com. Ammend went beyond Sumter in a picket boat & saw no piles."]

The Admiral has leave of absence but a letter came from him last night stating that he is entirely well again and fuller of fight than I have seen him before. He denounces the newspapers and says if they hound him on to attack before he is ready they will be the first to denounce him if he fails. Altogether it seems as if we must admit that his career at Port Royal is up to this point a failure, as Gen. Terry & Colonel Hawley said this morning at breakfast. They were very bitter & I thought unjust. I hope Smith will come down here & give me some idea of the way Army men feel about the matter.

October 25, 1863. Terry and Hawley were here this afternoon and I presented them to the President. They said in answer to his inquiry why Charleston was not shelled that they preferred to save their fire for service against Johnson & Moultrie when the Navy moves, rather than burst their guns now by throwing a few shell into the city.[13] A very sensible conclusion as it appears to me. They had a long talk & came away much pleased with the Tycoon.

Pit Halstcd walked up with me.[14] He says the President won over Ames and Brandegee by his friendly candid manner and the fair way in which he met their complaints and requests. He seems to think that Chase is going to pack the Convention.

Puleston came in after Pit had gone, drank a glass of wine and talked. He gave a most graphic account of the way Curtin received the news of Little Mac's letter (against his election as Governor). *Et tu Brute* was not a circumstance.

He also gave a very funny account of the way Chase effusively cultivated him the other day, "with Presidency glaring out of both eyes," said the wily Doctor. "Poor devil, he has no more show than that chair." Which remains to be seen.

[13] Charleston remained in possession of the Confederates until Feb. 18, 1865. It was one of the main centers for blockade-running.
[14] Possibly Murat Hasted.

October 26, 1863. Sent the Sanitary Fair the autograph of the Proclamation [15] and wrote Boker letter (dated 24) accepting the gold medal and honorary membership of the Philad[a] Union League.[16]

Dined with Fox and Wise. Afterwards visited a wonderful telegraph man named Beardsley & finished the evening with Canterbury & initiating those two innocent youths into the Harveyan mysteries of stewed oysters.

October 28. The President today wrote a letter to Schofield in relation his alleged arming of returned rebels in Missouri, in which he said that the Government here had done the same thing frequently. He orders Schofield to give attention to the matter; if things are wrong, right them; protect the polls from any interference by either citizens or soldiers.

The President added, "I believe, after all, those Radicals will carry the State & I do not object to it.[17] They are nearer to me than the other side, in thought and sentiment, though bitterly hostile personally. They are utterly lawless—the unhandiest devils in the world to deal with—but after all their faces are set Zionwards."

L[t] Col. Smith, A.A.G., Dep[t] of the South, spent the afternoon & evening with me. He thinks Dahlgren is dreadfully broken in health & spirit. That except in the event of the Navy forcing their way in, the Army's work is done. That now the only practicable advance is by sapping along the left bank of the Stono, with the gunboats covering our left flank.

Benham has gotten a friend, Prof. Martin, to submit a plan through Sumner of an approach by way of Dewee's Inlet to the North side of the city which Smith says is wholly impracticable by reason of preparations of the enemy.

---

[15] The original, engrossed Emancipation Proclamation, signed by the President, was, as was customary, deposited and preserved in the Dept. of State. The draft sent to the Northwestern Fair for the Sanitary Commission at Chicago was, according to the letter of transmission ("Complete Works," II, 429), "the original draft" and was in Lincoln's handwriting to which was pasted a "printed part, cut from a copy of the preliminary proclamation, and pasted on, merely to save writing."

[16] *Ibid.*, II, 429.

[17] Missouri.

October 29. I went down to Willard's today & got from Palmer who is here a free ticket to New York and back for Walt. Whitman, the poet, who is going to New York to electioneer and vote for the Union ticket.

Saw Garfield & Hunter. Hunter is just starting for the West on a tour of inspection. I would give my chances for —— to go with him but Nicolay still stays in the Sunset & I am here with a ball and chain on my leg.

The President tonight wrote letters to several of the more prominent Senators & [undecipherable] of the Republican States, urging them to take care of a supposed plot of Gen. Etheridge. This crazy Tennesseean, who was kindly taken up by the Republicans & made clerk of the House, has turned malignantly Copperhead and now hopes to retain his clerkship by Copper votes. His plan for securing to the opposition the organization of the House is to take advantage of a foolish little law passed in the hurry of the concluding days of the last session (approved March 3, 1863) making certain specific requirements for credentials; and to throw out those State delegations which are principally Republican. He will of course post those Governors whose delegations are a majority Democratic & will leave in ignorance those who have a Republican preponderance in their delegations. This matter was suggested to the Pres^t some days ago by a man named Briggs who came with a great show of mystery which I thought humbug and had two audiences of the Pres^t. The President has taken occasion to checkmate any such rascality by sending to some of the Governors a specific form gotten up by himself which will cover the case. The members are to bring their ordinary certificates and these supplemental ones are to be procured by their Senators or some such and brought on in case of any rash question being made.

Garfield was with the President today. He spoke with much enthusiasm of Steedman at Chickamauga. He always mentions Rosecrans with kindness, even tenderness & says he is a man of such fixed convictions as to be frequently unreasonable in holding to them. At the battle of Chickamauga he became convinced that the field was lost & that his place was in the rear. It really seemed so. But when Garfield heard the firing steadily resumed on the left where Thomas was engaged, he was convinced that the left still stood & urged Rosecrans to stay & save the field. The General would not listen to such a suggestion & when Garfield begged permission himself to stay & join the battle on the left Rosecrans parted with him as if never expecting to see him again.

I told the Tycoon that Chase would try to make capital out of the Rosecrans business. He laughed & said, "I suppose he will, like the bluebottle fly, lay his eggs in every rotten spot he can find." He seems much amused at Chase's mad hunt after the Presidency. He says it may win. He hopes the country will never do worse.

I said he should not by making all Chase's appointments make himself *particeps criminis*.

He laughed on & said he was sorry the thing had begun, for though the matter did not annoy him his friends insisted that it ought to. He has appointed Ferry Fox, Com^r for Tennessee & has promised Plantz the District Attorneyship of Florida. I told him Plantz went down with but two ideas, to steal money for himself & votes for Chase. He thinks the matter a devilish good joke. He prefers letting Chase have his own way in these sneaking tricks than getting into a snarl with him by refusing him what he asks.

Wise says that at the time the President made up his mind to provision Fort Sumter he sent Wise to New York to make the necessary preparations. They were to be made quietly. Therefore he got Aspinwall to provide a ship & applied to C.H. Marshall to provision her. He declined saying it would certainly inaugurate civil war and the publication of the fact would prevent the negotiation of a loan on any terms.

I went tonight to Willard's: found there Palmer, Webster, Murphy, Smalley, and other New York Republicans. They have been working like beavers & seem in fine feather. They say they shall carry the State without doubt. They have sent home 10,000 men from the Army to vote. They say every facility has been afforded them. Surgeon General Barnes has acted, they say, "like a trump," exerting himself to carry out their wishes. A wonderful change for Barnes, who formerly rejoiced in a very Copperish head.

October 30, 1863. Dennison came this morning to urge the sending of Rosecrans to Missouri.

Theodore Tilton sends an abusive editorial in the *Independent* & a letter stating he meant it in no unkindliness.

I spent the evening at Dahlgren's—took Col. Ned Smith up with me. There were there the Duchess Luciguano and Captain DiLacy of the Italian Army, Miss Dahlgren, Miss Maury & Mrs. Goddard. The President & Mrs. Lincoln went to see "Fanchon." About midnight the President came in. I told him about Dennison's note and asked if D. had not always been a Chase man. He said "Yes, until recently, but he seems now anxious for my reelection."

I said Opdyke was expected here today & told the President the story of Palmer and Opdyke. He went on and gave me the whole history of the visit they made to Springfield, Barney, Opdyke & Hopboon—of the appointment of Barney—of the way Opdyke rode him—of his final protest & the break.

I said, "Opdyke now was determined to have the Custom House cleaned out."

"He will have a good time doing it."

He went on telling the history of the Senate raid on Seward—how he had & could have no adviser on that subject & must work it out by himself—how he thought deeply on the matter—& it occurred to him that the way to settle it was to force certain men to say to the Senators *here* what they would not say elsewhere. He confronted the Senate & the Cabinet. He gave the whole history of the affair of Seward & his conduct & the assembled Cabinet listened & confirmed all he said.[18]

"I do not now see how it could have been done better. I am sure it was right. If I had yielded to that storm & dismissed Seward

[18] In Dec., 1863, following the failure of Burnside at Fredericksburg a Republican senatorial caucus delegated nine senators to wait on the President to urge the dismissal of Seward on the ground that he was giving Lincoln poor advice on military matters. Lincoln arranged for the caucus committee and the Cabinet to meet together. Seward and Chase offered their resignations, but at the request of the President resumed their duties.

the thing would all have slumped over one way & we should have been left with a scanty handful of supporters. When Chase sent in his resignation I saw that the game was in my own hands & I put it through. When I had settled this important business at last with much labor & to entire satisfaction, into my room one day walked D.D. Field & George Opdyke and began a new attack upon me to force me to remove Seward. For once in my life I rather gave my temper the rein and I talked to those men pretty damned plainly. Opdyke may be right in being cool to me. I may have given him reason this morning."

"I wish they would stop thrusting that subject of the Presidency into my face. I don't want to hear anything about it. The *Republican* of today has an offensive paragraph in regard to an alleged nomination of me by the mass meeting in New York last night."

Received a more than usually asinine letter from Stoddard who is in New York stock-jobbing & writes to me pretending he is working for the election.

November 1, 1863. This evening Gen¹ Schenck, accompanied by Gen¹ Garfield & Judge Kelley, came in to insist upon some order which would prevent disloyal people from voting at the ensuing Maryland election. Before going into the President's room (Kelley & Garfield sitting with me in the anteroom) Kelley spoke very bitterly of Blair's working against the Union party in Maryland.

After they were gone I handed the President Blair's Rockville speech, telling him I had read it carefully, and, saving a few intemperate and unwise personal expressions against leading Republicans which might better have been omitted, I saw nothing in the speech which could have given rise to such violent criticism.

"Really," says the President "the controversy between the two sets of men, represented by him and by Mr. Sumner, is one of mere form and little else. I do not think Mr. Blair would agree that the States in rebellion are to be permitted to come at once into the political family & renew the very performances which have already so bedeviled us. I do not think Mr. Sumner would insist that when the loyal people of a State obtain the supremacy in their councils & are ready to assume the direction of their own affairs, that they should be excluded. I do not understand Mr. Blair to admit that Jefferson Davis may take his seat in Congress again as a Representative of his people; I do not understand Mr. Sumner to assert that John Minor Botts may not. So far as I understand Mr. Sumner he seems in favor of Congress taking from the Executive the power it at present exercises over insurrectionary districts, and assuming it to itself. But when the vital question arises as to the right and privilege of the people of these States to govern themselves, I apprehend there will be little difference among loyal men. The question at once is presented in whom this power is vested: and the practical matter for decision is how to keep the rebellious populations from overwhelming and outvoting the loyal minority."

I asked him if Blair was really opposed to our Union ticket in Maryland. He said he did not know anything about it—had never asked: he says Crisfield plainly told him he was opposed to the Administration.

I spoke of Fox having said that Union men must divide on the question of the Blair and Sumner theories & that I could see no necessity for it. He agreed. He says Montgomery Blair came to him today to say that Frank has no idea or intention of running for Speaker—that Frank wishes to know what the President desires him to do & he will do it. The President will write to Frank his ideas of the best thing to do: for Frank to come here at opening of Congress; say publicly he is not candidate for Speaker; assist in organization of the House on Union basis & then go back to the field.

If Frank Blair does that, it will be the best thing for his own fame he has recently done. He is a glorious fellow & it is pitiable to see him the pet of traitors or lukewarm loyalists in Mo. and attacked, abused and vilified by his old friends and adherents.

I was pleased to learn from the President tonight that the Eleventh Corps did specially well in Hooker's night battle on the Tennessee.[19]

---

[19] Oct. 29 Hooker repulsed Longstreet's effort to dislodge the Union forces from a key position essential to holding Chattanooga.

November 2, 1863. This morning I met Kelley at Willard's at breakfast. He resumed the subject of his last night's talk about Blair. He says there is a combination on foot to make Blair Speaker and Etheridge clerk: that Pendleton was already out of the field: and that Etheridge was betting money liberally on Blair. I told him Blair was not a party to that arrangement or any such. As he seemed to insinuate his fears that the administration favored some such thing I told him I was for Colfax all the time & I believed the President was decidedly though he would think it highly indecorous for him to interfere in the matter.

Kelley says that he has no part in any Presidential intrigue; that he would prefer Abraham Lincoln for his own successor to any one; that he would be grieved if by the course of the Government itself he should be forced into an attitude of seeming hostility.

I came up and told the Pres^t the wrong and injurious impression Kelley had & he asked to see Kelley. I found him closeted with Garfield & Whitelaw Reid, who seemed a little disgruntled at my abrupt requisition. He came up with me talking in his effusive and intensely egotistic way about the canvass he had been making & speaking most bitterly of Blair's Rockville speech. He went in and talked an hour with the President.

After him came Schenck and the President fixed up a letter to Bradford about Schenck's election order, in which, while he guaranteed to all loyal people the right of voting for whom they pleased, he strongly intimates that the loyalty of the candidates is not a sufficient safeguard—that men elected by disloyal votes are not wholly to be trusted.

I saw Sam. Wilkeson today. He tells me he assisted at a somewhat formal conference of political people yesterday and the unanimous conclusion was that the Union nominee for the next Presidency must be Abraham Lincoln. And that as a necessary condition of reelection a reorganization of the Cabinet must be made. The feeling of the country on this matter demands it. He laid his finger mysteriously on his lips and flitted like an elderly owl into the Treasury Department.

The President says Butler has been tendered Foster's Department while Foster goes to relieve Burnside, who resigns. It is not yet known whether Butler will accept.

I asked about Rosecrans. The President says he sees no immediate prospect of assigning him to command: that he had thought, when the trouble and row of this election in Missouri is over, and the matter will not be misconstrued, of sending Rosecrans to Missouri and Schofield into the field. He says that it was because of Grant's opposition that Rosecrans is not in the Army of the Cumberland: when it was decided to place Grant in command of the whole military division, two sets of orders were made out, one contemplating Rosecrans' retention of the command of his own army & the other his relief. Grant was to determine that question for himself. He said at once that he preferred Rosecrans should be relieved—that he (R.) never would obey orders. This consideration of course involves a doubt as to whether Rosecrans should be placed in command of a district from which Grant must to a certain extent derive supplies & reinforcements on occasion.[20]

Tonight Schenck sent for copies of the correspondence between the Pres^t and Bradford. The Tycoon came into his room with the despatch in his hands, clad in an overcoat pure & simple reaching to his knees, & sleepily fumbled for the papers in his desk till he found them & travelled back to bed. I took the letters to the telegraph office & sent them off about midnight.

November 3, 1863. Judge Cartter was in my room this morning talking about Butler. "I am glad he is going there.[21] He will have N.C. in the Union before frost is out of the ground. He is the smartest damned rascal that ever lived. He grovelled in the dirt for years, cutting under everybody in the race of degradation till they got tired of following him; rolled himself in the dust, eating dirt, vainly working to get lower; and when he rose from his wallowing & shook from him the filth of his life's contamination he stood head & shoulders above everybody.

"At the Charleston convention he went out of sight; the Devil

[20] Grant assumed command of a newly created Department of the Mississippi, Oct. 20.
[21] to Fort Monroe.

got ashamed to own him."

He says Butler assigns as a reason for his former proslavery record that he wanted to run the thing into the ground & disgust his own party. *Credat Judæus.*

Passed the evening in the telegraph office reading the returns. Found on arriving there that Stanton and Fox [and] President were a little dubious about the result. But they afterwards discovered an error in their calculations which corrected evidently gave them the State. Sanford's last telegram assured them of success.

Stanton said the disheartening thing in the affair was that there seemed to be no patriotic principle left in the Democratic party: the whole organization voting, as solidly as usual, against the country.

Nov. 4, 1863. Very anxious all day about Maryland. Dined Plantz and Stickney.

Nov. 5, 1863. Maryland all right. Nicolay returned this morning from the West. . . .

I rode in the afternoon over to Georgetown Heights with A.L.

Nov. 7, 1863. The President passed the morning in disposing of cases of courts martial with the Judge Advocate Gen[1].

Gen. Butler called this morning to report on his way to assume command at F[t] Monroe. Nicolay & I spent the evening at Sec. Chase's.

CHAPTER X

November 8—November 20, 1863

Sunday, 8th November, 1863. The President tells me that Meade is at last after the enemy and Grant will attack tomorrow.[1]

Went with Mrs. Ames to Gardner's Gallery & were soon joined by Nico and the Prest. We had a great many pictures taken. Some of the Prest, the best I have seen. Nico & I immortalized ourselves by having ourselves done in group with the Prest.

In the evening Seward came in. He feels much easier about his son. He is very easy and confident now about affairs. He says N.Y. is safe for the Presidential election by a much larger majority, that the crowd that follows power have come over; that the Copperhead spirit is crushed and humbled. He says the Democrats lost their leaders when Tombs & Davis & Breckenridge forsook them and went South: that their new leaders, the Seymours, Vallandigham & Woods are now whipped and routed. So that they have nothing left. The Democratic leaders are either ruined by the war or have taken the right shoot & have saved themselves from the ruin of their party by coming out on the right side.

No party can survive an opposition to a war. The Revolutionary heroes were political oracles till 1812 and afterwards the soldiers of the latter war succeeded to their honors. They were a small & exclusive class. But we are hereafter a nation of soldiers: these people will be trying to forget years hence that they ever opposed this war. I had to carry affidavits to prove I had nothing to do with the Hartford Convention.[2] Now that party that gained eminence by the folly of the Federalists in opposing the war have

[1] An attack on Missionary Ridge, Chattanooga, which was actually postponed eighteen days more.

[2] The Hartford Convention met Dec. 15, 1814. While the resolutions actually adopted were moderate, the general tone was one of opposition to the War of 1812.

the chalice commended to their own lips.

He told the Democratic party how they might have saved themselves & their organization & with it the coming Presidential election—by being more loyal and earnest in support of the administration than the Republican party—which would not be hard, the Lord knows.

Hill Lamon tonight read us a slip from the Chicago *Tribune* in which they very strongly advocate A.L. for his own successor, an utterance, Hill says, stimulated by the prospect of a new Administration paper being started in Chicago pledged against grumbling.

Spent the evening at Butler's rooms at Willard's. Nice wife & very pretty daughter. Butler went away early in the evening after a discharge of bile at Mercier.

November 9, 1863. Spent the evening at the theatre with President, Mrs. L., Mrs. Hunter, Cameron and Nicolay. J. Wilkes Booth was doing the "Marble Heart." Rather tame than otherwise.

November 10, 1863. Went to Mt Vernon with an excursion I had gotten up for Miss Chase's bridesmaids. The party was Mrs. Ames, Miss Lander, Miss N. Chase, Miss Nichols, Miss Skinner, Albrecht & Bates, Capt. Ives, Johnson, Kitchin who backed out before starting, Nicolay, Maj. Garrard, & myself. . . .

November 11, 1863. Went to the Capitol this afternoon and looked at some pictures.

In the evening went to the theatre with Ulric Dahlgren, Stahel, Kent & Kirkland to see Wilkes Booth in Romeo. Wheatley took all the honors away as Mercutio. Went to Harvey's & afterwards to Willard's & drank a good deal. Dahlgren was very funny by the one-legged enterprise he displayed at making a night of it.

Finished the evening by a serenade of Miss Chase by the band of the 17th Infantry.

November 12, 1863. Genl Schenck came in this morning with Davis, Criswell, Evans, Hoffman, & others of the Maryland Emancipationists. He is a little severe on Bradford & Reverdy Johnson for their recent demonstrations in Maryland. Told a very good story on Corwin & congressional service.

Hanscom had a long yarn to tell me this morning about Chase's complicity with the enormous jobbing in the Treasury Dep^t. In the evening Miss Chase and Govr Sprague's wedding. A very brilliant looking party. Kate looked tired out and languid especially at the close of the evening when I went into the bridal chamber to say good-night. She had lost all her old severity & formal stiffness of manner, & seemed to think she had *arrived*. McDowell, Stahel, Schenck, Stonemen, Cameron, and others present. The President came for a few minutes.

[*Nov. 20, 1863.*] Nov. 18 we started from Washington to go to the consecration of the Soldier's Cemetery at Gettysburg. On our train were the President, Seward, Usher & Blair; Nicolay & myself; Mercier & Admiral Reynaud; Bertinatti & Capt Isola & Lt Martinez & Cora; Mrs. Wise; Wayne MacVeagh; McDougal of Canada, and one or two others. We had a pleasant sort of a trip. At Baltimore Schenck's staff joined us.

Just before we arrived at Gettysburg the President got into a little talk with MacVeagh about Missouri affairs. MacV. talked Radicalism until he learned that he was talking recklessly. The President disavowed any knowledge of the Edwards case. Said that Bates said to him, as indeed he said to me, that Edwards was inefficient and must be removed for that reason.

At Gettysburg the President went to Mr. Wills who expected him, and our party broke like a drop of quicksilver spilt. MacVeagh, young Stanton, & I foraged around for awhile—walked out to the college, got a chafing dish of oysters then some supper and finally loafing around to the Court House where Lamon was holding a meeting of marshals, we found Forney and went around to his place, Mr. Fahnestock's, and drank a little whiskey with him. He had been drinking a good deal during the day & was getting to feel a little ugly and dangerous. He was particularly bitter on Montgomery Blair. MacVeagh was telling him that he pitched into the Tycoon coming up and told him some truths. He said the

President got a good deal of that from time to time and needed it.

He says, "Hay, you are a fortunate man. You have kept yourself aloof from your office. I know an old fellow now seventy, who was private secretary to Madison. He has lived ever since on its recollection. He thought there was something solemn and memorable in it. Hay has laughed through his term."

He talked very strangely. Referring to the affectionate and loyal support which he and Curtin had given to the President in Pennsylvania, with references from himself and others to the favors that had been shown the Cameron party whom they regard as their natural enemies. Forney seems identified fully now with the Curtin interest, though when Curtin was nominated he called him a heavy weight to carry and said that Cameron's foolish attack nominated him.

We went out after a while following the music to hear the serenades. The President appeared at the door and said half a dozen words meaning nothing & went in. Seward who was staying around the corner at Harper's was called out, and spoke so indistinctly that I did not hear a word of what he was saying. Forney and MacVeagh were still growling about Blair.

We went back to Forney's room, having picked up Nicolay, and drank more whiskey. Nicolay sung his little song of the "Three Thieves" and we then sung John Brown. At last we proposed that Forney should make a speech and two or three started out, Shannon and Behan and Nicolay, to get a band to serenade him. I staid with him. So did Stanton and MacVeagh. He still growled quietly and I thought he was going to do something imprudent. He said, "If I speak, I will speak my mind." The music sounded in the street and the fuglers came rushing up imploring him to come down. He smiled quietly, told them to keep cool, and asked, "Are the recorders there?" "I suppose so of course," shouted the fugler. "Ascertain," said the imperturbable Forney. "Hay, we'll take a drink." They shouted and begged him to come down. The thing would be a failure—it would be his fault, &c. "Are the recorders congenial?" he calmly insisted on knowing. Somebody commended prudence. He said sternly, "I am always prudent." I walked down stairs with him.

The crowd was large and clamorous. The fuglers stood by the door in an agony. The reporters squatted at a little stand in the entry. Forney stood on the threshold, John Young & I by him. The crowd shouted as the door opened. Forney said, "My friends, these are the first hearty cheers I have heard tonight. You gave no such cheers to your President down the street. Do you know what you owe to that great man? You owe your country—you owe your name as American citizens."

He went on blackguarding the crowd for their apathy & then diverged to his own record saying he had been for Lincoln in his heart in 1860—that open advocacy was not as effectual as the course he took—dividing the most corrupt organization that ever existed—the Proslavery Dem. Party. He dwelt at length on this question and then went back to the eulogy of the President, that great, wonderful mysterious inexplicable man who holds in his single hands the reins of the republic; who keeps his own counsels; who does his own purpose in his own way, no matter what temporizing minister in his Cabinet sets himself up in opposition to the progress of the age.

And very much of this.

After him Wayne MacVeagh made a most touching and beautiful speech of five minutes and Judge Shannon of Pittsburg spoke effectively and acceptably to the people.

"That speech must not be written out yet," says Young. "He will see further about it when he gets sober," as we went upstairs. We sang more John Brown and went home.

In the morning I got a beast and rode out with the President's suite to the Cemetery in the procession. The procession formed itself in an orphanly sort of way & moved out with very little help from anybody & after a little delay Mr. Everett took his place on the stand—and Mr. Stockton made a prayer which thought it was an oration; and Mr. Everett spoke as he always does, perfectly—and the President, in a fine, free way, with more grace than is his wont, said his half dozen words of consecration, and the music wailed and we went home through crowded and cheering streets. And all the particulars are in the daily papers.

I met Gen¹ Cameron after coming in and he, MacV. and I went

down to dinner on board the U.C.R.R. car. I was more than usually struck by the intimate, jovial relations that exist between men that hate and detest each other as cordially as do those Pennsylvania politicians.

We came home the night of the 19th.

Nov. 20, 1863. The President called me today & read the following letter which he had written in answer to one from Chandler of Michigan, blackguarding Seward, Weed, Blair & entreating him to stand firm, and other trash which lunatics of that sort think is earnest and radical, the immediate cause of this righteous outburst being a paragraph from some newspaper stating that Morgan & Weed were in Washington urging upon the President a conservative policy for his Message.

Ex. Man. Wash[n]
Nov. 20, 1863

Hon Z. Chandler

My Dear Sir
    Your letter of the 15th marked "Private" was received today. I have seen Gov[r] Morgan & Thurlow Weed separately but not together, within the last ten days, but neither of them mentioned the forthcoming message or said anything so far as I can remember, which brought the thought of the message to my mind.
    I am very glad the elections this autumn have gone favorably and that I have not by native depravity, or under evil influences, done any thing bad enough to prevent the good result.
    I hope to stand firm enough to not go backward, and yet not go forward fast enough to wreck the country's cause.
Yours truly,

He has also written a short letter to Mr. Everett in reply to one from Mr. E., containing (both letters) mutual congratulations & civilities about the Gettysburg business.

CHAPTER XI

November 21—December 31, 1863

DIARY

Nov. 21. Schuyler Colfax was here last night. He is very sanguine about the Speakership; in fact almost absolutely certain about it. He was talking to the President this evening about the matter, Nicolay & I being present. He says there is some fear that Gen. Etheridge may attempt some outrageous swindle for the purpose of throwing out the Maryland votes by Gov. Bradford's aid. But does not think it will succeed.

He then related an interview between himself and Montgomery Blair. He had heard Blair was against him & so said he, "I went to see Blair about it. He said he was against me. I said I was glad to know where he stood; that I remembered two years ago when Frank was a candidate, when I could have been elected, I declined in Frank's favor and worked for him; that he, M.B., assured me that I should have their lifelong gratitude; that if this was a specimen of it I would give them a receipt in full. He said matters had changed since then—that I was now running as a Chase candidate. I said I was not running as a Presidential candidate at all; that the Presidential question should not be mixed up with the current questions of the day. That I did not call on him except to ascertain his position and to tell him he was free from that debt of lifelong gratitude. Now what I would not say to him, I will say to you, Mr. President."

"Don't say anything to me you do not wish to say," said the Tycoon.

Said Schuyler, "I wish only to say that wherever I have been this summer I have seen the evidences of a very powerful popular feeling in your favor and that I think it will continue unless you do something to check it in your message or public utterances or acts this winter."

After a while Nicolay & I left them & they talked for an hour or so longer. Colfax came out and talked freely for a while. He does not fully commit himself but he talks fairly enough and I think will be all right in the coming fight.

Nov. 22. Judd was in our room this morning. We had a good deal of talk about things in general. He is restless and unhappy in Europe. He feels so thoroughly at home in our politics that it seems a banishment to be out of the whirl.

He was recalling with immense delight his two great political feats of getting the Convention at Chicago & then seating the Convention.

This evening Seward read to the President a despatch from Cash Clay in which he discussed the whole field of American politics, European diplomacy, and the naval improvements of the century. This man is certainly the most wonderful ass of the age. He recently sent a despatch to Seward criticizing in his usual abusive and arrogant style the late oration of Sumner on Foreign Relations, concluding in regular diplomatic style by saying, "You will read this to Mr. Sumner and if he desires it, give him a copy."

Seward says, "It is saddening to think of the effect of prosperity on such a man. Had not we succeeded and he prospered he would always have been known as a brave, sincere, self-sacrificing and eloquent orator. I went all the way to Kentucky to see and to encourage him. It is prosperity that has developed that fearful underlying vanity that poisons his whole character."

I asked Mr. Seward if he had heard of the three revolutions of Matamoras of which we have been talking today. He said, "Yes. I have received a despatch about it from Govr Banks. I am surprised that a man so sagacious and cautious should have been on the point of doing so imprudent a thing."

"He was about to fire on them, then?" said the Pres^t.

"Yes," said Seward. "Our consul at Matamoras asked for protection and he brought his guns to bear on the castle for that purpose." I wrote to him at once that that would be war. That if our consul wanted protection he must come to Brownsville for it.[1] Firing upon the town would involve us in a war with the Lord knows who."

"Or rather," said the Tycoon, "the Lord knows who not."

I happened to mention the Proclamation of Emancipation and Seward said, "One half the world are continually busying themselves for the purpose of accomplishing proclamations & declarations of war, &c., which they leave to the other half to carry out. Purposes can usually better be accomplished without proclamations. And failures are less signal when not preceded by sounding promises.

"The slave states seem inclined to save us any further trouble in that way," he continued. "Their best men are making up their minds that the thing is dead. Bramlette has written an admirable letter in answer to some slaveholders who ask him how he, a pro-slavery man, can support a war whose result will be the abolition of slavery. He tells them the war must be prosecuted no matter what the result: that it will probably be the destruction of slavery & he will not fight against it nor greatly care to see the institution ended."

The President added, as another cheering incident from Kentucky, that Jerry Boyle had asked for permission to enlist three thousand negroes for teamsters, paying them wages and promising them freedom.

The President is very anxious about Burnside.

Nov. 23. Got news tonight of Grant's advance on the enemy at Chattanooga & Thomas' success. The President, who had been a little despondent ab^t Grant, took heart again.[2]

Nicolay went tonight to New York.

Nov. 24, 1863. A very remarkable editorial appeared this morning in the Baltimore *American* under the title "Shall the Gulf States

[1] Matamoras is opposite Brownsville, Texas, which was occupied by Union troops under Gen. Banks. Matamoras was taken by the Imperialists a short time after this incident.

[2] This refers to preparations for the Battle of Chattanooga which was won by Grant the next day. Thomas won at Lookout Mountain.

be allowed to retain a remnant of Slavery?" I took it in to the President to show it to him. He said he did not entirely agree with that view. He thinks that the enormous influx of slave population into the Gulf States does not strengthen slavery in them. He says, "It creates in those States a vast preponderance of the population of a servile and oppressed class. It fearfully imperils the life and safety of the ruling class. Now, the slaves are quiet, choosing to wait for the deliverance they hope from us, rather than endanger their lives by a frantic struggle for freedom. The society of the Southern States is now constituted on a basis entirely military. It would be easier now than formerly to repress a rising of unarmed and uneducated slaves. But if they should succeed in secession the Gulf States would be more endangered than ever. The slaves, despairing of liberty through us, would take the matter into their own hands, and, no longer opposed by the Government of the United States, they would succeed. When the Democrats of Tennessee continually asserted in their canvass of '56 that Frémont's election would free the negroes, though they did not believe it themselves, their slaves did; and as soon as the news of Frémont's defeat came to the plantations the dissappointment of the slaves flashed into insurrection."

Casey & Webster of Md. were in my room today. It is the most encouraging thing in the world in consideration of the thick complications of the time to see these slave-state fellows thoroughly emancipated from the influences of a life long superstition in relation to this Mud God, Slavery.

Casey has some good ideas about reconstruction, which are the result of careful observation. He says that some of the bitterest rebels are beginning to acquiesce in the necessity of submission. That, having submitted themselves, it is a point of honor to preach that doctrine, both to justify themselves & induce others to do likewise: and men soon begin to believe what they pertinaciously preach.

He explains the attitude of Kentucky on the slavery question by showing how in all the other border States, the element of enterprise and energy remains in them or comes to them. But in Kentucky the flower of her life has gone out to Illinois, & Indiana, & Missouri—her young, ambitious, liberal men—and left the decayed branches of old pro-slavery houses still there supreme. Yet even in those dry bones there is agitation and a man may today talk freely in a way that would have insured a tarry-feathery outfit a year or two ago.

Tonight the President said he was much relieved at hearing from Foster that there was firing at Knoxville yesterday. He said anything showing Burnside was not overwhelmed was cheering: "Like Sally Carter when she heard one of her children squall would say, 'There goes one of my young 'uns, not dead yet, bless the Lord.'"

TO J. G. NICOLAY

EXECUTIVE MANSION,
WASHINGTON, *November 25, 1863*

Grant's and Wilcox's despatches are so cheering this morning that I sent you a cautious despatch this morning. Hooker (Fighting Joe) (Fightinger than ever) has done gloriously; carried the north slope of Lookout Mountain and gobbled a thousand prisoners. Thomas & Sherman have also done all they attempted & Grant is to advance today along his whole line.

Burnside has sent a courier through to Wilcox and says he is all right as yet: is not hungry or thirsty & hasn't quite begun his share of the fighting.

Every thing looks well.

Don't, in a sudden spasm of good-nature, send any more people with letters to me requesting favors from L. I would rather make the tour of a small-pox hospital.

TO J. G. NICOLAY

EXECUTIVE MANSION,
WASHINGTON, *November 26, 1863.*

The newspapers of this morning have told you all you want to know & so I send no telegram. The news is glorious.[3] Nature was against us, but we won in her spite. Had not the rapid current and drift swept away Hooker's pontoons he would have utterly destroyed them.

Grant will immediately send a column to relieve Burnside & if possible destroy Longstreet.

The President is sick in bed. Bilious.

Yours
J.H.

DIARY

Nov. 26, 1863. Thanksgiving Day to which Grant's despatches this morning give glorious significance.

I heard a sermon from Dr. Hale [4] in which he argued that our national troubles originated from a spirit of anarchy—that the affliction will not have been in vain if the war begets reverence for law.

The President quite unwell.

I took tea at Wise's. Mr. Everett is there.

Coming home, had some talk with Sec'y Nation. He says the rebels steal the stores we send our prisoners at Richmond. He also read to me the despatches just received from Dana giving a glowing account of that miraculous charge up Mission Ridge. It was Titanic.

Nov. 27, 1863. I dined today at Wise's with Mr. Everett. He is a very delightful old gentleman in his personal and family relations. His talk to his grandchildren was very winning and graceful.

Nov. 28, 1863. The Secretary of State came in this morning and gave me his contribution to the President's Message, relating exclusively to foreign affairs.

He then said he had a matter to submit, which was strictly confidential. "I saw a great while ago that the President was being

---

[3] To the victories of the Battle of Chattanooga was added, Nov. 25, that of Missionary Ridge. The effect was to give the Federal troops possession of East Tennessee and thus open the way for the famous march of Gen. Sherman to Atlanta.

[4] Possibly Edward Everett Hale, who had just published "The Man Without a Country."

urged to do many things which were to redound to the benefit of
other men, he taking the responsibility and the risk. I preferred to
leave to these men the attitude they coveted, of running before
and shouting for the coming events: I preferred to stay behind, to
do with and for the President what seemed best, to share with
him the criticism and the risk and to leave the glory to him and
to God.

"Among other measures to unite good men and to divide the
opposition was the Loyal League Associations of the country. I
saw very early that they would be valuable in bringing over to our
side the honest War Democrats and I therefore encouraged them
as far as possible with my influence and my money. Soon I discovered a wheel within this enterprise—a secret Know Nothing
Masonic order with signs and pass words. They asked me for
money. They sent to me from California for charters. Not to make
trouble, I complied with all requests. You will see for what purpose this machine is being used." Here he handed me a scrap of
paper on which was scrawled in Thurlow Weed's handwriting,
"Loyal Leagues, into which Odd Fellows and Know Nothings
rush, are fixing to control delegate appointments for Mr. Chase."
Seward, still scribbling, said, "If you want to be cheated, join a
secret society. They are all swindles. If I have an idiosyncrasy, it
is a hatred of secrets. The Consul at London tells me that he has
received trustworthy information of an alliance between France
and the rebels: but his sources of information being secret, he cannot give his authority. I answer asking him what right he has to
have a secret from the President, concerning public affairs, and
directing him to lay his information, whatever it may be, before
the American Minister at London."

He handed me a paper upon which he had copied this extract.
"The more I reflect, the less I am inclined to trust the Pa. proposition. The public men of that State are queer."

I am to give both to the Pres^t.

Wayne MacVeagh was here this morning. I took him into my
private room and we wet our whistles. And talked politics. Wayne
is very bitter against Blair: especially for having insulted Curtin

by removing a Postmaster for favoring his election and assigning that as the only reason for doing so, Correy Walborne's sister being app^d in his place at Middletown. [Subsequently Hay added in the margin: "It seems on investigation that Blair did not assign any such reason for his action; but alleged that the P.M. was removed (as he was appointed) at the request of Gen. Cameron."] Wayne says the President will be reelected *if* he turns Blair out of the Cabinet, but with that dead weight we can't carry Pennsylvania. He says Chase is at work night and day, laying pipe. Bowen tells me that Chase sent for Tilton and manipulated him "all a summer's day" to get his influence in the *Independent* for him. But Tilton, vain and shallow as he is, was disgusted, and went home and wrote a strong Lincoln article.

DeFrees gives some amusing incidents of his energetic electioneering.

I sat by Gen. Spinner today at dinner. He says Fernando Wood sought an interview with the Secretary of the Treasury today and talked with him in private. The Secretary says he gave in his adhesion and announced his intention of supporting the Administration in all its war measures—"And the Secretary sucked it all in," added the General.

Sunset Cox, it is said, is also now on the war path, and all the foul birds that have [been] croaking treason all the summer, are flapping their unclean wings about holy places and trying to roost under the National Ægis.

[*December 9, 1863.*] The exciting canvass for Speaker closed on Saturday night, 5th December, by Washburne withdrawing and Colfax being nominated by acclamation. All day Sunday there was great excitement about Etheridge's course of action. He seemed at the close to grow nervous and shaky, to lose the defiant air with which he had started out, and to assume a complaining and injured tone—saying he was only obeying the law—he did not see the reason why the Republicans should be so vindictive against him.

The President sent for Colfax. I went for him and as we were riding up from the National, I referred to the attempts which were making to identify him with the Chase interest. He characterized them as unjust and unfounded and said that with as much justice Washburne could be called the Grant candidate. Lovejoy was in my room a good part of Sunday morning in his finest vein. He avows the deepest faith in A.L. and the firmest adherence, though there is nothing subservient about it. . . . Lovejoy says he is going in, and is going to vote, and if it comes to a question of muscle he can whip Etheridge.

Monday morning, 7ᵗʰ, we went up expecting a taste of a scrimmage but were disappointed. Etheridge was very quiet and reasonable. He left off a large number of names but entertained the motion to put them on the rolls when it was made, contrary to the protest of J. C. Allen of Illinois. Everything went on properly then. The vote was taken showing 20 majority on the side of the Government, Odell and Stuart and Morrison and a few others of whom better things were expected voting wrong. When this was over Washburne nominated Colfax for Speaker and a round of applause burst from the galleries. Pendleton nominated Cox and a shower of hisses came from the critics above. A singular contrast with the voices of the celestials a few years ago. Colfax was elected & made a neat speech, & we went home.

On Tuesday, 8ᵗʰ, the House organized and the joint committees waited on the President, but Usher had changed the rhetoric of his paragraph in the Message, spoiled eight pages of matter & forced the Message over till the next day.

Wednesday we went up with the document and it was read. We watched the effect with great anxiety.

Whatever may be the results or the verdict of history the immediate effect of this paper is something wonderful. I never have seen such an effect produced by a public document. Men acted as if the millennium had come. Chandler was delighted, Sumner was beaming, while at the other political pole Dixon & Reverdy Johnson said it was highly satisfactory. Forney said, "We only wanted a leader to speak the bold word. It is done and all can follow. I shall speak in my two papers tomorrow in a way to make these Presidential aspirants squirm." Henry Wilson came to me and, laying his broad palms on my shoulders, said, "The President has struck another great blow. Tell him for me, 'God bless him.'"

In the House the effect was the same. Boutwell was looking over it quietly and saying, "It is a very able and shrewd paper. It has great points of popularity: & it is right." Lovejoy seemed to see on the mountains the feet of one bringing good tidings. He said it was glorious. "I shall live," he said, "to see slavery ended in America." Garfield says, quietly, as he says things, "The President has struck a great blow for the country and himself." Kellogg of Michigan was superlatively enthusiastic. He said, "The President is the only man. He is the great man of the century. There is none like him in the world. He sees more widely and more clearly than anybody."

Judd was then watching with his glittering eyes the effect of his great leader's word. He was satisfied with the look of things. Said Lovejoy, "Some of Lincoln's friends disagreed with him for saying, 'A house divided, &c.'" "I did," said Judd. "I told him if we had seen the speech we would have cut that out." "Would you?" said Lincoln. "In five years he is vindicated."

Henry T. Blow said, "God bless Old Abe. I am one of the Radicals who have always believed in the President." He went on to talk with me about the feeling of the Missouri Radicals. That they must be reconciled to the President, that they are natural allies, that they have nowhere to go out of the Republican party, that a little proper treatment would heal all trouble as already a better feeling is developing. He thinks the promotion of Osterhaus would have a good effect.

Horace Greeley went so far as to say it was "devilish good!"

All day the tide of congratulation ran on. Many called to pay their personal respects. All seemed to be frankly enthusiastic. Gurley of Iowa came and spent several hours talking matters over. He says there are but two or three points that can prevent the renomination of Mr. Lincoln: Gen. Halleck, the Missouri business, Blair, may be the weapons which in the hands of the Radical and reckless German element, may succeed in packing a convention against him.

In the evening Judd, & Usher, and Nicolay and I were talking politics and blackguarding our friends in the Council Chamber. A great deal had been said about the folly of the Edwards-Bates letter, the Rockville Blair speech, &c., when the President came in. They at once opened on him and after some talk he settled down to give his ideas about the Blair business. He said:

"The Blairs have to an unusual degree the spirit of clan. Their family is a close corporation. Frank is their hope and pride. They have a way of going with a rush for anything they undertake: especially have Montgomery and the Old Gentleman. When this war first began they could think of nothing but Frémont: they expected everything from him and upon their earnest solicitation he was made a general and sent to Mo. I thought well of Frémont. Even now I think well of his impulses. I only think he is the prey of wicked and designing men and I think he has absolutely no military capacity. He went to Missouri the pet and protégé of the Blairs. At first they corresponded with him and with Frank who was with him, fully and confidently thinking his plans and his efforts wᵈ accomplish great things for the country. At last the tone of Frank's letters changed. It was a change from confidence to doubt and uncertainty. They were pervaded with a tone of sincere sorrow, and of fear that Frémont would fail. Montgomery showed them to me and we were both grieved at the prospect. Soon came the news that Frémont had issued his emancipation order and had set up a Bureau of Abolition, giving free papers, and occupying his time apparently with little else. At last, at my suggestion Montgomery Blair went to Missouri to look at and talk over matters. He went as the friend of Frémont. I sent him as Frémont's friend. He passed on the way Mrs. Frémont coming to see me. She sought an audience with me at midnight and taxed me so violently with many things that I had to exercise all the awkward tact I have to avoid quarrelling with her. She surprised me by asking why their enemy, Montgᵞ Blair, had been sent to Missouri. She more than once intimated that if Gen. Frémont should conclude to try conclusions with me he could set up for himself."

(Judd says "it is pretty clearly proven that Frémont had at that time concluded that the Union was definitely destroyed and that he should set up an independent Government as soon as he took Memphis and organized his army.")

"The next we heard was that Frémont had arrested Frank Blair and the rupture has since never been healed.

"During Frémont's time the *Missouri Democrat*, which had always been Blair's organ, was bought up by Frémont and turned against Frank Blair. This took away from Frank, after his final break with Frémont, the bulk of the strength which had always elected him. This left him ashore. To be elected in this state of things he must seek for votes outside of the Republican organization. He had pretty hard trimming and cutting to do this consistently. It is this necessity, as it appears to me, of finding some ground for Frank to stand on that accounts for the present somewhat anomalous position of the Blairs in politics."

Judd. "The opinion of people who read your Message today is that on that platform two of your ministers must walk the plank —Blair and Bates."

Lincoln. "Both of these men acquiesced in it without objection. The only member of the Cabinet who objected to it was Mr. Chase."

The Grand Council of the Union League met tonight and did nothing of moment.

The Officers of the Russian Fleet were entertained tonight by the Sec. of the Navy. They have vast absorbent powers and are fiendishly ugly. I grieve to say that Mme Lissovski is not an exception.

Dec. 10, 1863. Tonight the President, talking with Arnold and me, told a magnificent Western law story about a steam doctor's bill.

Joe Forrest came in while we were talking and gave some of the comments upon the Message. Dickey says it is a "damned cunning trick—a trap." Florence says it is "very ingenious: admirably calculated to deceive." The plainness and simplicity of the thing puzzles and confounds them. They are trying very hard to make a mystery of it and roll up a devil in its folds.

Sumner speaks of the Message with great gratification. It satisfies

his idea of proper reconstruction without insisting on the adoption of his peculiar theories. The President repeated what he has often said before that there is no essential contest between loyal men on this subject if they consider it reasonably. The only question is who constitutes the State? When that is decided the solution of subsequent questions is easy. He says that he wrote in the Message originally that he considered the discussion as to whether a State has been at any time out of the Union as vain and profitless. We know that they were, we trust that they shall be in the Union. It does not greatly matter whether in the meantime they shall be considered to have been in or out. But he afterwards considered that the 4th Section, 4th Article of the Constitution empowers him to grant protection to States *in* the Union and it will not do ever to admit that these States have at any time been out. So he erased that sentence as possibly suggestive of evil. He preferred he said to stand firmly based on the Constitution rather [than] to work in the air.

Talking about the Missouri matter he said, "I know these Radical men have in them the stuff which must save the State and on which we must mainly rely. They are absolutely uncorrosive by the virus of secession. It cannot touch or taint them. While the Conservatives, in casting about for votes to carry through their plans, are tempted to affiliate with those whose record is not clear. If one side *must* be crushed out & the other cherished there could be no doubt which side we would choose as fuller of hope for the future. We would have to side with the Radicals.

"But just there is where their wrong begins. They insist that I shall hold and treat Governor Gamble and his supporters—men appointed by loyal people of Mo. as rep's of Mo. loyalty, and who have done their whole duty in the war faithfully & promptly—who when they have disagreed with me have been silent and kept about the good work—that I shall treat these men as Copperheads and enemies to the Govt. This is simply monstrous.

"I talked to these people in this way when they came to me this fall. I saw that their attack on Gamble was malicious. They moved against him by flank attacks from different sides of the same question. They accused him of enlisting rebel soldiers among the enrolled militia, and of exempting all the rebels and forcing Union men to do the duty: all this in the blindness of passion. I told them they were endangering the election of Senator; that I thought their duty was to elect Henderson and Gratz Brown: and nothing has happened in our politics which has pleased me more than that incident." [5]

He spoke of the new-born fury of some of these men; of Drake stumping against Rollins in '56 on the ground that R. was an abolitionist; of *ci-devant* rebels coming here in the Radical convention. Not that he objected to penitent rebels being radical; he was glad of it: but fair play; let not the pot make injurious reference to the black base of the kettle. He was in favor of short statutes of limitations.

In reply to a remark of Arnold's about the improved condition of things in Kentucky & the necessity of still greater improvement and the good disposition of the Kentucky Congressmen, the President said he had for a long time been aware that the Kentuckians were not regarding in good faith the Proclamation of Emancipation and the laws of Congress but were treating as slaves the escaped freedmen from Alabama & Mississippi: that this must be ended as soon as his hands grew a little less full.

Horace Greeley wrote a letter today to Nicolay commending the Message.

I went to the theatre & saw the pretty, lithe Webbs. The Muskovites were in the proscenium boxes and were disgustingly tight and demonstrative.

Forney said yesterday he should nominate the President today in his two papers. He has thought better of it. The leader in the *Chronicle* this morning ends amusingly. It looks as if the closing sentence had been emasculated. I think he probably corrected it cutting out all positive recommendation, after it was set up.

The Union League Convention seems to be going on right. They reelected their present officers today, who are generally Lincoln men.

Gen. Agnew today reports that numbers of men are coming to

[5] Both were elected Senators.

him to take the oath prescribed in the Proclamation of Amnesty.
A very rapid working of the machine.

Dec. 11, 1863. Hawkins Taylor began again this morning on his
unending theme, the Missouri business. He says there is an industrious effort making to combine and solidify the whole German vote against the President on those questions—Halleck, Blair,
Bates.

He says Chase has lost strength by not insisting on the removal of
all the Conservative office-holders in Missouri.

Dec. 12, 1863. Nicolay & I went to the [theatre to] see the Webb
girls.

I met at the theatre S. S. Cox, who was speaking of the statesmanship and success of Gov^n Seward, attributing much to the bonhommie and affability of his manners. He says Seward sent for him
the other day and asked him if he wanted to retain his place on
the Committee on Foreign Relations, & if he wished to designate
what gentlemen on the Democratic side should be associated with
him, promising to speak to Colfax for him. This frank kindliness
seemed to have won Cox over very much personally. Seward is
unquestionably gaining in popularity very fast. Mercier said of
him the other day, "Il est très sage." The diplomatic body have all
apparently stopped blackguarding and those who do not like have
been forced to respect.

Dec. 13, 1863. The President, speaking today about Missouri matters, said he had heard some things of Schofield which had very
much displeased him: that while Washburne was in Missouri he
saw or thought he saw that Schofield was working rather ener-
getically in the politics of the State, and that he approached Schofield and proposed that he should use his influence to harmonize
the conflicting elements so as to elect one of each wing, Gratz
Brown and Henderson. Schofield's reply was that he would not
consent to the election of Gratz Brown.

Again when Gratz Brown was about coming to Washington he
sent a friend to Schofield to say that he would not oppose his

confirmation if he (S.) would so far as his influence extended, agree to a convention of Missouri to make necessary alterations in her State constitution. Schofield's reply, as reported by Brown to the President, was that he would not consent to a State convention. These things, the President says, are obviously transcendent of his instructions and must not be permitted. He has sent for Schofield to come to Washington and explain these grave matters.

The President is inclined to put Rosecrans in Schofield's place and to give Gen. Curtis the Department of Kansas. But Halleck and Stanton stand in his way and he has to use the strong hand so often with those impracticable gentlemen, that he avoids it when he can.

These Kansas people are a queer lot. Delahay is here all alive with the idea that there is a Chase conspiracy about the President of which Pomeroy is one of the head devils, while Pomeroy swears by the President night & morning. Jim Lane told Champ. Vaughn he was for the President's action in the Schofield case & requested him to so tell Schofield. Yet he raised a deuce of a bobbery in the Union League convention about the same matter, still disclaiming any personal hostility to the President in the matter.

I talked with Ray this morning to try to get Reid removed from his functions as Correspondent Western Ass^d Press. He is so outrageously unfair to the President and so servilely devoted to Mr. Chase.

Tonight Hackett arrived and spent the evening with the President. The conversation at first took a professional turn, the Tycoon showing a very intimate knowledge of those plays of Shakespeare where Falstaff figures. He was particularly anxious to know why one of the best scenes in the play, that where Falstaff & Prince Hal alternately assume the character of the King, is omitted in the representation. Hackett says it is admirable to read but ineffective on stage, that there is generally nothing sufficiently distinctive about the actor who plays Henry to make an imitation striking.

Hackett plays with stuffing of india rubber; says Shakespeare refers to it when he says "How now, blown Jack!" Hackett is a very amusing and garrulous talker. He had some good reminiscences of Houston, Crockett (the former he admires, the latter he thinks a dull man), McCarty and Prentiss.

Sickles and Wadsworth were in the room part of the evening.

I visited Mrs. L. Her sister, Mrs. Gen. Helm, is with her, just arrived from Secessia.

[*December 19, 1863.*] Tuesday, December 15th, the President took Swett, Nicolay & me to Ford's with him to see Falstaff in Henry IV. Dixon came in after a while. Hackett was most admirable. The President criticized H.'s reading of a passage where Hackett said, "Mainly *thrust* at me," the President thinking it should read "Mainly thrust at *me.*" I told the Pres^t I tho't he was wrong, that "mainly" merely meant "strongly," "fiercely."

The Pres^t thinks the dying speech of Hotspur an unnatural and unworthy thing—as who does not?

Thursday the Pres^t went to see the Merry Wives & Friday to Bayard Taylor.

One morning this week I went to the State Department to get Gantt's pardon to send to him by Gen. Rice. Found Seward very busy over the complications arising from the *Chesapeake* piracy. He said Sumner had just come in & said with great glee, "This proves my position to be correct that England was wrong in conceding belligerency to these people." "Of course," said Seward, "but how the devil does that help the matter?" Sumner was delighted to have his theory vindicated even by such trouble.

19th, Saturday. Seward has just received another idiotic despatch from Cash Clay abusing the Emperor Napoleon like a pickpocket.

Sunday, Dec. 20. Gen. Buford's funeral. Nicolay & I spent an hour with Gardner leaving our shadows on his glass.

Wednesday, Dec. 23, 1863. I took to the Senate today the nomination of Schofield as Major General. The President had previously spoken to some of the Senators about it. He is anxious that Schofield sh^d be confirmed so as to arrange this Missouri matter properly. I told Sherman, Wilson, Harris and Doolittle. Senator Foote also agreed to do all he could to put the matter properly through. But on the nomination being read in executive session, Howard of Michigan objected to its consideration and it was postponed. Sherman and Doolittle tell me it will certainly go through when it is regularly taken up.

Lane came up to see the President about it, and told him this. Lane is very anxious to have the Kansas part of the plan at once carried out.

Morgan says that Gratz Brown gave to Sumner to present to the Senate the Radical protest against Schofield's confirmation, and that Sumner presented it today. The President sent for Sumner but he was not at his lodgings.

The President is very much disappointed at Brown. After three interviews with him he understood that Brown would not oppose the confirmation. It is rather a mean dodge to get Sumner to do it in his stead.

Brown and Henderson both agree on Rosecrans. The Pres^t thinks he will get on very well for the present, besides doing a good thing in the very sending.

General Banks writes the President a letter saying that Shipley and Duvant & Co. claim exclusive charge of the quasi-civil administration of affairs in Louisiana: that with proper management Louisiana can be made a free State in sixty days, with as little trouble as it would take to make and execute a dog law in Massachusetts. The President writes him in reply:

Ex. Man. Was^h *Dec. 24, 1863*

M. G. Banks

Yours of the 6th ins^t has been rec^d and fully considered. I deeply regret to have said or done anything that c^d give you pain or uneasiness. I have all the while intended you to be *master* as well in regard to reorganizing a State government for La., as in regard to the military matters of the Dep^t and hence my letters on reconstruction have been nearly, if not quite all addressed to you. My error has been that it did not occur to me that Go^v Shipley or any one else w^d set up a claim to act indepen^{ly} of you: & hence I said nothing expressly upon the point. Language has not been guarded at a p^t where no danger was thot of. I now tell you that in ev'y dispute with whomsoever you are master. Go^v Shi^y was app^d to *assist* the com^n of the Dep^t and not to thwart him or act $indepen^{dly}$ of him. Instructions have been given directly to him, merely to spare you detail labor, and not to supercede y^r authority. This, in its liability to be misconstrued, it now seems was an error in us. But it is past. I now distinctly tell you that you are master of all, and that I wish you to take the case as you find it, & give us a free State reorganization of La. in the shortest possible time. What I say here is to have a reasonable construction. I do not mean that you are to withdraw fr. Texas, or abandon any other military measure, that you may deem important. Nor do I mean that you are to throw away available work already done, for $reconstruct^n$, or that war is to be made upon Govr Shipley, or anyone else, unless it be found that they will not cooperate with you, in that case, & in all cases you are master while you remain in command of the Dep^t.

My thanks for yr. successful & valuable operations in Texas.

Yours as ever

A. LINCOLN

Gen. Banks, writing to the $Pres^t$ under the date N[ew] O[rleans], 16 Dec., answered the $Prest^s$ letter of the 5th more at length, saying he is impelled to make certain statements for the information of the $Pres^t$.

That he is only in partial command in N.O. "There are not less than *four* distinct gov^{ts} here, claiming and exercising original and independent powers, based upon instructions received directly fr. $Wash^n$, and recognizing no other authority than their own. They claim and exercise civil & military powers. Sometimes to the very serious injury of the public service. It cannot be necessary that such conflicting authority sh^d exist and it certainly cannot be exercised consistently with the interests of y^r administration. If it be necessary, I have nothing to say; but in that event the separate powers sh^d be distinctly defined: if not, the power of y^r Gov^t sh^d be concentrated somewhere so that somebody sh^d be responsible for the results. I have never asked increase of authority, but as y^r letter implies a responsibility in some matters, which

I did not understand were committed to me, I think it my duty to you personally and to your Government officially to represent my position and the difficulties I encounter in other relations than those referred to in my letter of the 6th ins^t which relates to the reconstruction of the State Gov^t in Louisiana only."

I. Relates incident of the civil authority seizing a vessel that he was loading for the Texas expedition, that he afterwards had to retake forcibly occasioning trouble and delay & a reprimand fr. the Court to officers executing his (B.'s) order.

II. The circumstances attending the recapture of the steamer *Leviathan*. The unpopularity of Military Power in the Courts. The Judge of the Court, Mr. Dowell & his financial operations— Dist. Atty crazy.

III. The Dis^t Court of one of the city districts, of which there are 6, recently decided that the Mil. Authorities h^d no power here agst judicial decree: that the Courts were established by the Mil^y Govr in pursuance of powers rec^d from Washⁿ and therefore no Mil^y order c^d stand agst judgment of these local Courts.

IV. City Courts assuming authority of all offences of soldiers or officers & abolition of the Courts.

V. Police in the hands of civil authorities & ill-disposed towards the army.

VI. The 6,000 families supported by charity still on our hands & the funds that supported them taken possession of by the Treasury Dep^t.

VII. Mil. Governor assumes the guaranty of the voters[?].

VIII. Gen. Halleck has already informed Gen. B. that his authority is supreme. But he does not wish to be wasting his time and strength in quarrelling with these people. Let powers of the different officers be more closely defined, or concentrated into single hands with direct responsibilities. Specially that what is called "the State Gov^t" be lifted out of its nets.

A year since he assumed command: the improvement so manifest as to give him consolation for suffering & labor.

Apologizes for trespassing, but hopes that the near approach of peace & the restoration of the country fr. its greatest peril will serve as an anodyne for all suffering & sorrow.

*   *   *   *

The President last night had a dream. He was in a party of plain people and as it became known who he was they began to comment on his appearance. One of them said, "He is a very common-looking man." The President replied, "Common looking people are the best in the world: that is the reason the Lord makes so many of them."

Waking, he remembered it, and told it as rather a neat thing.

December 24, 1863. Last night Nicolay went to Philadelphia to spend Christmas with Kelley. K. rather surprised us the other day at dinner by saying, in the course of a tirade against Blair, "This man calls himself the distinctive friend of Lincoln & says that the opposition to him is opp^n to the Pres^t. No man shall go from my district to Convention who is not pledged to Lincoln first, last & all the time. I honor and admire Mr. Chase; Lincoln out of the way, I should be proud to support him. But the Lord has given us this man to keep as long as we can."

O'Neill of Phila^{da} said something very similar to me the other day.

I dined today with S. S. Cox. He spoke of Greeley's foolish Chase explosion the other night at Wendell Phillip's Cooper Institute meeting & said Chase was working night and day. He has gotten nearly the whole strength of the New England States. If there is any effort made in Ohio, he can be beaten there. He has little strength in his own State.

I asked him whom his party would nominate.

C. "General McClellan. We will run McClellan. He is our best ticket. He lost some prestige by his Woodward letter. But it was necessary. He never could have gotten the nomination without it."

"You don't agree with the *Herald* on Grant?"

C. "Grant belongs to the Republicans. We can't take him after his letter to Washburne. But for that we might have taken him.

The Republicans won't take him either. They have got his influence and have no further use for him.

"If I were a soldier I should much prefer commanding the U.S. Army for life to four years in the Executive Mansion. I think Grant would."

C. "So would McClellan, I know."

I met him again tonight in the theatre. He says he is getting tired of Washington. He wants to spend a few years in Europe. He will go if McClellan is next Pres^t: thinks he will anyhow. Says it is delightful to be in the minority, you are not bored by your people for offices. "Glad you like it," quoth I. "We will try to keep you so."

Dec. 25, 1863. A lonesome sort of Christmas. I breakfasted, dined and supped alone. Went to the theatre & saw "Macbeth" alone. Came home and slept alone.

The President today got up a plan for extending to the people of the rebellious districts the practical benefits of his proclamation.[6] He is to send record books to various points to receive subscriptions to the oath, for which certificates will be given to the man taking the oath. He has also prepared a placard himself giving notice of the opening of the books and the nature of the oath required.

He sent the first of these books to Pierpoint to use in Virginia. The second he will probably send to Arkansas.

The Pres^t was greatly amused at Greeley's hasty Chase explosion and its elaborate explanation in the *Tribune*. He defended Govr Chase from Phillips' unjust attacks, saying that he thought Chase's banking system rested on a sound basis of principle, that is, causing the capital of the country to become interested in the sustaining of the national credit. That this was the principal financial measure of Mr. Chase in which he (L.) had taken an

---

6 Proclamation of Amnesty and Reconstruction, Dec. 8, 1863: full pardon and restoration of property, except slaves, for those who will subscribe to oath of allegiance. When in any southern state, Virginia excepted, not less than a number equal to 10% of votes cast in 1860 presidential election, take the oath and establish a state government, it will be recognized.

especial interest. Mr. C had frequently consulted him in regard to it. He had generally delegated to Mr. C. exclusive control of those matters falling within the purview of his dep^t. This matter he had shared in to some extent.

Usher said that there had been some symptoms of antagonism developed by the bankers of N.Y. against the proposed system of National Banks and that Mr. Hutton backed by Cisco & others would put the matter through.

The President read to us a paper he had written last summer during the days of bitterest opposition to the draft, arguing its constitutionality and expediency. He was a little curious to know what could have been the grounds taken by the Sup. Court of Pa. in deciding otherwise. The matter seemed so clear to him that he wondered how there could be any other side to it.

Dec. 28, 1863. The President yesterday went down the river to P^t Lookout to visit Gen. Marston. He returned about dusk. He says that Gen. M. represents a strong feeling of attachment to the Union or rather disgust for the rebellion existing among his prisoners—a good many of whom are Northern men & foreigners, the victims of conscription: from one-third to one-half ask that they may not be exchanged and about one half of this number desire to enter our Army, having, poor devils, nowhere else to go & nothing else to do. The bill just introduced in the Rebel Congress which will probably become a law, holding permanently all soldiers now in the army, will doubtless greatly increase the disaffection.

Peck was here this evening. The Indiana State Convention meets in Mass Assembly of the people on the 22nd of February to nominate delegates to the Union Convention for Presidential Selection. P. does not understand this clearly. He will cause the Illinois Convention to be called two days before, if it is thought advisable. Morton is a trickster & has been bitten himself by the White House Gadfly.

I rec^d tonight letters from Paige & Stickney asking me to come down to Florida and be their Representative in Congress.

Talked with the President about the matter of the reconstruction of Florida. He wants me to take one of his Oath books down to P^t Lookout and get the matter going there and after that he will appoint me a Commissioner to go to Florida and engineer the business there. By their meeting at St Augustine the other day there seems a prospect of getting the State under way early next spring. I will go down & form my plans after I get there, as to my own course.

Dec. 31. Spent the evening at Forney's. There was quite a gathering of political people early in the evening which thinned as the night wore on. Shortly after 11 o'clock Gen. Martindale issued a military order that no man should leave the room this year. Forney made several very ebrious little speeches. He talked a great deal about the President. The love of the people for him; his unconscious greatness; the vast power he wields and the vast opportunity afforded to a diseased ambition. "If the old man knew the loving thoughts and prayers that are rising for him tonight from millions of hearts, the unconditional confidence and the loyalty to his person that is felt throughout this land, he could do or be anything he wished. But thank God he is incapable of abusing this trust, and the freedom of our institutions render impossible a devotion to any man at variance with the spirit of our Government."

He said he was for Lincoln because he couldn't help it.

When any one asks, "who are you for [for] Pres^t?" he says, "Nobody. Not for Lincoln, he never asked me & don't want me. When I go to see him he asks me what is the last good joke I have heard.

"Lincoln is the most truly progressive man of the age, because he always moves in conjunction with propitious circumstances, not waiting to be dragged by the force of events or wasting strength in premature struggles with them."

Some Treasury people were there who winced with all the sensibility their copious libations had left them.

He made a dead set at me and demanded the Administration policy for the coming year. I said a half dozen words promising confidentially that the course of the Administration should be like Hooker's fight at Lookout Mountain, above the clouds. The mists of prejudice and passion and popular indecision seemed at last beneath our feet, and we might hope to finish the business in the higher sunshine.

We sung a good deal of John Brown and a little of other things.

I dined at Buhler's with Goover, Philp Eastman & Young. Goover is a most amusing blackguard with a queer history.

CHAPTER XII

January 1—January 9, 1864

DIARY

January 1, 1864. I did not attend the reception today, laboring all the morning under a great disgust.

I left Willard's yesterday and went to live at [the] Club today.

January 2, 1864. POINT LOOKOUT [1] The President and Secretary of War today (January 2, 1864) commissioned me to go down to Lookout Point and deliver to Gen. Marston the book of oaths and the accompanying blanks and explain to him the mode in which they are to be used. Gen. Butler was ordered by telegraph to meet me there and consult as to the manner of carrying out the President's plan for pardoning and enlisting the repentant rebels. I bore a letter for Gen. Butler's instruction.

I went on board a little tug at the 7th Street Wharf, and rattled and rustled through the ice to Alexandria where I got on board the *Clyde,* most palatial of steam tugs: fitted up with a very pretty cabin and berths heated by steam and altogether sybaritic in its appointments.

The day was bitterly cold and the wind was malignant on the Potomac. I shut myself up in my gorgeous little cabin and scribbled and read and slept all day. The Captain thought best to lay to for a while in the night, so we put in at Smith's Creek and arrived at Point Lookout in the early morning. (*3d.*) I went to the headquarters of the General accompanied by a young officer who asked my name & got it. I felt little interest in his patronymic & it is now gone into the oblivion of those ante-Agamemnona. It was so cold that nobody was stirring. A furry horse was crouching by

[1] The following account of a three-day trip to Point Lookout would appear to have been written after Hay's return, although the phrasing does not so indicate.

the wall. "Hello Billy! Cold. Ain't it?" said my companion. Billy was indignantly silent. We stumbled on, over the frozen ground, past the long line of cottages that line the beach built by the crazy proprietor of the land who hoped to make here a great watering place which would draw the beauty & fashion of the country away from Long Branch & make Newport a Ranz des Vaches.[2] We came up to the snug looking frame house, which had been the dwelling of the adventurous lunatic. A tall young man with enormous blond mustaches and a general up-too-early air about him, hove in sight and my guide & friend introduced me. "Yes, I have heard of you, Mr. Hale. I got a despatch from the General saying you would be here. When did you arrive Mr. Kay? Rather cold weather. Any ice on the River, Mr. Day?" All this in a voice like the rumbling of distant thunder, measured & severe, and with a manner of preternatural solemnity. "The general will soon be up, Mr. Hayes," my mild insinuations as to my agnomen having brought him that near to my christening, at last.

He disappeared and coming back, beckoned me out. I followed him across the little entry into a room opposite. There stood, in the attitude in which, if comfort ever were deified, the statue should be posed—parted coat-tails—a broad plenilunar base exposed to the grateful warmth of the pine wood-fire—a hearty Yankee gentleman, clean shaven—smug and rosy—to whom I was presented & who said laconically, "Sit there," pointing to a warm seat by a well-spread breakfast table. I had an appetite engendered by a day and night of river air and I ate breakfast, till the intelligent contraband who served us caught the infection and plied me with pork steaks till hunger cried quarter. The General told a good yarn on a contraband soldier who complained of a white man abusing him. "I doesn't objick to the pussonal cuffin', but he must speck de unicorn."

The General's flock are a queer lot. Dirty, ragged, yet jolly. Most of them are still rebellious but many are tired and ready to quit, while some are actuated by a fierce desire to get out of the prison and by going into our Army avenge the wrongs of their

---

2 Point Lookout, which had been converted into a camp for prisoners of war, is on the Maryland side of the Potomac where it empties into Chesapeake Bay.

forced service in the rebel ranks,

They are great traders. A stray onion—a lucky treasure-trove of a piece of coal—is a capital for extensive operations in Confederate trash. They sell and gamble away their names with utter recklessness. They have the easy carelessness of a punchman about their patronymics. They sell their names when drawn for a detail to work, a great prize in the monotonous life of every day. A small-pox patient sells his disease to a friend who thinks the path to Dixie easier from the hospital than the camp. The traffic in names on the morning of Gen. Butler's detail of 500 for exchange was as lively as Wall Street on days when Taurus climbs the zenith or the "Coal Hole" when gold is tumbling ten per cent an hour.

They live in a 30-acre lot fenced around by themselves. They put up the fence with great glee, saying "they would fence out the d—d Yankees & keep respectable."

Rather a pleasant place on a pleasant day is P^t Lookout. Today it was dreary and cold. I could not but think of the winter life of the sanguine lunatic who built the little village intended for the summer home of beauty & chivalry & destined for the malodorous abode of the diseases and the unfragrant belongings of a great hospital in busy war times.

My little boat got frightened at the blow that freshened in the evening and I sent her up to snooze the night away in Smith's Creek.

In the dusk of the evening Gen. Butler came clattering into the room where Marston & I were sitting, followed by a couple of aides. We had some hasty talk about business. He told me how he was administering the oath at Norfolk; how popular it was growing; children cried for it; how he hated the Jews; how heavily he laid his hand on them: "A nation that the Lord had been trying to make something of for three thousand years & had so far utterly failed." "King John knew how to deal with them—fried them in swine's fat."

After drinking cider we went down to the *Hudson City,* the General's flagship: his wife, niece and excessively pretty daughter, tall, statuesque & fair and named by a happy prophecy of the blonde beauty of her maturity, Blanche, were there at tea. I sent my little web-footed sulky word to get home as she could and sailed with the Butlers for Baltimore.

At night after the ladies had gone off to bed—they all said *retired* but I suppose it meant the same thing in the end—we began to talk about some queer matters. Butler had some odd stories about physical sympathies: he talked also about the Hebrew jurisprudence & showed a singular acquaintance with Biblical studies: his occasional references to anatomy & physiology evidently surprised the surgeon to whom he respectfully deferred from time to time. He talked till it grew late & we dispersed to bed. I slept on the guards, a pleasant bedroom but chilly, & listened, till I slept, to the cold & shuddering roar of the water under the wheels.

[*4th.*] At Baltimore we took a special car & came home. I sat with the Gen[1] all the way and talked with him about many matters: Richmond & its long immunity. He says he can take an army within thirty miles of Richmond without a skirmish & supply them there without any trouble: from that point the enemy can either be forced to fight in the open field south of the city or submit to be starved into surrender.

He was very severe on McClellan for his action about the New Orleans expedition. He says that before the exp[n] was resolved on by the Pres[t], McC. said it w[d] require 50,000 men: after it was resolved on he said 5,000 w[d] be enough. He said he did not like to attack McC. *nil nisi bonum,* &c., but he might have to exploit that matter sometime.

I told him of the night of October 21.[3]

He gave me some very dramatic incidents of his recent action in Fortress Monroe smoking out adventurers & confidence men, testing his detectives and matters of that sort. He makes more business in that sleepy little Department than anyone w[d] have dreamed was in it.

---

[3] There is no entry for October 21, 1861. The incident referred to is probably the one recorded under the date of Nov. 13, 1861, *ante,* pp. 34–35.

Copy of letter to Gen. Butler

EXECUTIVE MANSION.

WASHINGTON. *Jan. 2, 1863* [*1864*]

MAJOR GEN¹ BUTLER

The Secretary of War and myself have concluded to discharge of the prisoners at Point Lookout, the following classes:

1. Those who will take the oath prescribed in the Proclamation of Dec. 8ᵗʰ and by the consent of Gen. Marston will enlist in our service.
2. Those who will take the oath and be discharged and whose homes lie safely within our military lines.

I send by Mr. Hay this letter and a blank book, and some other blanks, the way of using which I propose for him to explain verbally, better than I can in writing.

Yours very truly,

A. LINCOLN

January 8, 1864. Nicolay and I visited tonight the Secretaries of the Interior and of the Treasury. Usher talked about the vacancy occasioned by the death of Caleb B. Smith. Said he understood Smith to be for him, when he was asking it for himself. Otto is an admirable man for the place but Usher does not want to lose him from the Department.

We found at Chase's a most amusing little toy, "The Plantation Breakdown." The Sec. and his daughter were busily engaged exhibiting it to some grave and reverend old fellows who are here at the meeting of the Society of Arts & Sciences. In the course of conversation the Secretary said to me, "It is singularly instructive to meet so often as we do in life and in history, instances of vaulting ambition, meanness and treachery failing after enormous exertions and integrity and honesty march straight in triumph to its purpose."

A noble sentiment, Mr. Secretary.

January 9, 1864. Cameron has written to the President that the entire Union force of the Pa. Legislature, House and Senate, have subscribed a request that the President will allow himself to be reelected, and that they intend visiting Washington to present it. He says, "I have kept my promise."

The indications all look that way. The loud Lincoln men, who are useful only as weather gauges to show the natural drift of things, are laboring hard to prove themselves the original friends of the Pres^t. Mark Delahay is gassing eternally about the Chase plot to ruin him and Lincoln. He says Pomeroy is to be at the head of the New Frémont party that is soon to be placed in commission. And much of this. On the other hand, Wayne MacVeagh who dined with me today says that the stragglers now seem to get ahead of each other in the nomination. The New Hampshire occurrence startled the Union League of Philad^a. They saw their thunder stolen from their own arsenals. They fear their own endorsement will be *passée* before long and are now casting about to get some arrangement for putting him in nomination at once.

Wayne told a very funny story about Forney & Cameron in conversation about politics on the train. Forney bibulously insisting that if he had beaten Cameron for the Senate there would have been no war.

CHAPTER XIII

January 13—March 24, 1864

DIARY

Jan. 13, 1864. I received today my comm^n as A.A.G. from the War Department & accepted it taking the oath of allegiance before Notary Callan.

Made a visit or two.

Went into the Tycoon's room and announced myself ready to start.

"Great good luck and God's blessing go with you, John."

"How long will you stay? One month or six months?"

NEW YORK, *Jan. 14.* Custom House politics.

Mrs. J. Wood in evening.

Jan. 15. On board the Fulton.

The embarcation of the 54th Boys—variety of complexions—red-heads—filing into their places on deck—singing, whistling, smoking and dancing—eating candy & chewing tobacco. Jolly little cuss, round, rosy & half white, singing

> Oh John Brown dey hung him
>> We're gwine to jine de Union Army
> Oh John Brown dey hung him
>> We're gwine Dixie's land.

> Way down by Jeemes' River
>> Old massa's grave is made
> And he or me is sure to fill it
>> When he meets de black Brigade.

> We're gwine to trabbel to de souf
>> To smack de rebels in de mouf.

Sung by a tall cadaverous fellow:

> Now in de Southern Section
> Dey rose a insurrection
> And so all de country is a flamin'
> But we're gwine to put 'em down
> With the sword of Ole John Brown
> Or come back by de happy land of Canaan.
>
> Oh Oh Oh
> Listen to me now
>
> De Fifty-fourth boys is a coming
> God Bless de whole Capoodle
> Of de fighting Yankee Doodle
> And save 'em in de happy land o' Canaan

At two o'clock the captain decides that he cannot sail for the fog and the passengers dispersed for a few hours furlough on shore.

Sunday, 17 Jan. The morning services. The Chaplain. His efforts to convince the young fellows on board that they were totally & utterly depraved without a singular good impulse or quality.

Wednesday, Jan. 20. 1864. HILTON HEAD, S.C. On arriving at Hilton Head yesterday afternoon, I found that Gen. Gillmore's Headquarters were now at Hilton Head. I went on shore, met Col. Smith & made an appointment to be presented to Gen. G. later. Took tea at the Port Royal House & was told by the gentlemanly proprietor that I had better forage on my friends for a bed. Was presented to the Gen[1] & delivered my letter to Gen. G. He seemed perplexed rather & evidently thought he was expected to undertake some immediate military operations to effect the occupation & reconstruction. He dwelt on the deficiency of transportation in the Dep[t] & the immobility of his force for purposes of land attack. He has only now after great efforts succeeded in mounting a reg[t] of infantry for cavalry service, &c., &c.

I told him it was not the President's intention to do anything to embarrass his military operations—that all I wished from him was an order directing me to go to Florida & open my books of record for the oathes, as preliminary to future proceedings.

He said we would speak farther of it. Meanwhile I will wait for my papers, delayed at New York.

Spent the evening with Col. Smith & Gen¹ Turner, & slept on a cot, my feet hanging like icicles over its lower end.

Major Dorman of Florida came in this morning. He is rather severe on the measures initiated by our friends the tax collectors to reconstruct the State. He says the people of the State, if they can be reached and protected, are ready to come back: but the movement must come from the people, and the State must be occupied by our troops. That he knows all about them & can do more than any one for this purpose: and asked me to take tea with him.

* * * *

Jan. 21. The General directed me to say to the President that he would cordially cooperate in carrying out the President's wishes.

I had considerable talk with the Gen¹ this evening. He spoke of his dispersing the Secesh convention at Frankfort, & [undecipherable]. He says, "I hope we will get enough voters out of the territory already in our hands in Florida: if not, we will occupy some more territory."

He seems frankly and sincerely anxious that the President's intentions shall be fully carried out.

Talking with Gen. Turner, he said, "An officer may plot and plan and figure forever, without result: what is needed is for a man to stand by & say 'Go in.'"

He says Dahlgren lost caste with the sailors for being seasick. He stood it as long as he could but had to yield to it or die.

After Ammen had made his reconnoissance, Dahlgren seemed struck with a new idea: said "We can go in any time, whenever we please, but must not go in without a plan: must get up plan first." This to Terry.

Turner says Dahlgren never seemed to have plan: accepted readily any suggestion made by Gen. G. Never suggested modification or change.

Jan. 22, 1864. Morning in the Photograph Gallery. Wrote a letter to Gen. Banks asking authority to open book at Key West. . . .

Jan. 31, Sunday. The 62^d Reg^t veterans reenlisting went down to the Atlantic this morning with all possible pomp & circumstance escorted by two brigades who formed on the two sides of the prin. street: between them came the veterans, bearing palmettoes, palm canes, mementoes of all sorts, and a few leading pets. Tattered & stained flags. The change in bearing—they go home men and soldiers. The music especially enlivening. Band played "Sweet Home." Marching home up the beach—the black Reg^t 8th U.S. The sand trodden level as a floor—Army shoes.

February 1st & 2nd. Evening of Feb. 1st Gen. Turner & I got on board a noisy little tug at wharf which took us to the *Ben Deford*. We went up stairs & drank a few whiskey punches & then to ship.

In the morning found ourselves off Stono—tide too low to let us over the bar—were rowed ashore—Gen. Terry, Turner & I.

Stopped at lower end of Folly for an ambulance—rode to Gen. Terry's Headquarters & took horses to ride to Lt House Inlet—crossed in a boat & walked up to Col. Davies. Col. D. full of a plan for capturing the Sumter Garrison.

We went in ambulance to Wagner. The sound of firing had been heard all the morning. It grew more frequent & Davies told us it was directed at a stranded blockade runner. Just as we got in sight of Wagner, a white smoke appeared in the clear air (the fog had lifted suddenly) and a sharp crack was heard. It seemed as if a celestial popcorn had been born in the ether. "There's a shell from Simkins," said Turner. We went on & there were more of them. As we got to Wagner, we got out & sent the ambulance to a place of safety under the walls. They were just making ready to discharge a great gun fr. Wagner. The Gen^s clapped hands to their ears. The gun was fired & the black globe went screaming close to the ground over the island, over the harbor, landing and bursting near the helpless blockade runner stranded half way from F^t Beauregard to Fort Moultrie. We walked up the beach. Heretofore we had from time to time seen little knots of men gathered to look at the fight, but now the beach was deserted—once in a while you w^d see a fellow crouching below a sandhill keeping a sharp lookout. We soon came to Batteries Seymour, Barton & Chatfield which were firing vigorously.

We mounted the parapet & took a good look at the steamer. She was already a good deal damaged by our shell amidships.

The enemies' fire was getting pretty warm. They had the range perfectly. Most of the shell burst in or over the works, but the men were so well protected that all the time we were there but 3 were hit and they were said to be imprudent. The men dodged & broke to cover at the flashing of the enemies' batteries. But the officers exposed themselves with perfect insouciance.

The shells had singular voices. Some screamed frightfully: some had a regular musical note like Chu-chu-weechu-weechu-*brrr* and each of the fragments a wicked little whistle of its own. Many struck in the black marshy mud behind us burying themselves & casting a malodorous shower into the air—others burrowed in the sand. One struck the face of Chatfield while I was standing on the parapet with a heavy thud—& a moment afterward threw a cloud of sand into the air. I often saw in the air a shell bursting—fierce jagged white lines darting out first like javelins—then the flowering of the awful bud into full bloom—all in the dead silence of the upper air—then the crack & the whistle of the fragments.

Col. Drayton took us to see the great 300-pounder Parrot. At a very little distance an ugly looking hole where a shell had just burst—beside the gun, traces in the sand hasty trampling & wagon wheels—dark stains soaking into the sand—a poor fellow had just had his leg taken off by a piece of a shell.

I saw them putting a crushed and mangled man into an ambulance. He was still & pale. The driver started off a merry trot. A captain said, "Dm you, drive that thing slower."

Two or three young fellows were playing with their horses in the parade. The horses joining in the fun threw riders over their heads & started off.

The ill-starred boat got badly pounded. Her machinery & works battered in. She seemed sinking before we left. The Navy were off nearly two miles but still made passable shooting. Their ricochet shots, however, were generally failures.

*   *   *   *

Came back to Terry's H^dquarters. He had sent a puzzling despatch to his brother. *Envoyer acheter du Ouiskie pour moi.* It had gone through. We took nips & went.

Feb. 4. Gen. Seymour today had a review of the corps which is to invade Florida. 6,000 men black & white, infantry, artillery & mounted infantry.

*   *   *   *

[JACKSONVILLE.] *Feb. 9, Tuesday.* Woke with a frowsy sense of having passed a bad night. Some neat lunatic proposes a wash and others with sleepy meekness accede. We wash & breakfast.

*   *   *   *

We came to Jacksonville, gay with flags & busy with shipping, at noon. I landed & found no Genl, no staff, no means of information. Ignorance the densest.

*   *   *   *

Feb. 10. Yesterday I had a number of copies of the Proclamation posted through the town. The few citizens gathered around— the lettered reading, the unlettered listening with something that looked like a ghost of interest.

Rode out with Reese and Place & Walker to place the works for defense of the town. One by the site of Wright's work. One small battery looking down the Panama Road and another, if necessary, by an old church (which must be removed) which will dominate the Panama Road and the crossing at the cemetery. We rode out beyond our furthest pickets unquestioned. The troops had evidently been foraging in the woods. We saw in one place the carcass of a cow & in another the head of a hog, neatly relieved, looking as if that much had just grown out of the ground. We rode on till

we came to a little settlement. Saw a newborn calf, heard the bay-
ing of dogs, the cackling of poultry: rode up to the house fragrant
with apple bloom. No soul near. Everything in order: as if that
instant occupied. Called: no one answered. They were probably
hidden in the bushes. Evident traces of some refinement in the
house: books on the centre table, &c. We rode away leaving the
strange solitude. Surrounded the marsh. Some beautiful specimens
of southern flora. Came out on cemetery road, but couldn't cross
the causeway as bridge was gone. Passed a Hebrew graveyard D.C.
5619, & coming home again saw a negro sergeant copying the
Proclamation.

At 2½ P.M. General Gillmore & Staff came clattering into the
cabin of the *Ben Deford*. They seemed greatly elated by the success of the expedition & were full of Col. Henry's achievement in
the capture of the artillery beyond Camp Finegan.

In the afternoon Lt Michir came in with his railroad train from
Baldwin. He had 4 mules for locomotive, who had a playful habit
of humping themselves & casting off their riders. He had a young
woman on board to whom he showed the usual courtesies of R.R.
conductors.

Feb. 11. By direction of Gen. G. I went to the prisoners confined
in the guardhouse, read to them the Proc^n & said I had come to
inform them "of this Executive act & extend to you its benefits. I
have in my possession a book for the record of oathes. I have certificates entitling those signing the book to the benefits of the act. If
you sign you will be released & allowed to return to your towns if
they are not, &c. If not, you will be sent north as prisoners of war,
for exchange. By signing it you will entitle yourselves to all y^r
rights as citizens of the U.S.

"It is a matter for y^r own choice. There is to be neither force nor
persuasion used in the matter. It is a matter that you must decide
for y^{r}selves.

"There has been some doubt expressed as to whether you will
be protected. I am authorized to promise that you will be. We
occupy present. Men enough.

"Inducement is peace & protection & reestablishment of y^r State Gov^t." When I had finished the little I had to say they crowded around me asking innumerable questions. I got away & had an office fixed up in the quartermaster's block & waited for my flock. They soon came, a dirty, dirty swarm of grey coats & filed into the room, escorted by a negro guard. Fate had done its worst for the poor devils. Even a nigger guard didn't seem to excite a feeling of resentment. They stood for a moment in awkward attitudes along the wall. I could not but think that the Provost had made a mistake & sent me his whole family, as Alsop said he thought 8 or 10 of them could be induced to take the oath of allegiance. But I soon found they had come up in good earnest to sign their names. They opened again in a chorus of questions which I answered as I could. At last a big good-natured fellow said, "There's questions enough. Let's take the oath." They all stood up in line & held up their hands while I read the oath. As I concluded, the negro sergeant came up, saluted, & said, "Dere's one dat didn't hole up his hand."

They began to sign—some still stuck and asked questions—some wrote good hands, but most bad. Nearly half made their mark.

The captured crew of the *St Mary's* came in. Said they were aliens & owed no allegiance, & I sent them suddenly back to the guardhouse.

I sent in the evening (in the *Cosmopolitan's* cutter) Judge Alsop over to the west bank of the river to see Sheriff Bowden, a very intelligent cracker who is said to be loyal.

Feb. 12. Alsop returns saying that Bowden will follow him at once & take the oath of allegiance.

Received orders from the General to go to St Augustine with despatches for Col. Osborne.

*   *   *   *

My first days' operations in Jacksonville were such as to give very great encouragement. I enrolled in all 60 names—some of them men of substance and influence. The fact that more than 50 per cent of the prisoners of war were eager to desert & get out of the service shows how the spirit of the common people is broken. Everybody seemed tired of the war. Peace on any terms was what they wanted. They have no care for the political questions involved. Most of them had not read the oath & when I insisted on their learning what it was they would say listlessly, "Yes, I guess I'll take it." Some of the more intelligent cursed their politicians & especially South Carolina, but most looked hopefully to the prospect of having a government to protect them after the anarchy of the few years past. There was little of what might be called loyalty. But what I build my hopes on is the evident weariness of the war & anxiety for peace.

The leading man of the town, Judge Burritt, is deeply exercised about the reconstruction. He has courted so long the triple-headed Cerberus, the World, the Flesh, & the Devil, that he finds it very hard to shift to a new object of exhaustive devotion. He hangs like Mahomet's coffin beyond loyalty & rebellion. Between the Gillmore who is here & the Finegan that may return he knows not how to choose. If he is true to Gillmore he may get cotton. If he is false to Finegan he may stretch hemp.

He has given dinner to Swift & tea to Dorman & has powerful allies at Headquarters. But Quincy, not knowing much law, has an awkward devotion that insists that a man must be loyal or disloyal. So over the head of the Judge hangs like a Damocles sabre my awful oath. I think he will, like the jugglers of Siva, conclude to swallow it.

*   *   *   *

[St. Augustine.] *Feb. 15.* Established my office in the Dist. Atty's office of the U.S. Court Room. After dinner swore a few persons.

*   *   *   *

Feb. 16. Dined at Mrs. Gardner's who has a beautiful avenue of orange trees.

Received a good many signatures. The Colonel recd orders to take the 24th Mass. to Jacksonville. Leaving Col. Otis here. I think I will go with them & get thence to Fernandina.

In the evening Mr. Oliveros came in & spent the shank thereof.

He is a shrewd old fellow without education or refinement but full of practical hard sense. He gave a short lecture on orange culture which is just now specially interesting to me. . . . He gave a most humorous account of the effect of muck manure on a farm near here, producing enormous turnips, which afterwards became the nursery of early water-melons that sold lucratively—"The trick of a Northern man," he added simply. Indeed I find among these people everywhere a quiet & almost unconscious admission of the superiority of the North. A Northern house—a Northern farm—a Northern apparatus of any kind.

We got him to talking politics & it seemed he w^d never stop. He had very little to say of recent affairs: his heart was in the past. If we asked him how anyone stood on the great questions he w^d say, "He is a good Whig," or "a bitter Democrat."

Feb. 17. Today in anticipation of the *Hunter's* going I gave up my business to Col. Otis.

Yesterday I met in the Plaza, Buff—with his friend Parcitti. He introduced him as "one of our strong Union men." Parcitti cringed & grinned, & shook my fist with snaky fingers. They have here a very uncommon breed of scoundrels. The greatest liars & most fawning stab-you-in-the-back rascals you could find unhung in any southern climate. Buff tells his constituents that any one signing my oath signs his death warrant: & fawns snakily on every one with Army buttons. He shall sign my oath himself or vote nevermore.

[JACKSONVILLE.] *Feb. 18. Thursday.* We arrived at Jacksonville about dusk. I went out to loaf & met some of the 24^sters whom I joined & we went to Col. Hartwell's quarters. There we learned that a military execution was about to take place. Four negroes had committed a rape on a woman in the neighborhood. After a while we heard the dead march sounding & a reg^t marching by. Going out I saw the 5th [Reg.?] in line in the open square. Went in. In the middle of the square a gallows was erected. It was light enough to define the gallows clearly against the sky. A cart drove in & after pulling & hauling & swearing was backed under the gallows: the poor devil stood upright apparently engrossed by the trivial details: wanted more rope &c. His sentence was read, the noose adjusted, he said a few words to the crowd & the cart beginning to move he jumped up & tried to break his neck but failed & gasped & jerked & struggled dreadfully. His stentorian breathing could have been heard over the square. A man jumped up to his shoulders & hung on him swinging. No effect. Another man got on: he still gasped. At last they raised him up & jerked him down hard: & he ceased struggling & after a while the crowd dispersed.

We foraged for supper.

Feb. 19. I got my baggage on board the *Price* & filled up the time to ten o'clock in tramping around. I passed by the hanging place & saw the poor devil still fluttering his rags in the wind—his head horribly oblique, his eyes staring wide, his mouth open & his blackened tongue protruding. A curious crowd of negroes, boys & crackers lingered around him, some who had been there last night taking a permanent station near him & detailing with intense relish to those less favored the hideous show of the night before.

Found the work by the old redoubt pretty well advanced and the one by the church staked off ready to begin.

Went to examine Record book and found a large no. of citizens had signed, some of position and influence.

Got on board & started down the river about ten. . . .

We got to the mouth of the Harbor & went to the *Ben Deford* & spent the afternoon. I boarded the *Haughton,* got Place to tea & gassed the evening.

[HILTON HEAD.] *Feb. 21.* Seymour has seemed very unsteady and queer since the beginning of this campaign. He has been subject to violent alternations of timidity & rashness, now declaring Florida loyalty was all bosh, now lauding it as the purest article extant, now insisting that Beauregard was in his front with the whole Confederacy & now asserting that he could whip all the rebels in Florida with a good brigade.

28th Feb. Sunday. The *Arago* came in this morning. The papers of the 23rd & 24th attack my coming here as a political trick.[1] Q.A.G.[2] is much troubled at it.

I had some talk with Turner. He thinks I had better stay. He gave me in full his idea of the present campaign. This is Gen. G.'s birthday. He called us all together & we drank a glass of wine with him.

*   *   *   *

[Fernandina.] *March 1.* I opened my book this morning & got a few more names. Some refused to sign, on the ground that they were not repentant rebels: or that it was in Stickney's office.

The *Dictator* came in this afternoon & reported to me for orders. I will start for Key West in the morning.

Henshaw sends a note asking me for *amour de Dieu* to send him some gin from Key West.

I am very sure that we cannot now get the President's 10th & that to alter the suffrage law for a bare tithe [3] would not give us the moral force we want. The people of the interior would be indignant against such a snap judgment taken by incomers & would be jealous & sullen.

Stickney said today, looking at States which have declared for Lincoln, "No power on earth can prevent his election."

[Fernandina.] *St. Patrick's Day.* I breakfasted on board the *Arago* like a fighting cock.

I read from Gen. Gillmore's letter-book that—

On Decem. 22, 1863, Gen. Halleck informs Gen G. that he is authorized by the Sec. of War to undertake any expedition he chooses with the force at his disposal.

Jan. 14. Gen G. writes to the Sec. of War that he intends to oc-

---

[1] The alleged political trick was by means of a costly military expedition, which had ended in defeat, to secure Florida delegates for Lincoln's renomination at the coming Baltimore Convention. "John Hay," p. 49.

[2] Gen. Gillmore.

[3] The proclamation of Dec. 8, 1863 had offered recognition to a state government only when the number of those taking the oath equalled one tenth of the number of those who had voted in the 1860 election.

cupy the west bank of the St John's & to revive trade and business in that region, & on the

15th Jan., 1864, he says the same thing to Gen. Halleck.

I arrived at H.H. Jan 19, 1864.

On the 22nd of January Halleck writes that as an outlet for cotton & a place for recruiting the expedition may pay. As a purely military measure he don't think much of it.

And on 31st Jan. Gen Gillmore writes to Halleck showing that the purposes of the expedition are:

1st To afford an opening for trade,
2nd To cut off largely enemies' supplies & railroad facilities,
3^d To obtain recruits,
4th To comply with wishes of the loyal citizens & enable them
    under protection to organize the State Gov^t.

It is this last expression, an evident afterthought, added after the rest was planned, which Gen. Halleck has used so much to the disadvantage of the expedition, of Gen. Gillmore, the President and myself.

I spoke to the General about it: he said he added that clause to show Gen. Halleck that the expedition w^d incidentally favor the reconstruction of the State, and w^d thereby advance the cause which the Pres^t has at heart.

I could not but be struck with the honor and loyalty and soldierly candor at the bottom of a blunder so great, as that of supposing that a cause w^d find favor in Gen. Halleck's eyes, because it advanced the cause which the Pres^t has at heart.

[WASHINGTON.] *March 24. 1864.* I arrived at Washington this morning finding Nicolay in bed at 7 o'clock in the morning. We talked over matters for a little while & I got some ideas of the situation from him.

After breakfast I talked with the President. There was no special necessity of presenting my papers as I found he thoroughly understood the state of affairs in Florida and did not seem in the least annoyed by the newspaper falsehoods about the matter. Gen. Halleck, I learn, has continually given out that the expedition was the

President's and not his (Halleck's). So Fox tells me. The President said he had not seen Gillmore's letters to Halleck but said he had learned from Stanton that they had nothing to bear out Halleck's assertion. I suppose Halleck is badly bilious about Grant. Grant, the Pres^t says, is Commander in Chief & Halleck is now nothing but a staff officer.[4] In fact, says the President, "when McClellan seemed incompetent to the work of handling an army & we sent for Halleck to take command he stipulated that it should be with the full power and responsibility of Commander in Chief. He ran it on that basis till Pope's defeat: but ever since that event, he has shrunk from responsibility wherever it was possible."

The Radicals are acting very ugly. Gratz Brown says they will beat Lincoln in any case. Peck says they have no voting strength.

March 25, 1864. Spent part of last evening talking with Secretary Chase. He seems deeply interested just now in negroes, believing it to be the best thing for the slave states & the surest safeguard against a rebel reaction after the war. I mentioned my plan for a convention in Florida which he heartily approved.

A bad day—rain & wind & weather. Nicolay goes to New York tonight.

Blair, talking about the Missouri muddle, spoke of the President's *laissez faire* policy with the Radicals there, as resembling the Irishman's with the skunk: "Let him alone and the d—d little thing will stink itself to death."

Hawkins Taylor says that Jim Lane will beat Carney on his election & that Pomeroy has ripped up his own bowels by his recent course.

---

[4] Congress by law, Feb. 29, 1864, revived the grade of Lieut.-General. Grant was ordered to report to Washington where, Mar. 10, he was placed in supreme command.

CHAPTER XIV

March 26—April 28, 1864

DIARY

March 26, 1864. Colonel Webster is here, very anxious to have the Marylanders in the Army allowed to come home and vote. He says the vote will be very close & without the soldiers, the State may be lost. Stanton says the troops must not leave on the eve of action.

Frank H. Underwood came in this morning to get a rec^n to Gillmore to allow him to saw-mill at Jacksonville.

Grant writes a despatch fr. H^d Q^r of the Army suggesting a very extensive spring campaign. That Shreveport being taken by Banks, he should then move against Mobile. Rosecrans & Steele should reinforce him in this as heavily as possible and if necessary Sherman add something to his force. That Gillmore should keep what he has in the South, holding all his available force mobilized to assist Grant when he begins to operate against Lee.

Seward says Wykoff is in town to sell out the *Herald* to the highest bidder. S. is bored by him but will not see him.[1]

March 27, 1864. I had a little talk with Stanton this morning. He says Gillmore has rather lost in popular favor recently but without any merited blame: that he had done all he promised. He is a little severe on the Navy.

He speaks very freely in favor of the President on the Pres^{tial} fight.

I went to church & was badly bored.

[1] Meaning, presumably, that Wykoff, as agent for James Gordon Bennett of the *N. Y. Herald,* was seeking some sort of promises from candidates for the nomination, and that Seward would not see him.

Saw General Grant: a quiet, self-possessed and strong-sense look-ing man. He pleased me by the prompt way in which he heard what I had to say about Gillmore & answered.

Dined with Sumner at the Hoopers. S. says that matters look well with France—that Drouyn de L'Huys sent for Dayton the other day & said Max. w^d not affiliate with the rebels.[2]
General Hunter was in my room today. He is very anxious to go into the field. They have offered him one or two administrative departments but he will not accept them. He wants to fight.

He spent a great while with Grant in the West. He has a very good opinion of him. He says he is a cool man: industrious, discreet and enterprising: able to hold his own plans and purposes and profit by the errors of the enemy.

March 30. I spent the early part of this evening at Mr. Welles: a very large infusion of fogy there; fine old fellows with nine stripes on the coat sleeve. All the Admirals and Commodores on the Wilkes court martial [3] were there: Mrs. General Grant also. I went from there to Forney's, where a party was assembled to meet For-rest. I got there late; after the toasting & speeching of the great Edwin was over, but heard some recitations from him & McCul-loch and from Dan Dougherty of Philadelphia who was by far the cleverest and brightest of the party: his Spring Garden reminis-cences were full of character. Dougherty toasted Sickles who re-sponded—first paying a most graceful compliment to Forrest as a representative of American genius (the old fellow surlily eyeing him, with his head abased like a Buffalo Bull). Then went off into the general issues of the war: saying by nature, habit & education he was a sympathizer with rebels & rebellions; that he had studied this thing at its beginning; that this was different from all other

[2] Maximillian, although accepting the crown of Mexico in 1863, did not reach Vera Cruz until May 28, 1864.
[3] Admiral Charles Wilkes, who as captain of the *San Jacinto* in Nov. 1861, had removed Mason and Slidell from the Trent, subsequently was assigned to blockade duty where he was promoted and then demoted on a technicality. He engaged in a long controversy with Secretary Welles, was court-martialled, suspended from the service, but in 1866 made a rear admiral on the retired list.

rebellions in the fact that it was a reaction against liberty, conspiracy of the strong vs. the weak, of privilege against freedom, of Aristocracy vs. Democracy. He concluded by expressing his belief that the nation would come out of the struggle stronger than ever before, purified & strengthened, with its only element of discord eliminated.

Once or twice during Sickles' careful little speech Forrest applauded. Forney was delighted, & clinched the thing by referring to it in a little speech—claiming Forrest as one of us.

March 31, 1864. A ball at the National: very neat little thing. I was congratulated by chuckled-headed boys who have been a week or two in the service, on being "one of us." Johnson & Kinney had a dirty little muss.

I adjourned to the Patent Office about 2 in the morning & saw the fag end of the dance there—clouds of dust & crowds of demi-monde & base mechanicals. A small policeman in constant hot water guarding the entrance to the hats, &c.

April 2, 1864. The Kentucky Congressmen in my room with Rousseau. Enter Jim Lane, Rousseau addressing him with Kentucky cordiality; after Jim goes Rousseau turns to his friends evidently pluming himself on the magnanimity which he displayed in speaking to James.

They talked on about men and things. Sumner was discussed: "Why," said Rousseau, "let him come out to Kentucky & see our different way of living & he w^d never be satisfied again with the mean and low life of New England. He w^d find such a noble, free-hearted hospitality thar that he c^d never bear his life at home again. There is nothing now to take him to Boston: so he always spends his vacations here. It w^d be different if he visited Kentucky once." Clay quietly extinguished the argument by saying, "He has been at Ky., and at my house, & here he scarcely knows me."

Sunday, April 3, 1864. Dined at Lamon's, & spent part of the evening with Lorings. The oldsters veering round to the heavy patriotic & the youngsters still vehemently secesh.

April 4, 1864. "Der Freischutz" at Grover's, & April 5th "Martha." The President and Mrs. Lincoln attended. On the 4th the President wrote a political letter to Hodges of Ky., that will be published in due time. The Radicals will attack him like Arabs on the strength of it.[4]

April 7, 1864. Tonight private theatricals at Maunsell B. Fields'. Seward, Chase, Stanton, were there, with their families. Major Hetzel, recently dismissed the service, played the Gens d'Armes in a Major's uniform.

DRAFT IN DIARY

TO C. G. HALPINE

April 13, [1864]

MY DEAR HALPINE

I thank you for y'' kind and most unjust letter. I did call at your lair on Bleecker Street and you were not at home—nor was M. la Generale. I am too old a soldier to pass through y'' camp without reporting.

I thank you for offering to set me right with the pensive public. But the game is not worth so bright a candle. The original lie in the *Herald* was dirty enough & the subsequent commentaries were more than usually nasty.[5] But the Tycoon never minded it in the least and as for me, at my age, the more abuse I get in the newspapers the better for me. I shall run for constable some day on the strength of my gory exploits in Florida.

I am stationed here for the present. I fear I shall not get away soon again. I have a great deal to do. It is the best work that I can do if I must stay here.

I am, yours—

DIARY

April 24, 1864. Today the President, loafing into my room, picked up a paper and read the Richmond *Examiner's* recent at-

---

[4] The text of the letter to A. G. Hodges is published in "Complete Works," II, 508–9. A review of Lincoln's changing policy on emancipation.

[5] Reference to criticism of Hay's Florida assignment. *Ante,* p. 165.

tack on Jeff. Davis. It amused him. "Why," said he, "The *Examiner* seems ab^t as fond of Jeff as the *World* is of me."

Ives has returned to the Navy Yard: was here this morning.

E. Lyulph Stanley, son of Lord Stanley, has been here for a week. I took him over to Arlington & showed him the African. He asked more questions than I ever dreamed of in similar circumstances. He applied a drastic suction to every contraband he met with & came back with brain and note-book crammed with instructive miscellany. He has been exhausting everybody the same way: till his coming is dreaded like that of the schoolmaster by his idle flock. He is a most intelligent gentleman—courteous & ready—a contrast to most Englishmen in his freedom from conceit & prejudice.

He leaves town today. I gave him my autograph book: our exchanged *cartes* "like two young shepherds very friendly & pastoral."

Tonight Gen. Burnside came up with me from Willard's to see the President. They talked about the opening campaign more than anything else. The despatch of Admiral Lee that had just been rec^d, containing the news of the fall of Plymouth, Burnside tho't bogus.

He gave some interesting reminiscences of the siege of Knoxville (Tad laughing enormously whenever he saw his father's eye twinkle, though not seeing clearly why).

Burnside & Sigel are the only ones in motion in accordance with the order for a general movement on the 23^d.

April 25, 1864. This morning Burnside came in with Foster, a fine handsome fellow who *looks* like a soldier at least, & seemed to think the Plymouth matter was more serious than he considered it last night.

If I can get away during this campaign, I think I will go either with Burnside or Gillmore.

[*April 28, 1864?*] On the evening of the 25th Fox, who had been frequently telegraphed by Butler to come down to F^t Monroe, determined to go & asked me to go with him. We started from the Navy Yard at 5:30, passing Willard's while Burnsides's splendid column was moving down 14th Street across the Long Bridge into Virginia. This is the finest looking & best appointed force I have ever yet seen. A little gorgeous & showy, reminding one of the early regiments who went shining down to Bull Run & the Peninsula as if to a picnic. The 3ᵈ N.J. Cavalry looked fine and yellow in their new cloaks & gold-braided breasts. The officers looked so superbly outlandish that it surprised one to hear them speaking in a Yankee accent, pure American, as Cash Clay calls it. The black regiments looked well & marched better than others: as in fact they always do.

We went down the river among the twilight "shadders" and got some fish and dined off shad roe and shad. Fox had brought with him some of his choice Oolong tea. He told us of a present that a Chinese grandee once made to the crew of a ship he was on of a chest apiece of their fine tea, and that the crew, not liking, sold for common tea & the officers drank, gradually growing to like it, until one day a tea-taster came in and, smelling the exquisite bouquet, exclaimed that they were drinking a tea which would impoverish a millionaire to use habitually.

We got to Fortress Monroe in the morning & Welles & I visited the *Iroquois,* Capᵗ Raymond Rodgers, while Fox went to see the General. Coming ashore we skirmished for some time about the walls of the Fortress before we could find the right entrance. We went in: saw Schaffer, and Kent who was loafing around with an air intensely *ennuyée,* and who said, "There are plenty of indications here which to a green hand wᵈ presage an early movement: but we blasé fellows don't seem to see it; we are familiar with large promise & scanty performance."

Joined Butler & Fox on the ramparts. Butler said he was walking there for the first time in several months, preferring to take necessary exercise on horseback. He spoke highly of the negro troops—especially of their walking powers: they start off & trot slouchingly without wasting any muscle in grace of action, he said, illustrating the shuffling step on the ramparts, bending his knees & dragging his feet over the oniony grass. He spoke of the delight with which Bob Ould ate the good dinners he got while at the fort—saying that one breakfast he got at Schaffer's w^d have cost $2,000 in Richmond.

At Gen. Butler's suggestion we went to the rip-raps. On the way to the boat we met Gens. Vogdes, Foster & Kautz, whose troops are at Yorktown, where is also Turner and Terry. The rip-rap is a flattened ellipse—a splendid piece of masonry so far, to which two more stories are to be added—one being already completed. The old wall, whose sinking caused the change & delay in the fort's construction, is still to be seen, the roughness & imperfect workmanship contrasting sharply with the finish & magnificence of the work of today. Butler is anxious to be allowed to fire at the work from Old Point to test its strength before the building goes any farther. He told me of a remarkable shot that was made from F^t Wool (rip-raps) at the rebel flagstaff, Sewall's Point.

We went back, joined by Admiral Lee & Capt Barnes, and started up to luncheon. Major Davis was good enough to give us somewhat to sustain life, a better luncheon than one c^d easily get in Washington. We called on *Madame la Generale,* a most courteous and kindly lady, and then loafed awaiting the issue of the conference of General, Secretary & Admiral. My own enterprise was a failure, owing to Gillmore's not having arrived and Turner having gone to Yorktown.

I had a good deal of talk with Schaffer, one of "the best staff a man was ever blessed with—Strong, Turner, Schaffer, & Weitzel" as Butler says. Schaffer is sanguine about the coming movement.[6] "We will fasten our teeth," he says "on Lee's line of supplies & he must leave his positions to come and beat us off," relying on Grant's not being the man to let that be done quietly.

We went up to Yorktown, accompanied by Admiral Lee: met there Capt Babcock & visited Baldy Smith who returned to the cabin of the *Baltimore* and passed several hours in conference.

Fox seemed troubled sorely by the prospect. He fears the details have not been sufficiently studied; that the forces are to bulge ahead and get badly handled; that they rely on help from the Navy

[6] Grant's spring campaign called for closing in on Lee and the capture of Richmond. This entry is made a week before the beginning of the Battle of the Wilderness.

in places where the Navy cannot possibly help, but rather "will be as useless as an elephant with his trunk unscrewed & his tusks unshipped"; that going up the James between the precipitous banks, a few riflemen on the banks will produce a panic that nothing can remedy. He seemed surprised that the Navy sh^d not have been informed of the intended movement until today, or that Grant sh^d have sanctioned, & concluded that G. must be letting the thing slide on without suggestion from him, to squelch it before it was consummated, or, relying upon his other plans, might have given this column up to the fate of a reconnaissance in force which will have accomplished its object if it diverts from *his* front a force large enough to destroy it.

We arrived off the Arsenal at 4½ on the 27th and, finding our way barred by a grounded schooner, we got upon the wharf & walked to the avenue. We ate shad & fired vainly at vagrant birds on the way up the river.

CHAPTER XV

April 28—June 6, 1864

28th April, 1864. Had considerable talk with the Pres^t this evening. He understands that the day arranged for Grant's movement is to be the 2nd prx.—Monday. Sherman has asked for a little more time—says that he can't fully come up to his part in the programme before the 5th. Sigel is at work on his.

The stories of Grant's quarreling with the Secretary of War are gratuitous lies. Grant quarrels with no one.

The Pres^t tells a queer story of Meigs. When McClellan lay at Harrison's landing,[1] Meigs came one night to the President & waked him up at Soldiers' Home to urge upon him the immediate flight of the Army from that point—the men to get away on transports & the *horses to be killed* as they c^d not be saved. "Thus often," says the President, "I who am not a specially brave man have had to sustain the sinking courage of these professional fighters in critical times.

"When it was proposed to station Halleck here in general command, he insisted, to use his own language, on the app^t of a General-in-Chief who sh^d be held responsible for results. We appointed him & all went well enough until after Pope's defeat,[2] when he broke down—nerve and pluck all gone—and has ever since evaded all possible responsibility—little more since that than a first-rate clerk."

Granville Moody was here this evening & told a good story ab^t Andy Johnson & his fearful excitement when Buell was proposing

[1] July–August, 1862.
[2] Second Battle of Bull Run, August 30, 1862.

to give up Nashville to the enemy. He found him walking up &
down the room supported by two friends. "Moody, I'm glad to see
you," he said. The 2 friends left & he & Moody were alone. "We're
sold, Moody, we're *sold*," fiercely reiterating. "He's a traitor,
Moody," and such. At last suddenly, "Pray! Moody!" And they
knelt down & prayed, Andy joining in the responses like a Methodist. After they had done he said, "Moody, I feel better. Moody
I'm not a Christian—no church,—but I believe in God, in the
Bible, all of it, Moody, but *I'll be damned if Nashville shall be
given up.*"

The Pres[t] was much amused by a story I told him of Gurowski.
The venomous old count says, "I *de*spise the anti-Lincoln Republicans. I say I go against Lincoln, for he is no fit for be President: di say di for one term (holding up one dirty finger), bimeby
di brat Lincoln, den di for two term (holding up two unclean
digits): di is cowards and *Ass!*"

A despatch just rec[d] from Cameron stating that the Harrisburgh
had elected Lincoln delegates to Baltimore properly instructed.

The President assents to my going to the field for this campaign
if I can be spared from here.

Jim Lane came in a few days ago with a telegram announcing
his complete victory over the Carney-Pomeroy men—the happiest
fellow out of jail. He read over the list of elected delegates to
Baltimore, himself & Wilder being among them, and added, "All
vindictive friends of the President." The adjective is especially
felicitous.

April 30, 1864. The President this morning read me his letter
to Gen. Grant, an admirable one, full of kindness & dignity at
once.[3] It must be very grateful to Grant on the eve of battle.

Fry's nom[n] that has been delayed for several days was signed
today. Fry has been removing provost marshals without consultation & has stirred up hot water in Pennsylvania. I warned

[3] Text in "Complete Works," II, 517. A letter of assurance and confidence before the
opening of the spring campaign.

him of the trouble he was causing & he said the Secretary had authorized him to make removals where he saw fit.

Fry now thinks that Butler and Lee are moving in the dark. That their destination will be changed at the last moment. He thought the movements down there were inexplicable on any other theory. He told Halleck so, on arriving here, at which he grinned, & said they had not got their orders yet.

Tonight came in Swett and Lamon anxious about their line of stocks. Well might they be!

The President came loafing in as it grew late and talked about the reception which his Hodges [4] letter has met with. He seemed rather gratified that the *Tribune* was in the main inspired by a kindly spirit in its criticism. He thought of & found & gave to me to decipher Greeley's letter to him of the 29th July, 1861. [5] This most remarkable letter still retains for me its wonderful interest as the most insane specimen of pusillanimity that I have ever read. When I had finished reading, Nicolay said, "That w^d be nuts to the *Herald*. Bennett w^d willingly give $10,000 for that." To which the Pres^t, tying the red tape round the package, answered, "I need $10,000 very much but he could not have it for many times that."

The President has been powerfully reminded, by General Grant's present movements and plans, of his (President's) old suggestion so constantly made and as constantly neglected, to Buell & Halleck, et al., to move at once upon the enemy's whole line so as to bring into action to our advantage our great superiority in numbers. Otherwise by interior lines & control of the interior railroad system the enemy can shift their men rapidly from one point to another as they may be required. In this concerted movement, however, great superiority of numbers must tell: as the enemy, however successful where he concentrates, must

4 Not in Hay Papers.
5 Text in N. & H., IV, 365-6. Extracts: "You are not considered a great man. . . . If the Union is irrevocably gone, an armistice . . . ought at once to be proposed. . . . If it is best for the country and for mankind that we make peace with the rebels at once and on their own terms, do not shrink even from that."

necessarily weaken other portions of his line and lose important positions. This idea of his own, the Pres[t] recognized with especial pleasure when Grant said it was his intention to make all the line useful—those not fighting could help the fighting. "Those not skinning can hold a leg," added his distinguished interlocutor.

It seems that Banks' unhappy Red River Expedition was undertaken at the order & under the plan of Gen. Sherman, who, having lived at Alexandria, had a nervous anxiety to repossess the country. Grant assented from his confidence in Sherman & Halleck fell into the plan.[6] Had not this wasteful enterprise been begun, Banks w[d] now be thundering at the gates of Mobile & withdrawing a considerable army from Sherman's front at Chattanooga.

Sherman has asked for an extension from the 2nd to the 5th to complete his preparations against Dalton. He says that Thomas' and Schofield's armies will be within one day's march of Dalton by tonight, and that McPherson will be on time.

A little after midnight as I was writing those last lines, the President came into the office laughing, with a volume of Hood's works in his hand, to show Nico and me the little caricature "An unfortunate Bee-ing," seemingly utterly unconscious that he with his short shirt hanging above his long legs & setting out behind like the tail feathers of an enormous ostrich was infinitely funnier than anything in the book he was laughing at. What a man it is! Occupied all day with matters of vast moment, deeply anxious about the fate of the greatest army of the world, with his own fame & future hanging on the events of the passing hour, he yet has such a wealth of simple bonhommie & good fellowship that he gets out of bed & perambulates the house in his shirt to find us that we may share with him the fun of one of poor Hood's queer little conceits.

May 5, 1864. Last evening Grant telegraphed that he was across the Rapidan, dating 1.30 P.M., & wished Butler to be so informed.

[6] N. & H., VIII, 285 ff. Seward wished to have Texas made secure on account of the French threat in Mexico. Halleck urged the occupation of northern Texas by way of the Red River. Banks was defeated, April 8. Grant was very impatient to have Banks close the campaign, thus freeing troops for Sherman's use in his drive on Atlanta.

Butler said the evening before, "I am ordered to move at 8 A.M. tomorrow & shall obey the order."

This evening while I was sitting in the President's room, came in Gen. Clay Smith & Ashley. They were talking about some matters that drifted into politics. Smith said nothing cᵈ beat Lincoln. Ashley did not give in his adhesion, but denounced the Frémont-Cleveland movement as foolish and ruinous: he said that Frémont was in New York personally soliciting signers to the *Cleveland Call;* [7] that he sent for him (A) & he wᵈ not go to see him; that Frémont was an ass, &c.; that when he was a candidate in '56 at first no one imagined he was going to be elected—he was nominated because they did not want to damage a better man by having him beaten, but that before the canvass ended they feared F. would be President. A. says he has a natural affinity for scoundrels. A. seems to be inclined to support the regular nominees, but I suppose he will make up his mind on that point after the Convention meets. I never see him now without thinking of *Prof. Ashley, the Great Biologizer.* A great fine animal nature—unabashed cheek and a cheery manner are good stock in trade for a mesmerist. The long-haired vegetarians always make a sad hash of it when they attempt it.

DIARY

May 9, 1864. Received today the first despatches from Grant.

The President thinks very highly of what Grant has done. He was talking about it today with me and said, "How near we have been to this thing before and failed. I believe if any other general had been at the head of that army it would have now been on this side of the Rapidan.[8] It is the dogged pertinacity of Grant that wins." It is said that Meade observed to Grant that the enemy seemed inclined to make a Kilkenny-cat fight of the affair, & Grant answered, "Our cat has the longest tail."

[7] A call for a political convention at Cleveland which met May 31 and nominated Frémont for President.

[8] Battle of the Wilderness in which Grant, though unable to claim a clear victory, did not, as Lee had expected, retreat across the Rapidan.

May 13, 1864. Early this morning Nesmith came in with Ingalls' spread-eagle despatch—which "Nez" in the worst possible taste published in the papers—Seward and the President in the room together reading telegrams. Nesmith, on hearing that Grant had said, "I will fight it out on this line if it takes all summer," told an awful backwoods story which is a miracle of pertinency.

Jim Lane came into my room this morning and said the President must now chiefly guard against assassination. I pooh-poohed him & said that while every prominent man was more or less exposed to the attacks of maniacs, no foresight could guard against them. He replied by saying that he had by his caution & vigilance prevented his own assassination when a reward of one hundred thousand dollars had been offered for his head. Bruce, who was sitting near, who has lost his contest in the House & who consequently is disposed to take rather cynical views of things, observed, when Lane had left, that he was probably anxious to convince the President that his life was very precious to *him* (L.)

May 14, 1864. Carney has written a very impertinent letter to the President in relation to troops for Kansas, which the President today in a very characteristic letter answers & nullifies.

Kelley was here this morning. He is much disgusted with the recent foolish and injurious action of Anna Dickinson. He says also that Miller McKim and other distinguished radical abolitionists are entirely satisfied that the President is (in Kelley's own words) "the wisest radical of them all," which accounts for Garrison's speech at the recent anniversary.

The President came in last night in his shirt & told us of the retirement of the enemy from his works at Spottsylvania & our pursuit. I complimented him on the amount of underpinning he still has left & he said he weighed 180 pds. Important if true.

Pomeroy has recently asked an audience of the President for the purpose of getting some offices. He is getting starved out during the last few months of dignified hostility and evidently wants to come down. He did not get any.[9]

---

[9] Senators Pomeroy and Lane of Kansas did not get on together. The President withheld patronage from Pomeroy. The latter, Feb., 1864, secretly had issued the famous Pomeroy Circular proposing Chase for the nomination.

I have not known the President so affected by a personal loss since the death of Baker, as by the death of General Wadsworth. While deeply regretting the loss of Sedgwick, he added, "Sedgwick's devotion and earnestness were professional. But no man has given himself up to the war with such self-sacrificing patriotism as Gen¹ Wadsworth. He went into the service not wishing or expecting great success or distinction in his military career & profoundly indifferent to popular applause, actuated only by a sense of duty which he neither evaded nor sought to evade." [10]

20 May, 1864. Last evening I spent at Charles Eames', where we went to drink tea with Mrs. Julia Ward Howe, who has been reading some very remarkable essays here during the past week. One on "Moral Trigonometry," whatever that may mean: one on the French revolution which she calls by the somewhat affected title "Equalities." This evening she read again; a practical discourse on Life, full of admirable promptings and suggestions. She is rather the most remarkable woman I have ever met: she carries the greatest head piece without getting top heavy.

I spent the latter part of the evening at Chase's to hear Teresa Carrino play the piano: a wonderful child—babyish, infantile, with a child's smile & a man's power over the keys. The company was rather noticeable for the absence of uniforms—my buttons showing in solitary splendor.

The company to hear Mrs. Howe was oddly composed: Lorings, Julians, Ashleys, Chase, Philp, &c.

21 May, 1864. Jim Lane brot up today & introduced Mr. Fishback, the new Senator from Arkansas—a rather decent looking person from the West. The Congressional delegation from there was lying about my office in an orphaned sort of way most of the morning, oppressively patronized by Stoddard who wants them to recommend him for marshal of the State.

Music on the grounds in the afternoon. Some good women &

---

[10] Gen. Wadsworth offered his services in 1861 as aide to Gen. McDowell. He became military governor of Washington in '62. In that year he had been an unsuccessful candidate against Seymour for gubernatorial nomination in New York.

some not so good. I passed the early part of the evening in Georgetown, & the latter part at the theatre, where I saw Banci's "Relief
of Lucknow," a very telling sensation play.

22 May, 1864. Grant has marched by the left flank down the
left bank of the Mattapony to Bowling Green & Lee has shifted his
position to meet him there. The town is full of silly rumors that
Lee is skedaddled & such trash.

Butler is turning out much as I thought he would—perfectly
useless & incapable for campaigning. He quarrels with Gillmore
& Smith & makes rather a nuisance of himself.

I said to the President today that I thought Butler was the only
man in the Army to whom power would be dangerous. McClellan
was too timid & vacillating to usurp. Grant was too sound and cool
headed & too unselfish; Banks also. Frémont would be dangerous
if he had more ability & energy.

"Yes," says the Ancient, "he is like Jim Jett's brother. Jim used
to say that his brother was the damndest scoundrel that ever lived,
but in the infinite mercy of Providence he was also the damndest
fool."

The Germans seem inclined to cut up rough, about the removal of Sigel from command in the Shenandoah. They are heap-
ing up wrath against themselves by their clannish impertinence in
politics.

24 May, 1864. I yesterday discovered that Doolittle and Randall
were urging the app^t of R.'s brother for the Tax Com^n in Fla.
I arranged it to have R. go to Louisiana & Smith to Fla. I feared
trouble in Fla. if Randall went down, from the legacy of the Reed
matter.

Doolittle is a fine instance of the result of industry, steadiness
of mind & common sense applied to politics. He attends rigorously
to his business: is a leading man in his party and yet finds a great
deal of time for literary culture and improvement. During the
last year he has become quite proficient in French. He thinks very
small beer of the "Dutch Revolt." Gurowski says if Lincoln is
nominated, he will take the stump.

I saved the life of a poor devil at F^t Monroe today: two innocent little sisters came down begging it: the Judge A.G. made a favorable report & we put him in jail.

Seward and Cameron spent the evening with the President. Seward has prepared the answer to Winter Davis' guerilla Res^n and it will go up tomorrow.[11] It seems perfectly satisfactory to the Pres^t & Nicolay. I think it will subject the Adm^n to a good deal of rancorous and foolish attack at this time. Davis' Res^n, though expressing the feelings of almost every American citizen, was introduced from the worst motives; still these motives can not be gracefully explained by our Government to France.

Despatches from Dana & Grant show them making fine time. Warren has been behaving finely at the crossing of the North Anna. Things look better than it was rumoured with Butler. Meigs & Barnard say he can hold his position with 10,000 men.

May 31, 1864. Despatches from Grant show the country apparently clear of the enemy to the Chickahominy. I hope the evil portent of that stream may not avail against our little Western General.

Stager telegraphs today that the Cleveland Convention, which has been rather a small affair every way, has adjourned after nominating Frémont and Cochrane.

Cochrane came down here some time ago & volunteered to the President the information that he was going up to Cleveland to try to forestall and break up that bolting institution.

June 1. Ashley was in my room this morning, talking to E.C. Ingersoll, & saying that he wrote to all his counties urging the endorsement of the President. An old preacher who opposed Lincoln's endorsement on the ground that he had not crushed the rebellion in three years was met & squelched by the suggestion that the Lord had not crushed the devil in a much longer time.[12]

[11] April 4, the House unanimously adopted a resolution expressing disapproval of the occupation of Mexico by France. At the White House this resolution appears to have been regarded as designed to embarrass the administration.

[12] The diary omits comment on the disappointing events of the next few days. Grant failed at Cold Harbor, June 3, in his frontal attack on Richmond.

June 5. For a day or two the House has been full of patriots on the way to Baltimore who wish to pay their respects & engrave on the expectant mind of the Tycoon, their images, in view of future contingencies. Among the genuine delegations have come some of the bogus & the irregular ones. Cuthbert Bullitt is here with Louisiana in his trousers pocket. He has passed thro' New York & has gotten considerably stampeded by the talk of the trading pettifoggers of politics there. He feels uneasy in his seat.

The South Carolina delegation came in yesterday. The Pres^t says, "Let them in." "They are a swindle," I said. "They won't swindle me," quoth the Tycoon. They filed in: a few sutlers, cotton-dealers, and negroes, presented a petition & retired.

Florida sends two delegations: neither will get in. Each attacks the other as unprincipled tricksters.

Lamon hurt himself badly yesterday by falling from his carriage on the pavement. I went to see him this morning, found him bruised, but plucky. Says he intends to go to Baltimore tomorrow. Says he feels inclined to go for Cameron for Vice Pres^t on personal grounds. Says he thinks Lincoln rather prefers Johnson or some War Democrat as calculated to give more strength to the ticket.

Nicolay started over today in company with Cameron.

Puleston dined with me at the Club. He says very many of the New Yorkers are talking Grant. Says Penn^a w^d prefer Hancock for Vice.

Whitely (reporter of *Herald*) says Chase told him the other day that he now for the first time in his life agreed with the N.Y. *Herald* in politics. It is thought that he may in the hope of obtaining preferment from Grant (if the popular will points to Grant) advocate him for Pres^t in opp^n to Lincoln. The *Post* corresp^n pledges him, however, to the Baltimore nominee.

Talking with Swett tonight, found he was talking Holt for Vice Pres^t. I suggested to him that two Kentuckians from adjoining States were rather crowding his ticket.

I spent part of the evening at Lorings where I met all there is left of that magnificent young fellow, Col. Bartlett.[13] Then went

---

[13] Col. Bartlett, severely wounded and losing a leg in 1862, was made a colonel; wounded again in Wilderness campaign.

down to Eames: saw Count Gurowski come into the parlor & go
growling out because I was there & then talked to the male Eames
who thinks I ought to write verses and get married. Then went
to [undecipherable] where were some heterogeneous foreigners,
musicians, singers & vagrom people & passed the rest of the evening pleasantly with music and potables.

June 6. House full of delegates: Steve Hurlbut here from the
West.

Got a letter from Nicolay at Baltimore—answered by mail &
telegraph. The President positively refuses to give even a confidential suggestion in regard to Vice Pres^t, platform or organization.

Everybody comes back from Convention tired but sober. Nicolay says it was a very quiet Convention. Little drinking—little
quarreling—an earnest intention to simply register the expressed
will of the people and go home. They were intolerant of speeches
—remorselessly coughed down the crack orators of the party.

TO J. G. NICOLAY

EXECUTIVE MANSION, WASHINGTON, *June 6, 1864.*

Yours of yesterday just received & read to the President. Swett
is unquestionably all right in regard to the President, but his
presentation of Col. Holt's name is entirely of his own suggestion.
He seemed not to have considered the bad effect of the contiguity
of Illinois & Kentucky on his proposed ticket until I called his
attention to it last night. He has never even mentioned Col. Holt's
name to the Pres^t for the place designated.

The President wishes not to interfere in the nomination even
by a confidential suggestion. He also declines suggesting anything
in regard to platform or the organization of the Convention. The
Convention must be guided in these matters by their own views
of justice & propriety.

Do not infer from what I have said above that the President
objects to Swett presenting Col. Holt's name. He is, and intends
to be absolutely impartial in the matter.

CHAPTER XVI

June 9—June 18, 1864

DIARY

[*June 17, 1864.*] Thursday night, June 9, the President came into my room just before bed time and said that Rosecrans had been sending despatches requesting that an officer of his staff might be sent to Washington to lay before the Pres^t matters of great importance in regard to a conspiracy to overthrow the government. He asked for this permission on account of the outrage committed upon Major Bond of his Staff who was some time ago court martialed for coming to Washington under General Rosecrans' orders. Recently Gov. Yates has joined in Rosecrans' request, asking that Sanderson shall be sent for. "If it is a matter of such overwhelming importance," said the President, "I don't think Sanderson is the proper person to whom to entrust it. I am inclined to think that the object of the General is to force me into a conflict with the Secretary of War and to make me overrule him in this matter. This at present I am not inclined to do. I have concluded to send you out there to talk it over with Rosecrans and to ascertain just what he has. I would like you to start tomorrow."

He gave me, in the morning before I was out of bed, this note to deliver to Rosecrans.

EXECUTIVE MANSION
WASHINGTON, *June 10, 1864.*

MAJOR GENERAL ROSECRANS

Major John Hay, the bearer, is one of my Private Secretaries, to whom please communicate in writing or verbally, anything you would think proper to say to me.

Yours truly,
A. LINCOLN

Friday afternoon, June 10, I left Washington and passed through Harrisburgh at midnight, Pittsburgh noon of the 11th, through Mingo, Cadiz, to Cincinnati, where I arrived on Sunday morning. I washed my face and went out. Saw a plain old church covered with ivy and congratulated myself that there I would find some decent people worshipping God *comme il faut:* and was horribly bored for my worldliness. After dinner, where I met a rascally looking Jew who was dining with a gorgeous lovette, and who insisted on knowing me & recognizing me from a picture in *Harper's Weekly*—I strolled out to make visits. The Andersons were not at home, except young Larz. I plunged into the bosom of a peaceful family and demanded to see the wife of a quiet gentleman on the ground that she was a young lady now travelling in Europe. He commiserated my wild and agitated demeanor and asked me to dinner.

I left Cincinnati Sunday evening & came to St. Louis about 11 o'clock Monday morning. The road is a very pleasant one, though rather slow. I sat and wrote rhymes in the same compartment with a brace of whiskey smugglers.

I reported to General Rosecrans immediately upon my arrival. After waiting some time in an anteroom, full of officers, among them Gen. Davidson, a young, nervous, active looking man, [and] Gen. Ewing whom I had known before [as] a man of great coolness and steadiness of judgement, Rosecrans came out and took me to his room. I presented my letter; he read it & nodded. "All right—got something to show you—too important to talk about—busy just now—this orderly business—keep me till 4 o'clock—dine with us at the Lindell—½ past five—then talk matter over at my room there. Hay, where were you born? How long have you been with the President? &c." And I went away. He is a fine, hearty, abrupt sort of talker, heavy-whiskered, blond, keen eyes, with light brows and lashes, head shunted forward a little, legs a little unsteady in walk.

We dined at the Lindell quietly at 6 o'clock, Rosecrans, Major Bond and I. The General was chatty and sociable; told some old Army stories; and drank very little wine. The dinner had nothing to tempt one out of frugality in diet, being up to the average badness of hotel dinners.

From the dining room I went to his private room. He issued

orders to his intelligent contraband to admit no one. He seated himself in a queer combination chair he had—which let you lounge or forced you to a rigid pose of business, as you desired—and offered me a cigar. "No? Long-necked fellows like you don't need them. Men of my temperament derive advantage from them as a sedative and as a preventive of corpulence." He puffed away & began to talk, in a loud easy tone at first, which he soon lowered, casting a glance over his shoulder and moving his chair nearer.

There is a secret conspiracy on foot against the Government, carried forward by a society called the Order of American Knights or, to use their initials, O.A.K. The head of the order, styled the high priest, is in the North, Vallandigham, and in the South, Sterling Price. Its objects are in the North, to exert an injurious effect upon public feeling, to resist the arrest of its members, to oppose the war in all possible ways: in the Border States to join with returned rebels and guerilla parties to plunder, murder, and persecute Union men, and to give to rebel invasion all possible information and timely aid. He said that in Missouri they had carefully investigated the matter by means of Secret Service men who had taken the oaths, and they had found that many recent massacres were directly chargeable to them: that the whole order was in a state of intense activity—that they numbered in Missouri 13,000 sworn members, in Illinois 140,000. In Ohio & Indiana almost as large numbers and in Kentucky a very large and formidable organization.

That the present objective point was the return and the protection of Vallandigham.[1] He intends, *on dit*, that the district convention in his district in Ohio shall elect him a delegate to the Chicago Convention. That he is to be elected and come over from Canada & take his seat, and if the Government should see fit to rearrest him, then his followers are to unite to resist the officers and protect him at all hazards.

A convocation of the order was held at Windsor, Canada, in the month of April under his personal supervision: to this came delegates from every part of the country. It is not definitely known what was done there.

[1] a fugitive in Canada.

The Grand Commander of the order for the State of Missouri is Hunt, the Belgian Consul whose exequator was recently revoked on account of his pleading his consular privilege against enrollment. For a long time Rosecrans had been informed that treasonable meetings and practices were carried on under the mask of this fellow's consular office. He set his spies to watching him. One of them gained Hunt's confidence by exhibiting to him forged credentials from Sterling Price and thus obtained from him copies of their books of ritual and organization. He also followed Hunt on a journey he made from St Louis and ascertained that he went directly to Windsor for a conference with Vallandigham. On such evidence as this he was arrested. The day I arrived in St Louis R. rec^d a despatch from the Sec. of War, directing him to release Hunt and give him up his papers. He answered protesting against the order and requesting that it be withheld until my arrival in Washington. R. says the order resulted from a lying despatch sent by one Johnston, a St Louis secessionist, a brother of Joe.

An important part of the plot in the Border States is the protection and encouragement and organization of rebels from Kirby Smith's & other armies coming North as spies or as pretended deserters. Some coming out of the bush, as the Missourians phrase it, with grass in their hair & the oath in their pocket—to plunder, steal, persecute and kill, and stand ready for insurrection and revolt.

Rosecrans has made some arrests and has alarmed the leaders in St Louis. Some of them fled at the first intimation of trouble: among them George Washington Wiley, &c.

This is the substance of what Rosecrans told me in the course of the evening.

Later, Sanderson came in and added some things to R.'s recital. He laid special stress on the disclosures made by one Lieutenant Rolla on the staff of Forrest, a woman who has served in disguise throughout the war. She has been attached to Forrest in all his campaigns except the last, being then a prisoner. She has served as chief ordinance officer and has made several trips to St Louis, coming in the dress of a woman and succeeding through the influence of the order in getting everything needed, purchased and sent over the lines. While recently a prisoner at Fort Pillow, a spy, a pretended

refugee, approached her and said that Forrest sent him to her to tell
her to keep up heart—that he would soon be there to rescue her:
that she disclosed this fact to the Com^{dt}, that he removed her before
the massacre took [place]. She now alleges that she has no wish to
return to the rebel service: pretends to be very grateful for the kindness shown her by Sanderson in her sickness and imprisonment: and
talks and writes pretty freely about the subject in hand. Sanderson
says he surprised her into an involuntary admission of her knowledge
of the order by giving her some of the signs, stroking his beard,
shading his eyes with his hand, &c. She asserts, as in fact all do, that
death is the penalty of disclosure, and it is this consideration more
than any other that causes Rosecrans' attempt to envelope the matter in such profound mystery.

I went over to Sanderson's office and he read to me his voluminous
report to Rosecrans in regard to the workings of the order and
showed me some few documents, among them a letter from Vallandigham to the Abbé McMastin, dated June 1, in which he at
first complains that "orders issued" are not properly executed—hints
at a scarcity of funds—expresses himself a little dubious as to his own
action in relation to the Chicago Convention—and concludes by referring to the "Household of Faith."

We went back and finished the evening at Rocecrans' rooms. I
said I would go back to Washington & lay the matter before the
President as it had been presented to me and I thought he would
look upon it as I did, as a matter of importance. I did not make any
suggestions: I did not even ask for a copy of Sanderson's report or
any of the papers in the case, 1. because my instructions placed me
in a purely receptive attitude & 2nd because I saw in both R. & S. a
disposition to insist on Sanderson's coming to Washington in person
to discuss the matter without the intervention of the Secretary of
War. Two or three motives influenced this, no doubt. Rosecrans is
bitterly hostile to Stanton: he is full of the idea that S. has wronged
him & is continually seeking opportunities to thwart and humiliate
him: then, Sand^{n} himself is rather proud of his work in ferreting out
this business and is not unwilling to come to Wash^{n} & impress the
Pres^{t} with the same sense: then they wish a programme for future
operations determined, & finally they want money for the Secret

Service fund.

Gen. Rosecrans wrote a letter to the President Monday night, which I took on Tuesday morning & started back to Washington.

R. talked about many things with perfect freedom and frankness. He told me about Thomas' conduct on being assigned command after Perryville and again after Chickamauga: that Thomas told him, R., that if R. were removed from command of the Army of the Cumberland, he did not wish to remain in it. That he (R.), persuaded him to accept the command.

He says further that Sherman informed him on Grant's authority that he, Grant, did not know why Rosecrans was removed. (In one sense this is true. Grant had nothing to do with the supercession of R. by himself. But he did object to having R. in the same department with him, saying he would not obey orders, & he has since repeated the same criticism upon him.)

I had bad luck coming back. I missed a day at Springfield, a connection at Harrisburgh, and one at Baltimore, leaving Philadelphia five minutes after the President and arriving at Washington almost as many hours behind him. I saw him at once and gave him the impressions I have recorded above. The situation of affairs had been a good deal changed in my transit, by the avatar of Vallandigham in Ohio.[2] The President seemed not over well pleased that Rosecrans had not sent all the necessary papers by me, reiterating his want of confidence in Sanderson, declining to be made a party to a quarrel between Stanton and Rosecrans, and stating in reply to Rosecrans' suggestion of the importance of the greatest secrecy, that a secret which had already been confided to Yates, Morton, Brough, Bramlette, & their respective circles of officers could scarcely be worth the keeping now. He treats the Northern section of the conspiracy as not especially worth regarding, holding it a mere political organization, with about as much of malice and as much of puerility as the Knights of the Golden Circle.

About Vallandigham himself, he says that the question for the Government to decide is whether it can afford to disregard the contempt of authority & breach of discipline displayed in Vall's un-

[2] *Post,* p. 193.

authorized return: for the rest, it cannot but result in benefit to the
Union cause to have so violent and indiscreet a man go to Chicago
as a firebrand to his own party. The President had some time ago
seriously thought of annulling the sentence of exile but had been
too much occupied to do it. Fernando Wood said to him on one
occasion that he could do nothing more politic than to bring Val.
back: in that case he could promise him two Democratic candidates for President this year. "These war democrats," said F.W.,
"are scoundrelly hypocrites: they want to oppose you & favor the
war at once which is nonsense. There are but two sides in this fight:
yours & mine—war & peace. You will succeed while the war lasts, I
expect, but we shall succeed when the war is over. I intende to keep
my record clear for the future."

The President said one thing in which I differ from him. He says,
"The opposition politicans are so blinded with rage seeing themselves unable to control the politics of the country that they may
be able to manage the Chicago Convention for some violent end, but
they cannot transfer the people, the honest though misguided
masses, to the same course." I said, "I thought the reverse to be true:
that the sharp managers would go to Chicago to try to do some clever
and prudent things such as nominate Grant without platform: but
that the bare-footed Democracy from the heads of the hollows, who
are now clearly for peace, would carry everything in the Convention
before them. As it was at Cleveland; the New York politicians who
came out to fugle for Grant could not get a hearing. They were as
a feather in the wind in the midst of that blast of German fanaticism.
I think my idea is sustained by the action of the Illinois Convention
which endorses Val. on his return [3] & pledges the party strength to
protect him. In the stress of this war politics have drifted out of the
hands of politicians & are now more than ever subject to genuine
popular currents."

The President said he would take the matter into consideration

[3] Vallandigham, June 14, in disguise returned from Canada by way of Detroit and
made his way back to Ohio where he was at once nominated delegate to the Democratic Convention in Chicago. He there and thereafter became a recurring embarrassment to the Democrats.

and would write tomorrow, the 18th, to Brough & Heintzelman about Val. and to Rosecrans at an early day.

June 18, 1864. The Illinois Copp[s] are troubled about the Val. apparition. Billy Morrison said to me this morning, "How much did you fellows give Fernandy Wood for importing that fellow?" Joe Forrest tells me that Allen is also uneasy about it.

I spent the evening at Seward's. He began by asking me if Val. had come back by consent of the Government. I said I thought it too marked an exercise of good sense to be ascribed to the Administration. I considered it a visible interposition of Divine Providence ag[st] the [harmonious?] Democracy. [" 'If I didn't know I'd tell you,' Seward once said to a man who asked him a question of State importance." The foregoing appears in the margin of the page at this point.] He said V.'s friends seem to be preparing for a war with the gov[t] on his account: that we probably will not oblige them until something more decisive comes from Grant or Sherman. That of course the Government must take cognizance of the matter in time. I told him his Belgian Consul Hunt had been arrested on account of complicity with the conspiracy which thus results, and that an order fr. Wash[n] had gone forward for his release. He seemed surprised at this; said Blondell had represented that Hunt had been arrested for pleading his consular privilege ag[st] the enrollment, and that Rosecrans had not denied that this was the case; but that if Hunt had been guilty of these treasonable practices he must be held and tried for them.

Later in the evening, talking to his dog, he said "Midge, what do you conclude about the Major? Did you ever notice that the dog is the only animal that gains his impressions of the persons he meets by studying their faces? The other day I was driving pretty rapidly; a large Newfoundland dog lay in the street, taking his *dolce far niente;* he had just time to get out of the way by a movement which was unpleasantly hurried. Instead of attacking the horses, or us who were in the carriage, he addressed himself to the driver, who was farther from him than either, as the cause of the trouble; defied him with a loud voice, and dared him to come down and have it out in a fair fight. No man could have acted with more discretion & spirit."

CHAPTER XVII

June 21—July 1, 1864

DIARY

June 21, 1864. Today the President started down the river with Fox to have a talk with Gen. Grant and Admiral Lee.

General Gillmore arrived at Willard's today. He is very much cut up by Butler's mean and ungenerous blow in ordering him to the rear in the midst of a campaign like this. Brooks says that Butler has quarreled with every general officer who had been thrown in contact with him. Wright, Terry, &c. Wright is especially severe upon him. Wright had been ordered by Butler, who was very far in the rear, to take a position which had been ascertained by reconnaissance to be enfiladed from both sides by the enemies' batteries. Wright sent a despatch to Butler announcing his readiness to move and adding this statement of fact. Butler replied, "I ordered you to fight: you answer with an argument." Wright appealed at once to Meade to relieve him from Butler's command. An insult like that from a man who never smelt powder to one who has been in half the battles of the war is almost incredible.

Butler's whole course down there seems marked by the two faults which seem inseparable from civilian generals (excepting those who have a natural aptitude for military affairs, which B. has not): too great rashness & too great timidity in constant alternation. His ignorance of war leads him constantly to require impossibilities from his subordinates and to fear impossibilities from the enemy.

June 23, 1864. The President arrived today from the front, sunburnt and fagged but still refreshed and cheered. He found the Army in fine health, good position and good spirits; Grant quietly confident: he says, quoting the Richmond papers, it may be a long

summer's day before he does his work but that he is as sure of doing
it as he is of anything in the world. Sheridan is now on a raid, the
purpose of which is to sever the connection at junction of the Lynch-
burg & Danville R.R.'s at Burk's, while the Army is swinging around
to the south of Petersburg and taken possession of the roads in that
direction.

Grant says he is not sufficiently acquainted with Hunter to say
with certainty whether it is possible to destroy him: but that he has
confidence in him that he will not be badly beaten. When McPherson or Sherman or Sheridan or Wilson is gone on any outside expedition he feels perfectly secure about them, knowing that while
they are liable to any of the ordinary mischances of war there is no
danger of their being whipped in any but a legitimate way.

Brooks says of Grant that he seems to arrive at his conclusions
without any intermediate reasoning process—giving his orders with
the greatest rapidity & with great detail. Uses the theoretical staff
officers very little.

June 24, 1864. Today a resolution came from the Senate asking
information about War and Treasury Orders concerning exporta-
tion of arms to Mexico. I did not like to act without consulting Seward, so took the paper to him, asking if it would be well to send
copies to Sec⁸ War & Treasury or not. He said, "Yes, send the Resolution to the Secretary of War, a copy to the Secretary of the Treasury,
asking reports from them, and then when the reports are in—

("Did you ever hear Webster's recipe for cooking a cod? He was
a great fisherman & fond of cod. Someone once asking him the best
way to prepare a cod for the table, he said, 'Denude your cod of his
scales, cut him open carefully, put him in a pot of cold water, heat
it until your fork can pass easily through the fish, take him out,
spread good fresh butter over him liberally, sprinkle salt on the
butter, pepper on the salt, and—send for George Ashmun and me.' ")

"When the reports are in let me see them."

He got up, stumped around the room enjoying his joke for awhile,
then said, "Our friends are very anxious to get into a war with
France, using this Mexican business for that purpose. They don't
consider that England and France would be together surely in that

event. France has the whiphand of England completely. England got out of the Mexican business into which she had been deceived by France, by virtue of our having nothing to do with it.[1] They have since been kept apart by good management, and our people are laboring to unite them again by making war on France. Worse than that, instead of doing something effective, if we must fight, they are for making mouths and shaking fists at France, warning & threatening and inducing her to prepare for our attack when it comes."

Carpenter, the artist, who is painting the picture of the "Reading the Proclamation" says that Seward protested earnestly against that act being taken as the central and crowning act of the Administration.[2] He says slavery was destroyed years ago: the formation of the Republican Party destroyed slavery; the anti-slavery acts of this administration are merely incidental. Their great work is the preservation of the Union, and in that, the saving of popular government for the world. The scene which should have been taken was the Cabinet Meeting in the Navy Department where it was resolved to relieve Fort Sumter. That was the significant act of the Administration: the act which determined the fact that Republican institutions were worth fighting for.

June 25, 1864. General Gillmore called to take leave of the President this morning: he goes to New York. He told me another incident of Butler's brutality. Col. Sewell, Gillmore's engineer officer, was engaged under Butler's order, building a little field work that a sergeant could have superintended as well. While Gillmore had an extensive line of works in process of construction. G. asked for Sewell to return. Butler replied, "If Gen. Gillmore feels himself incompetent to execute the duties devolving upon him, he can ask the assistance of Gen. Weitzel or Col. Comstock." Gillmore returned the despatch for "the correction of a mistake in it," & Butler quietly put it in his pocket.

[1] Oct. 31, 1861 England, Spain and France signed a convention with a view to joint intervention in Mexico. In April, 1862, England and Spain withdrew, suspecting the ulterior motives of Napoleon III.

[2] "Lincoln Reading the Emancipation Proclamation to the Cabinet" is now in the Capitol.

Fox, who has an old grudge against Gillmore for becoming popular by his operations on Morris Island instead of Dahlgren, abuses both Gillmore & Butler. Says B. is an elephant on the hands of the authorities. My only hope is that he will quarrel with Grant & be sent to F^t Monroe.

June 30, 1864. This morning, the President sent for me saying, "When does the Senate meet today?"

"Eleven o'clock."

"I wish you to be there when they meet. It is a big fish. Mr Chase has resigned & I have accepted his resignation. I thought I could not stand it any longer."

"Is it about the Field matter?" [3]

"Yes."

"Who is to be his successor?"

"Dave Tod. He is my friend, with a big head full of brains."

"Has he the skill and experience necessary for such a place?"

"He made a good Governor, and has made a fortune for himself. I am willing to trust him."

I arrived at the Senate door while the Chaplain was praying. When he ceased I delivered the message and went back to the Executive Mansion. In an hour the excitement rolled up our way. Mr Hooper came in, much excited. He feared the effect on our finances. He says it is not about the Field matter because Cisco has withdrawn his resignation. Ashmun looks at it coolly, does not think the bottom has fallen out. *Washburne does.* I never knew a man more stampeded. He says it is a great disaster: at this time, ruinous; this time of military unsuccess, financial weakness. Congressional hesitation on question of conscription & imminent famine in the West. Chittenden came over to say that there was a movement for a general resignation in the Department: that he would stay until Tod came and got things started, although intending for some time past to resign as soon as possible.

In the afternoon I talked over the matter with the President. He

---

[3] Chase had recommended Maunsell B. Field to succeed John J. Cisco as assistant treasurer of the United States, a position which, notwithstanding the title, ranked in importance above that of assistant secretary of the Treasury, the position which Field had held.

said that Chase was perfectly unyielding in this whole matter of Field's appointment: that Morgan objected so earnestly to Field that he could not appoint him without embarrassment & so told the secretary, requesting him to agree to the appointment of Gregory Blatchford or Hillhouse or some other good man that would not be obnoxious to the Senators. The Secretary still insisted, but added that possibly Mr Cisco would withdraw his resignation: the President answered that he could not appoint Mr Field but w^d wait Mr Cisco's action. Yesterday evening a letter came from the Secretary announcing first the intelligence that Mr Cisco had withdrawn his resignation. This was most welcome news to the President. He thought the whole matter was happily disposed of. Without waiting to read further he put the letters in his pocket & went at his other work. Several hours later, wishing to write a congratulatory word to the Secretary, he took the papers from his pocket, and found to his bitter disappointment the resignation of the Secretary. He made up his mind to accept it. It meant, "You have been acting very badly. Unless you say you are sorry, & ask me to stay & agree that I shall be absolute and that you shall have nothing, no matter how you beg for it, I will go." The President thought one or the other must resign. Mr Chase elected to do so.

The Finance Committee, to whom was referred the nomination of Tod, came down in a body to talk to the President. He says, "Fessenden was frightened, Conness was mad, Sherman thought we could not have gotten on together much longer anyhow, Cowan & Van Winkle did not seem to care anything about it." They not only protested against any change but objected to Tod as too little known and experienced for the place. The President told them that he had not much personal acquaintance with Tod; had nominated him on account of the high opinion he had formed of him while Governor of Ohio: but that the Senate had the duty & responsibility of considering & passing upon the question of fitness, in which they must be entirely untrammelled. He could not in justice to himself or Tod withdraw the nomination.

Mr Hooper talked with me for some time this afternoon. He says he feels very nervous & cut up about today's work. That he had been for some time of the opinion that Mr Chase did not see his way entirely clear to raising the money necessary; that this supplementary demand sent in at the close of the session, after everything had been granted which he had asked, looked like an intention to throw an anchor to windward in case he was refused, that he might say, "If you had given me what I asked, &c." Like McClellan on the Peninsula continually asking for reinforcements which did not exist: "I (H.) woke up this morning feeling a little vexed that Mr Chase had done this at this time, attempting to throw unfair responsibilities on Congress; but now this comes to relieve him of all responsibility in the most remarkable manner; I would not have lifted the responsibility from him for anything. It may be that Tod knows so little of the work before him that he will accept. It is an enormous work and the future is troubled. You have the great practical problem regularly recurring, to raise one hundred millions a month: I do not clearly see how it is to be done. This matter of finance is a very special one: in its larger sense entirely distinct from banking. The bankers generally attack Mr Chase. Chase has the faculty of using the knowledge and experience of others to the best advantage: that has sufficed him hitherto; but a point has been reached where he does not clearly see what comes next; and at this point the President allows him to step from under his load." Hooper did not seem to anticipate any fall in securities or rise in gold, but rather the contrary, thinking that gold must go down anyhow.

Fox is the only man who seems to be jolly over it. Fox & Rush Plumley, the two antipodes. Plumley said when he heard of it, "That is right—the judgments of God are sure." Fox says Morgan says a weight has been lifted from the financial heart.

In Congress and on the street there is a general feeling of depression and gloom. It looks like a piece of ratting on the part of Chase, to some; like a triumph of the Blairs, to other idiots; like a dangerous symptom of general decay and break-up of the Administration to most. I cannot help regarding the financial future with foreboding. For some months the feeling has grown upon me, and this incident convinces me, that Chase is anxious to stand from under the ruin.

Harrington is acting.[4] The little man was astounded this morning at his appointment. He is in a constant twitter, occasionally
subdued by a vague sense of dignity and responsibility suddenly
enveloping him. He rises to the level of the occasion by opening
his eyes like saucers, pursing his lips, & speaking in a basso profundo.

Tonight the aspect of affairs is changed by Tod's declining by
telegraph on account of bad health. I, thinking the Senate might
hold an executive session tonight & reject him, thought it well
to go up & inform them, to which the President assented. I told
Fessenden who told everybody and the comment was universal,
"Not such a fool as I thought he was." "Shows his sense."

Hooper thinks that this imbroglio will slough off from the Union
party a large and disastrous slice.

If the President has made a mistake (as I think he has) in allowing Chase to shirk his post of duty, Chase's leaving at this time is
little less than a crime.

July 1, 1864. I went in at half-past ten this morning to see the
President. He gave me a nomination. He said, "I have determined
to appoint Fessenden himself." I said, "Fessenden is in my room
waiting to see you." "Send him in & go at once to the Senate."

I delivered the message to the Senate & it was instantly confirmed,
the executive session not lasting more than a minute, & returned
to the office. There I met Abe Wakeman in high glee. He thought
it a great thing to do: that henceforward the fifty thousand Treasury
agents would be friends of the President instead of enemies. I
could not help pouring some cold water on his enthusiasm.

Going to the Senate as usual early this afternoon I saw several
who seemed very well pleased. At the House it was still better.
Washburne said, "This appointment of Fessenden is received with
great éclat. The only fear is that he will not accept. The general
feeling in Congress is in favor of Boutwell in case Fessenden declines. If the President cares for any expression from Congress a
very strong one could be sent up for Boutwell." Coe of New York

4 Acting Secretary of the Treasury.

was here about the Gold Bill which was repealed today. He visited
the President & was by him set upon Fessenden to aid in insisting
on his accepting the place. The President said so to Howe also &
to Diven & to Ashmun and others. A strong delegation of Congress
waited upon Fessenden today to add their request that he would
accept.

The President says, "It is very singular, considering that this appointment of F.'s is so popular when made, that no one ever mentioned his name to me for that place. Thinking over the matter
two or three points occurred to me. *First,* he knows the ropes
thoroughly: as Chairman of the Senate Committee on Finance he
knows as much of this special subject as Mr Chase. 2nd, he is a man
possessing a national reputation and the confidence of the country.
3^d, he is a radical—without the petulent and vicious fretfulness of
many radicals. On the other hand I considered the objections: the
Vice President & Sec. Treasury coming from the same small state
—though I thought little of that: then that Fessenden from the state
of his health is of rather a quick & irritable temper: but in this
respect he should be pleased with this incident; for, while for some
time he has been running in rather a pocket of bad luck—such as
the failure to renominate Mr Hamlin which makes possible a contest between him & the V.P., the most popular man in Maine for
the election which is now imminent, & the fact of his recent spat
in the Senate where Trumbell told him his ill-temper had left him
no friends—this thing has developed a sudden & very gratifying
manifestation of good feeling in his appointment, his instant confirmation, the earnest entreaties of every body that he may accept
& all that. It cannot but be very grateful to his feelings. This
morning he came into this room just as you left it. He sat down &
began to talk about other things. I could not help being amused by
seeing him sitting there so unconscious and you on your way to the
Capitol. He at last began to speak of this matter, rather supporting
McCulloch for Secretary. I answered, 'Mr Fessenden, I have nominated you for that place. Mr Hay has just taken the nomination to
the Senate.' 'But it hasn't reached there—you must withdraw it—
I can't accept.' 'If you decline,' I replied, 'you must do it in open

day, for I shall not recall the nomination.' We talked about it for some time and he went away less decided in his refusal. I hope from the long delay, that he is making up his mind to accept. If he would only consent to accept & stay here and help me for a little while, I think he would be in no hurry to go."

The President yesterday told me he had a plan for relieving us to a certain extent financially: for the Government to take into its own hands the whole cotton trade and buy all that [is] offered; take it to New York, sell for gold, & buy up its own greenbacks. Harrington talked somewhat the same doctrine to me last night.

I am glad the President has sloughed off that idea of colonization. I have always thought it a hideous & barbarous humbug & the thievery of Pomeroy and Kock have about converted him to the same belief.[5] Mitchell says Usher allows Pomeroy to have the records of the Chiriqui matters away from the Department to cook up his fraudulent accounts by. If so, Usher ought to be hamstrung.

The President says, what Chase ought to do is to help his successor through his installation, as he professed himself willing to do in his letter to me; go home without making any fight and wait for a good thing hereafter, such as a vacancy on the Supreme Bench or some such matter.

This evening I referred to Wilkeson's blackguardly misstatements in today's *Tribune* & asked if I might not prepare a true statement of facts to counteract the effects of these falsehoods. He answered, "Let 'em wriggle."

[5] In 1862 the President received authority to provide for the colonization of negroes in some tropical country. Chiriqui, in the northwestern corner of the state of Panama, was favored for one colony. Bernard Kock proposed a colony on the Ile A'Vache, Haiti, and from Lincoln secured a contract to colonize 5,000 negroes at $50 a head. Shortly thereafter Kock was disclosed as irresponsible and dishonest. A new contract was made under which Kock accompanied as governor about 500 negro emigrants. The Ile A'Vache colony became a scandal, Kock was expelled by the colonists, and the latter repatriated by the U. S. Govt. N. & H., VI, 356–66.

CHAPTER XVIII

July 4—July 14, 1864

DIARY

July 4, 1864. Today Congress adjourned at noon. I was in the House for a few minutes before the close. They read the Declaration of Independence there in spite of the protest of Sunset Cox that it was an insurrectionary document & would give aid & comfort to the rebellion.

In the President's room we were pretty busy signing & reporting bills. Sumner was in a state of intense anxiety about the Reconstruction Bill of Winter Davis.[1] Boutwell also expressed his fear that it would be pocketed. Chandler came in and asked if it was signed. "No." He said it would make a terrible record for us to fight if it were vetoed. The President talked to him a moment. He said, "Mr Chandler, this bill was placed before me a few minutes before Congress adjourns. It is a matter of too much importance to be swallowed in that way." "If it is vetoed it will damage us fearfully in the Northwest. It may not in Illinois; it will in Michigan and Ohio. The important point is that one prohibiting slavery in the reconstructed States."

Pres^t. "That is the point on which I doubt the authority of Congress to act."

Chandler. "It is no more than you have done yourself."

President. "I conceive that I may in an emergency do things on military grounds which cannot be done constitutionally by Congress."

Chandler. "Mr President I cannot controvert y^r position by argument, I can only say I deeply regret it."

[1] The Davis Bill would have enacted what was later accomplished by the Thirteenth Amendment, as well as undo Lincoln's program of reconstructing state governments under the proclamation of Dec. 8, 1863. The President pocketed the bill.

Exit Chandler.

The President continued, "I do not see how any of us now can deny and contradict all we have always said, that Congress has no constitutional power over slavery in the States." Mr Fessenden, who had just come into the room, said, "I agree with you there, Sir. I even had my doubts as to the constitutional efficacy of your own decree of emancipation, in such cases where it has not been carried into effect by the actual advance of the Army."

Pres^t. "This bill and this position of these gentlemen seems to me to make the fatal admission (in asserting that the insurrectionary States are no longer in the Union) that States whenever they please may of their own motion dissolve their connection with the Union. Now we cannot survive that admission, I am convinced. If that be true, I am not President, these gentlemen are not Congress. I have laboriously endeavored to avoid that question ever since it first began to be mooted & thus to avoid confusion and disturbance in our own counsels. It was to obviate this question that I earnestly favored the movement for an amendment to the Constitution abolishing slavery, which passed the Senate and failed in the House.[2] I thought it much better, if it were possible, to restore the Union without the necessity of a violent quarrel among its friends, as to whether certain States have been in or out of the Union during the war: a merely metaphysical question and one unnecessary to be forced into discussion."

Seward, Usher, and Fessenden seemed entirely in accord with this.

After we left the Capitol I said I did not think Chandler, man of the people and personally popular as he was, had any definite comprehension of popular currents and influence—that he was out of the way now especially—that I did not think people would bolt their ticket on a question of metaphysics.

The Pres^t answered, "If they choose to make a point upon this I do not doubt that they can do harm. They have never been friendly to me & I don't know that this will make any special dif-

[2] A Joint Resolution proposing an amendment to the Constitution to abolish slavery having passed the Senate, failed of the necessary two-thirds majority in the House, May 31, 1864.

ference as to that. At all events, I must keep some consciousness of being somewhere near right: I must keep some standard of principle fixed within myself."

Stanton talking about Harper's Ferry was thinking of sending for Alex. McCook to take command there.[3] I suggested Gillmore who is on a visit to his family at New York. Mr Seward concurred, thinking Gillmore the best man.

The President thinks with decent management we [can] destroy any enemy who crosses the Potomac. Stanton says he would be sure of that if he could rely entirely upon Hunter.

July 5, 1864. I went this morning to get places at the Canterbury. I found the lower boxes taken, but they told me at the office that G.C. S[mith] who had taken the one I wanted would probably not occupy it, as he generally sat on the stage. I went down to the National to see him about it, was directed to his room & went there alone. Mr. Goodloe, his nephew, opened the door & on my telling him what I wanted, he asked me into the room where were 3 Canterbury girls. We had some Bourbon whiskey which the sprightly ladies drank like little men. One of them, overcome by her emotions, retiring for ten minutes or so, and then came back to be joked by the envious others.

I dined with Malet, Kennedy, & Bob L. and went to the Canterbury in the evening. The room was hot and we took off our coats & sat comfortably in the box. Smith's was occupied but I saw him sitting in the flies, fanning the legs of a dancing girl. The show was the Bushwhackers of the Potomac, filthy & not funny except in its burlesque of Beau Hickman. There is a sentinel discovered pacing in front of the Capitol by moonlight. He is quickly shot by the heavy man, the Bushwhacker, who informs the audience that another Yankee has gone to his long home—that he (the B.) has a Union wife & "cherishes a lustful passion" for his sister: both these ladies coming on the stage opportunely, he kills the one & requests the other to fly with him. She objects and a miserable hangdog creature comes on the scene in the garb of a lieutenant who of

---

[3] Gen. Early crossed the Potomac, July 6, and threatened Washington.

course points his finger in defiance at the Bushwhacker who sneaks off saying he will have revenge. We then have a haunted hut & an apparition of Washington—a flash-ball—an indecent scene in which some african [effaced] strip Beau Hickman's trousers from him— a few bloody fights & a final apotheosis of everybody who has been killed in the play, while the bloody Bushwhacker of course dies miserably.

There was a pic-nic yesterday, in the President's grounds, of the negroes of Washington. They were very neatly & carefully dressed, very quietly & decently behaved: the young fellows buckishly & the young girls like ill-bred boarding school maids. There were many of both sexes, perfectly white and blue-eyed.

July 7, 1864. Today I went to the Attorney General to talk over the matter of Chamberlain's reappointment which has lapsed by the adjournment. The old judge was not in the best humor: in the first place, he considered his dignity infringed by the fact that neither Frasier nor Chamberlain had ever sent a line of report to him: second he did not think a court could have any show of juris- diction [over territory] then in the power of the army. He talked a long while and very earnestly in deprecation of the present over- riding of law and of judicial procedure in the military departments: the leasing of cotton plantations by Treasury agents & all that class of affairs. He seems in a decided and growing frame of discontent at the way things are going. The President says Judge Bates is per- suaded and tries to persuade him that the Baltimore Convention was thoroughly anti-Lincoln and though forced to nominate him did everything else in the interest of the opposition. The worthy old gentleman feels that he has fallen on evil times.

Friday, July 8, 1864. B.L. & I visited the Seward's last evening for a little while. The Secretary had the New York *Tribune* in his hands giving the reasons for Mr Chase's resignation: simply enough stated; that he wanted to appoint Mr Field, & the President desired him to select some other man on account of the political opposition to Mr Field. But he states disingenuously that he resigned because the President refused him an interview, thus showing a want of confidence in him. The Secretary went on to say that this statement was absurd, as nobody ever wanted to see the President who did not —that there was never a man so accessible to all sorts of proper and improper persons. He then continued his comments on the matter, very severely adverting to Chase's iron and unbending obstinacy in the matter of appointments and in matters strictly within the scope of the President's authority.

July 10, 1864. Sunday. A rather quiet day in spite of Wallace's defeat and the nearness of the enemy.[4] The usual flight of rumors but no special excitement.

I spent the evening—an hour at General Wright's, whose wife and daughter were waiting for their soldier and sure that the Capital would be safe when he got here, and an hour after at Malet's where were several Britons. When I got home I found Mr Whiton had been there, had stampeded the servants by leaving a message for me suggesting that Mr Lincoln should have a gunboat in readiness to leave in the morning as the enemy was in force within five miles. I went to bed.

A little after midnight R.T.L. came into my room & got into bed, saying Stanton had sent out for them all to come in [presumably from the Soldiers' Home].

July 11, 1864. The President concluded to desert his tormentors today & travel around the defenses. Gillmore arrived & reported. Wright & staff also came in.

At three o'clock P.M. the President came in bringing the news that the enemy's advance was at F^t Stevens on the 7th Street road. He was in the Fort when it was first attacked, standing upon the parapet. A soldier roughly ordered him to get down or he would have his head knocked off. I can see a couple of columns of smoke just north of the White House. It is thought to be Silver Spring in flames—I was at Mr. Blair's this evening; Fox says Gen. Wright tells him that Silver Spring is not burnt.

---

4 Gen. Lew Wallace was defeated by Gen. Early, July 9, at Monocacy Bridge only a few miles from the District line.

209

The President is in very good feather this evening. He seems not in the least concerned about the safety of Washington. With him the only concern seems to be whether we can bag or destroy this force in our front.

Part of Canby's troops are here.

Gillmore has been placed in command of them. Aleck McCook is in charge of the defences. There is a great plenty of Generals. Meigs has gone out for a spurt.

July 12, 1864. The President seemed in a pleasant and confident humor today. The news from Sherman, if confirmed, is good—that the enemy intend to desert Atlanta.[5]

The President again made the tour of the fortifications; was again under fire at F^t Stevens; a man was shot at his side.

The militia of the District are offering their services and the Department clerks are also enrolling themselves. In Judge Lewis' office 87 men enlisted and organized themselves in 15 minutes.

Last night the President's guard of Bucktails was sent to the front.

Mr Britton A. Hill called this evening, in great trepidation, and said he was apprehensive of a sudden attack on the Navy Yard.

July 13, 1864. The news this morning would seem to indicate that the enemy is retiring from every point.

The President thinks we should push our whole column right up the River Road & cut off as many as possible of the retreating raiders.

There seems to be no head about this whole affair. Halleck hates responsibility: hates to give orders. Wright, Gillmore & McCook must of course report to somebody & await somebody's orders which they don't get.

I rode out to the front this morning, R.T.L. and I. We visited Wright's Headquarters first. On the way out we found the road full of [a] block [of] men and women who had come out to see the fun & had been turned back by the hard-hearted guard.

---

[5] But they did not. Hood replaced Joseph E. Johnston in command of the Confederate army and took the offensive July 20, 22, and 28. The confederate losses were heavy but Hood did not evacuate Atlanta until Sept. 1.

At Crystal Spring we met young Capt O. W. Holmes, Wright's A.D.C. He joined us and we proceeded through the encampment, which was stretched in a loafer-like, gipsy style among the trees— the Artillery ready to move, the Infantry diffused through the brush—dirty, careless, soldierly in all else—every variety of style and manner among officers. We went to F^t Stevens & had a good view from the parapet of the battlefield of yesterday. Then went to McCook's headquarters and drank lager beer. The room was full of regulars from the bureaus at Washington.

We took a ride over to the Q^r Mrs Hdq^{rs} and lunched under the trees with General Rucker. Young Welles, who had been ordered to bury the rebel dead, got a squad of fifty contrabands under an old sapper & miner & we started for the field. Going down the road in advance of our squad we came to the toll gate & looking back saw them halted half way up the road. Sent an orderly back who returned with the information that they had stopped to speak to an old acquaintance. They came on & charged on a pile of picks and shovels. The Com^g Sapper then gave the order to those who were to carry the stretchers, "Chief mourners, to the rear as pall bearers. Get out y^r pocket hankerchers."

We soon came to the orchard through which our troops marched. The trees were riddled to pieces with musketry. It was here that our heavy loss took place.

We skirted around fences & country roads for an hour until I got tired of the fun and came home.

There were a few prisoners brought in to McCook: ragged & dirty but apparently hearty & well-fed of late. Most of them expressed themselves anxious to get out of the Army. Said they had been watching for a chance, &c., &c.

July 14, 1864. Nothing of importance yet. This evening as the President started to the Soldiers' Home I asked him *quid nunc* & he said, "Wright telegraphs that he thinks the enemy are all across the Potomac but that he has halted & sent out an infantry reconnoissance, for fear he might come across the rebels & catch some of them." The Chief is evidently disgusted.

CHAPTER XIX

August 25—*October* 13, 1864

TO J. G. NICOLAY

WARSAW ILLINOIS

Aug 25. 1864 [1]

MY DEAR NICO:

I arrived home yesterday, fagged. I have made an examination of something less than a hundred boarding schools and convents and we have at last, after a family council held last night, pretty well settled upon the Convent of the Visitation at St Louis.

I shall stay here until the term begins & go with Ellie there, and then come at once back to Washington early in September.

We are waiting with the greatest interest for the hatching of the big Peace Snakes at Chicago. There is throughout the country, I mean the rural districts, a good healthy Union feeling & an intention to succeed, in the military & the political contest, but everywhere in the towns, the Copperheads are exultant and our own people either growling & despondent or sneakingly apologetic. I found among my letters here, sent by you, one from Joe Medill, inconceivably impudent, in which he informs me that on the fourth

---

[1] There are no entries in the Hay diary, and no letters, aside from the report on the Greeley-Niagara Falls negotiation, from July 14 to August 25 when Hay wrote to Nicolay from Warsaw, Ill. where Hay was visiting his parents. The Greeley mission is fully covered in N. & H., IX, Chap. 8. This interval covers what was probably the darkest period of the war. Gen. Early's raid on Washington, which might easily have resulted in its capture if Early had pressed his initial advantage, was stopped July 11. However, three weeks later Early made a second raid in which he reached Chambersburg, Penn., which he burned. Grant's spring campaign to capture Richmond had been a failure. The Union losses in the Wilderness, Cold Harbor and Spotsylvania battles were appalling. Government loans were at 15%. Sherman, July 17, began his direct advance toward Atlanta which he reached but did not take July 24. The President issued a call for 500,000 volunteers, July 18, but volunteering was slow with the prospect that a draft would be applied in Sept. The Democratic convention was set for Aug. 29 in Chicago. There were several movements within the Republican ranks to ask Lincoln to withdraw as a candidate. The peace-at-any-price faction was stronger than at any previous time since '61.

of next March, thanks to Mr Lincoln's blunders & follies, we will be kicked out of the White House. The damned scoundrel needs a day's hanging. I won't answer his letter till I return & let you see it. Old Uncle Jesse is talking like an ass—says if the Chicago nominee is a good man, he don't know, &c., &c. He blackguards you & me—says we are too big for our breeches—a fault for which it seems to me either Nature or our tailors are to blame. After all your kindness to the old whelp & his cub of a son, he hates you because you have not done more. I believe he thinks the Ex. Mansion is somehow to blame because Bill married a harlot & Dick Oglesby is popular.

Land is getting up near the stars in price. It will take all I am worth to buy a tater-patch. I am after one or two small pieces in Hancock for reasonable prices; 20 to 30 dollars an acre. Logan paid $70,000 for a farm a short while ago, & everybody who has greenbacks is forcing them off like waste paper for land. I find in talking with well-informed people a sort of fear of Kansas property: as uncertain in future settlement & more than all, uncertain in weather. The ghost of famine haunts those speculations.

You were wrong in thinking either Milt. or Charlie Hay at all Copperish. They are as sound as they ever were. They of course are not quite clear about the currency, but who is?

Our people here want me to address the Union League. I believe I won't. The snakes would rattle about it a little & it w^d do no good. I lose my temper sometimes talking with growling Republicans. There is a diseased restlessness about men in these times that unfits them for the steady support of an administration. It seems as if there were appearing in the Republican party the elements of disorganization that destroyed the Whigs.

If the dumb cattle are not worthy of another term of Lincoln then let the will of God be done & the murrain of McClellan fall on them.

Yours truly

J.H.

[P.S.] My sister Mary is here & she & Charlie desire to be remembered.

WARSAW ILLINOIS.
Aug. 26, 1864

I this morning received Derby's circular with my interpolated title. Please send him the enclosed under your frank. He of course knows better.

It is reported here that Greeley, Raymond & the Ex. Com. are trying to run Lincoln off, having given up beat. Most of our people are talking like damned fools. My father on the contrary is the most sanguine man I have met. He says we will carry this State with a fair working majority. Some of the Dutch [Germans] are bit with the Frémont mania. But the returned soldiers are all for Lincoln, if they can be kept right till November.

The worst thing I have noticed is that prominent & wealthy Republicans who still continue all right in politics & go their length on the President, are getting distrustful of the issue and forcing off their greenbacks into land at fancy prices. One firm here have $80,000 in Gov^t bonds which they intend to keep, but they say, "if a Copperhead is elected in November, which is not impossible, we will lose it all by repudiation."

John T. Stuart is legging a little for Fillmore as the fogy candidate in the Convention which meets tomorrow. But I suppose they can't control the McClellan current. I wait the result with some interest—not very much, as I have scarcely a doubt as to what they will do. If the Cop^s do roll us over this fall, will it not make Kansas land a very unsafe speculation? I anticipate anarchy & disorganization of society if those devils get full control, especially in the Border States.

Has the appointment of Land Patent Secretary yet been made? Charlie Philbrick is perfectly steady now, I am told. I saw him when last in Springfield & he was straight as a string. If you could make it proper at y^r end of the line, I am very sure you could not get a man more thoroughly discreet & competent. He made a most favorable impression on me when I saw him—all of one evening. The subject was not mentioned by either of us. Stod. has been extensively advertising himself in the Western Press. His asininity which is kept a little dark under your shadow at Washington blooms & burgeons in the free air of the West.

If there were any reason for hoping for our national future, Gov^t securities w^d be the best possible investment. But it is the growing despondency that has driven lands so high that a poor man cannot buy.

TO J. G. NICOLAY

WARSAW ILLINOIS
September 7, 1864

I had hoped to be in Washington before this but have been unlucky in many things. I have not yet spent one single day in recreation but have been busy ever since I left New York. Have placed Helen at school and gotten back here; attended to some business of my father's which could not be postponed; spent all my money in railroad tickets and drawn a hundred more to get back & find myself at the end of my trip worse tired out than if I had staid at Washington. I am today quite sick. I had made an engagement with Charlie Philbrick to leave Springfield tomorrow night for Washington but am unable to keep it. Had a chill this morning. I have written to Charlie to go on without me.

If I am not in bed on Monday morning next, I will start for Washington. If I am, I cannot say when "I will arise & go (from) my Father—"

I have been struck more than ever this summer with the beauty of our river scenery. Charlie Hay & I had a plan for going to Nauvoo but failed for want of time. You will enjoy all that when you come. I have told my mother of your intended pilgrimage to the old haunts of the Mormons & she directs me to assure you of the pleasure with which she will welcome you when you come. You can certainly find no quieter place to write your romance this side of the Great Desert. There is absolutely no society here. You can pass a couple of months here entirely undisturbed by visitors. If I could come with you I could introduce you to all the pretty views and attractive bridle paths but if you come alone you could soon find them for yourself. I would give a great deal to pass a month here. But all this after the War.

The Republicans here are talking better and *sassier* since the nomination of McClellan.

DIARY

[WASHINGTON.] *September 23, 1864.* Senator Harlan thinks that Bennett's [2] support is so important, especially considered as to its bearing on the soldier vote, that it would pay to offer him a foreign mission for it, & so told me. Forney has also had a man talking to the cannie Scot who asked plumply, "Will I be a welcome visitor at the White House if I support Mr Lincoln?" What a horrible question for a man to be able to ask. I think he is too pitchy to touch. So thinks the Presd^t apparently: it is probable that Bennett will stay about as he is, thoroughly neutral, balancing carefully until the October elections, & will then declare for the side which he thinks will win. It is better in many respects to let him alone.

TO J. G. NICOLAY

EXECUTIVE MANSION,
WASHINGTON, September 24, 1864.

MY DEAR NICO.

Your despatch was just brought in. I took it to the President & he told me to tell you you had better loaf around the city a while longer. You need some rest & recreation & may as well take it in N.Y. as anywhere else. Besides you can't imagine how nasty the house is at present. You would get the "painter's cholic" in 24 hours if you came home now.

Politicians still unhealthily haunt us. Loose women flavor the anteroom. Much turmoil & trouble. But there are small compensations. The Youngs are here. They are pretty exceedingly. They have grown fat and fair.

The world is almost too many for me. I take a dreary pleasure in seeing Philbrick eat steamed oysters by the ½ bushel. He has gotten a haven of rest in the family of some decayed Virginian

2 of the *N. Y. Herald.*

gentry. Really a very lucky chance. Good, respectable & not dear. Schafer must be our resource this winter in clothes. If you don't want to be surprised into idiocy don't ask Croney & Lent the price of goods. A faint rumour has reached me & paralyzed me. I am founding a "Shabby Club" to make rags the style this winter. Write to me some morning while you are waiting for your cocktail & tell me how's things. Give my love to the fair you are so lucky as to know.

Yours truly
J.H.

[P.S.] Isn't it bully about Sheridan! ³

DIARY

September 24, 1864. This morning I asked the President if the report of the resignation of Blair were true.

He said it was.

"Has Dennison been appointed to succeed him?" ⁴

"I have telegraphed to him today—have as yet received no answer."

"What is Mʳ Blair going to do?"

"He is going up to Maryland to make speeches. If he will devote himself to the success of the national cause without exhibiting bad temper towards his opponents, he can set the Blair family up again."

"Winter Davis is taking the stump also. I doubt if his advocacy of you will be hearty enough to be effective."

"If he and the rest can succeed in carrying the State for emancipation, I shall be very willing to lose the electoral vote."

September 25, Sunday. 1864. Yesterday Nicolay, who has been several days in New York, telegraphed to the President that Thur-

---

³ Sheridan, who in the summer had been placed in command of the army in the Shenandoah Valley, drove Early out of Winchester, Sept. 19, and won again at Fisher's Hill, Sept. 22.

⁴ Lincoln requested Blair's resignation as Postmaster General when Gen. Frémont withdrew as the Union Party candidate. It was a political deal.

low Weed had gone to Canada and asking if he, N., had better return. I answered he had better amuse himself there for a day or two. This morning a letter came in the same sense. The President, when I showed it him, said, "I think I know where Mr W. has gone. I think he has gone to Vermont, not Canada. I will tell you what he is trying to do. I have not as yet told anybody.

"Sometime ago the Governor of Vermont came to see me 'on business of importance,' he said. I fixed an hour & he came. His name is Smith. He is, though you wouldn't think it, a cousin of Baldy Smith. Baldy is large, blond, florid. The Governor is a little dark phystey sort of man. This is the story he told me, giving General Baldy Smith as his authority.

"When General McClellan was here at Washington, Baldy Smith was very intimate with him. They had been together at West Point & friends. McClellan had asked for promotion for Baldy from the President & got it. They were close and confidential friends. When they went down to the Peninsula their same intimate relations continued, the General talking freely with Smith about all his plans and prospects: until one day Fernando Wood & one other politician from New York appeared in camp & passed some days with McClellan. From the day that this took place, Smith saw, or thought he saw, that McClellan was treating him with unusual coolness & reserve. After a little while he mentioned this to McC. who after some talk told Baldy he had something to show him. He told him that these people who had recently visited him, had been urging him to stand as an opposition candidate for President: that he had thought the thing over, and had concluded to accept their propositions & had written them a letter (which he had not yet sent) giving his idea of the proper way of conducting the war, so as to conciliate and impress the people of the South with the idea that our armies were intended merely to execute the laws and protect their property, &c., & pledging himself to conduct the war in that inefficient conciliatory style. This letter he read to Baldy, who after the reading was finished said earnestly, 'General, do you not see that looks like treason: & that it will ruin you and all of us?' After some further talk the General destroyed the letter in Baldy's presence, and thanked him heartily for his frank & friendly counsel. After this he was again taken into the intimate confidence of McClellan. Immediately after the Battle of Antietam Wood & his familiars came again & saw the General, & again Baldy saw an immediate estrangement on the part of McClellan. He seemed to be anxious to get his intimate friends out of the way and to avoid opportunities of private conversation with them. Baldy, he particularly kept employed on reconnoissances and such work. One night Smith was returning from some duty he had been performing & seeing a light in McClellan's tent he went in to report. Several persons were there. He reported & was about to withdraw when the General requested him to remain. After everyone was gone he told him those men had been there again and had renewed their proposition about the Presidency—that this time he had agreed to their proposition and had written them a letter acceding to their terms and pledging himself to carry on the war in the sense already indicated. This letter he read then and there to Baldy Smith.

"Immediately thereafter Baldy Smith applied to be transferred from that army.

"At very nearly the same time other prominent men asked the same, Franklin, Burnside and others.

"Now that letter must be in the possession of Fernando Wood, and it will not be impossible to get it. Mr Weed has, I think, gone to Vermont to see the Smiths about it."

I was very much surprised at the story & expressed my surprise. I said I had always thought that McClellan's fault was a constitutional weakness and timidity which prevented him from active and timely exertion, instead of any such deep-laid scheme of treachery & ambition.

The President replied, "After the battle of Antietam, I went up to the field to try to get him to move & came back thinking he would move at once. But when I got home he began to argue why he ought not to move. I peremptorily ordered him to advance. It was 19 days before he put a man over the river. It was 9 days longer before he got his army across and then he stopped again, delaying on little pretexts of wanting this and that. I began to fear he was playing false—that he did not want to hurt the enemy. I saw how he could intercept the enemy on the way to Richmond. I determined to make that the test. If he let them get away I would remove him. He did so & I relieved him.

"I dismissed Major Key for his silly treasonable talk because I feared it was staff talk & I wanted an example.

"The letter of Buell furnishes another evidence in support of that theory. And the story you have heard Neill tell about Seymour's first visit to McClellan all tallies with this story."

I went over to talk, with Fox about Wilmington.[5] I asked when operations w^d begin there, wanting to go as a volunteer. He says we hope to take it in October. Porter is gone to the West to hurry up his business there & put up the shutters & shut up shop & will then return and organize the expedition. Fox took Gillmore down to Grant for the land operations but Grant simply said he would assign an officer to that duty when the time came. Fox thinks Weitzel. The Army have to take the town this time—the Navy forced to be secondary by the shoal water.

It is a most important thing. Fox says in scripture phrase the rebellion is sustained "not by what entereth into their ports but by what proceedeth out." The rebel credit will collapse the day their cotton supply is stopped.

Sept. 26. Blair has gone into Maryland stumping. He was very much surprised when he got the President's note.[6] He had thought the opposition to him was dying out. He behaves very handsomely and is doing his utmost. He speaks in New York Tuesday night.

Blair in spite of some temporary indiscretions is a good and true man and a most valuable public officer. He stood with the President against the whole Cabinet in favor of reinforcing Fort Sumter. He stood by Frémont in his emancipation decree, though yielding when the President revoked it. He approved the Proclamation of January, 1863, and the Amnesty Proclamation, & has stood like a brother beside the President always. What have in-

---

[5] Wilmington, S. C., together with Charleston, were the two ports chiefly used by the blockade-runners.

[6] Lincoln's request for Blair's resignation was dated Sept. 23. Text in "Complete Works," II, 579.

jured him are his violent personal antagonisms and indiscretions. He made a bitter and vindictive fight on the Radicals of Missouri, though ceasing at the request of the Pres^t. He talked with indecorous severity of Mr Chase, and with unbecoming harshness of Stanton, saying on street-corners, "this man is a liar, that man is a thief." He made needlessly enemies among public men who have pursued him fiercely in turn. Whitelaw Reid said today that Hoffman was going to placard all over Maryland this fall, "Your time has come." I said, "He won't do anything of the kind, & moreover Montgomery Blair will do more to carry emancipation in Maryland than any one of those who blackguard him."

Nicolay got home this morning looking rather ill. I wish he would start off & get hearty again, coming back in time to let me off to Wilmington.

He says Weed said he was on the track of the letter and hoped to get it. The object of N.'s trip was to see Weed who has a plan for getting campaign money out of cotton—*taeterrima fons malorum*— N. says it won't do.

Forney writes a light and enthusiastic letter claiming Pennsylvania by 50,000.

Nicolay thinks we will carry New York. The New Jersey men promise their State & the Kentuckians pluckily swear they will be on hand with theirs.

September 29, 1864. Blair was introduced to the great War Meeting Tuesday night by Curtis Noyes. In the beginning of B.'s speech he said his own father suggested the propriety of his resignation to the President.

Webster has just returned here from the North. He says New York is absolutely safe; that Weed is advising his friends to bet; that Dean Richmond is despondent—saying the Democratic party are half traitors.

Things looked very blue a month ago. A meeting was held in New York (to which Geo. Wilkes refers) of Union men opposed to Lincoln, & it was resolved that he should be requested to withdraw from the canvass. But Atlanta & the response of the country to Chicago infamy set matters right. Weed says they sent for him to come & join them. He replied that his only objection to Mr Lincoln was his favor to such fellows as they & that he sh^d not join them against him. He also says that Ben. Butler in his last visit to New York spent several hours with him trying to get him to go in for him (Butler) on a new Buffalo or Cincinnati supplementary convention ticket. W. told him the question lay between Lincoln and McClellan.

Grant is moving on Lee. This morning early the Pres^t telegraphed to Grant expressing his anxiety that Lee should not reinforce Early against Sheridan. Grant answered that he had taken measures to prevent it by attacking Lee himself. He is moving in two columns: Ord's south, & Birney north of the James. Stanton was much excited on hearing the news & said, "He will be in Richmond tonight." "No," said the President, "Halleck, what do you think?" Halleck answered that he w^d not be surprised if he got either Richmond or Petersburg by the maneuver.

Gold was at 201 & fell to 96 on the news of Grant's being in motion.

Today Hooker leaves for the West. He takes charge of the Dep^t administered by Heintzelman. Heintzelman is busily engaged canvassing for McClellan & the President kindly takes off his hands the additional burden of military duty.

Oct. 2. Today I received a letter from Wm N. Grover saying certain of his friends had agreed to press his name for Judge of the District Court, Western Missouri, in place of Judge Welles. He adds, however, that in case Judge Bates, Attorney General, should desire the appointment he would not stand in his way, believing that Bates's appointment would be very advantageous & satisfactory to the Union people of the State. He requested me to make this known both to Mr Bates & the President. I read his letter to the President & at the same time referred to the recent indiscreet announcement made by Cameron, that in the event of a reelection the Pres^t w^d call around him fresh & earnest men. He said, "They need not be especially savage about a change. There are now only 3 left of the original Cabinet with the Government." [7] He added that he rather thought he would appoint Mr Bates to the vacant judgeship if he desired it. He said he would be troubled to fill his place in the Cabinet from Missouri, especially from among the Radicals. I thought it would not be necessary to confine himself to Missouri: that he might do better further South, by taking Mr Holt from Kentucky.

He did not seem to have thought of that before. But said at once, "That would do very well. That would be an excellent appointment. I question if I could do better than that. I had always thought, though I had never mentioned it to anyone, that if a vacancy should occur on the Supreme Bench in any Southern District, I would appoint him. But giving him a place in the Cabinet would not hinder that."

I told him I should show Grover's letter to Judge Bates, to which he assented.

Oct. 7. I showed Bates the letter today. He said some friends of his had previously spoken to him in the same sense; that he was friendly to Grover, thought well of him as a gentleman and a lawyer, and knew of no one whom he would sooner see appointed. That he would not take the office himself in any case. That he had earnest antagonisms in that state: he was fighting those Radicals there that stood to him in the relation of enemies of law and order. There was no such thing as an honest and patriotic American Radical. Some of the transcendental, Red-Republican Germans were honest enough in their moonstruck theorising; but the Americans impudently and dishonestly arrogate to themselves the title of unconditional loyalty, when the whole spirit of their faction is contempt of and opposition to law. While the present state of things continues in Missouri, there is no need of a Court—so says Judge Treat, and I agree with him.

Mr Nicolay has gone West to try to find some way of pacifying the Missouri muddle. McKee has been here to have the Post Office changed. Carl Schurz writes advising the same.

[7] These were Seward, Welles, and Bates. The latter resigned Nov. 24.

TO J. G. NICOLAY

WASHINGTON D. C., *October 8. 1864*

Nothing as yet ripples the surface.

Every body is anxious about next Tuesday's work.

Raymond went home the other day rather discouraged about money matters. If you should care to go out to the convent I send you the necessary introduction. Don't go, unless you want to.

The Surgeon General sends a very ready response to y^r note in behalf of Dr Porter. I send it to you that you may be armed to meet him.

If you come across Grover you may trust every word he says as to facts. As to sentiments, you can appreciate them yourself. He may be a little too hard on the Radicals & a little too conservative himself.

General Meigs has lost his only son—a very brilliant young engineer.

Miss Bacon was duly married on the 6th. You & I were not there. Public business.

DIARY

October 8. Today I got a letter from Grover protesting against an assessment which has been levied upon him by Jim Lane's advisory committee, & sending me instead a hundred dollars. I gave it to Harlan with an explanation which seemed unnecessary to him, as he said there was a general doubt as to Lane's entire fitness as a disbursing officer.

Last night Swinton of the *Times* was in my room several hours. He says Raymond went away a good deal discouraged about money matters.

Halpine is working for the County Clerkship & will get it if the newspapers are worth anything.

General Banks arrived yesterday morning. I visited him and his wife at Willard's last night.

October 9th, Sunday. Governor Dennison and General Banks spent a little while in my room this morning. Banks says there is no city on the continent more salubrious than New Orleans, properly cared for as it has been during our occupancy. The city is now thoroughly loyal, thoroughly in harmony with the country at large, in spite of all that has been said to the contrary. The national airs are forever sounding in the schools and streets: the national bunting floating in the air. Society is running now in loyal channels: the secession element must breathe loyal air or perish. When Banks went there the prominent resident families would invite officers to their houses on condition that they should not wear their uniform. When Gen. Grant came down from Vicksburg, only our officers' families & a few of the poorer classes attended his receptions. Banks says all this is changed. At his receptions & those of his prominent associates in command, the best society of the city crowded his drawing rooms.

The loyal feeling of common nationality has done much to break up the exclusion and demarcation existing between the French and American classes; the town is more American than ever before. The organization of the fire companies, which was formerly in rebel hands, has especially felt the influence of this change of sentiment until now that enormous organization can be relied upon thoroughly in the interests of the Government. In very many cases, it is not so much a change of sentiment and conviction, as a more intelligent perception of interests and probabilities. They see the experiment of rebellion has failed, that the national cause will triumph and that free labor affords to them a brighter and more progressive future. But still insist, many of them, that slavery was best for the negro, that secession was constitutional and other such worn-out maxims of the past.

I referred to the humiliating fact that while abroad the world was recognizing the fact of the rehabilitation of Louisiana and the convincing proof it afforded of the entire feasibility of the national plan of a permanent and conquered peace on the basis of freedom, there were many men and journals in the North, esteemed, able, and patriotic, who labored to prove that all this work was a failure. I referred to the *Evn^g Post* and others. He replied that the foundation of those attacks in the *E.P.* was neither honesty nor patriotism, but unsuccessful pecuniary projects—something I had not heard of before.

Cameron telegraphed last night that the magnificent demonstration in Philadelphia was the certain augury of victory on Tuesday. Thurlow Weed says he is easy about Pennsylvania but anxious about Indiana. DeFrees writes under date October 5 from Indiana that he thinks the state will be ours by a small majority. Illinoisans generally claim Illinois.

The President is fighting today to get time to write a letter to the Baltimore meeting but is crowded as usual by visitors.

P.S. Wrote the letter. I changed the word "posted" to "informed."

TO J. G. NICOLAY

EXECUTIVE MANSION,
WASHINGTON, *October 10, 1864*

Here are y^r mails for this morning. We are very busy. Mr. Matile is sick.

Pennsylvania fellows are very confident. You will know the result before this gets there.

Kelley was here this morning. He seemed to be in a great hurry, as he only staid 2 hours & a half, & didn't talk about himself more than 9/10^{ths} of the time.

DIARY

October 10, 1864. Kelley was here before breakfast. He says he will carry his district by 2,000 which will grow to 4,000 by November. He says we shall carry the State [Penn.] in spite of Cameron who is trying to manage the campaign with a view to elect himself Senator. He charges C. with working to defeat McClure. He says that Childs, a strong friend of Cameron, is trying to defeat him (K.), because he won't declare for Cameron as Sec. War instead of Stanton.

Washburne tells me that Kelley wants Judge Lewis made Sec. Interior in place of Usher to keep Cameron out of the Cabinet.

Kelley is getting more and more infatuated with himself. He told today a dull anecdote for the purpose of bringing in what some one said of him. "You, Judge Kelley, with your splendid voice, your fine address, your fervid & impassioned eloquence, are one of the most dangerous men of the time."

Yet the fellow has fine abilities and is devoted to the good cause of equal rights.

October 11, 1864. Newell handed me this morning an estimate from A. Cummings giving 18,900 as the probable majority on the home vote in Pennsylvania.

Thurlow Weed writes anxiously on the subject of the Navy vote. The President has been with Seward & Welles this morning and arranged about it.

Morgan writes about Vanderbilt's medal. I went over to the State Department & set the thing going. Leutze is to make the design.

I showed the President today W. E. Dodge's letter to Judge Davis, complaining of the effect of the Niagara Manifesto [8] & asking the President to explain it away, "And," says the Pres^t, "lose ten times as much on the other side." I got to discussing the matter with Dorsheimer who dined with me today & who has been talking somewhat freely with Holcombe. I told him I thought the President was right; that if he had shown any back-track inclinations in that matter our people w^d have lost heart and faith in the cause; that there was really no opportunity at that time for honorable peace; that an attempt coupled with the reception of Commissioners at Washington would have excited the vague hopes of the country & a failure which was inevitable w^d have occasioned a disastrous relapse, which w^d have demoralized public sentiment so as to have risked this canvass & campaign. So it was better to

[8] After the failure of the Niagara Falls conference in July, 1864, in which Greeley appears to have sought to place the President in the position of offering peace to the Confederacy, the Confederate commissioners published a letter addressed to Greeley in which they accused Lincoln of bad faith.

meet them on the threshold & let them and the world know where we stood.

When Joe Medill wrote me an impertinent letter (hoping I w^d read it to the President, which hope was fallacious), denouncing the Niagara note of the President, I c^d not but think how loudmouthed w^d have been his denunciation of Lincoln's recreancy to principle if he had not made the condition of which these croakers now complain.

Montgomery Blair was here for a while this afternoon. He gives a most graphic picture of the fight in Maryland for the mayoralty, & Winter Davis' plottings & plannings, Swann's speech last night, &c.

I was mentioning old Mr Blair's very calm and discreet letter of October 5 to the Pres^t today, contrasting it with Montgomery's indiscretions, & the President said, "Yes, they remind me of ——.[9] He was sitting in a bar-room among strangers who were telling of some affair in which his father, as they said, had been tricked in a trade, and he said, 'That's a lie!' Some sensation. 'What do you mean?' 'Why the old man ain't so easy tricked. You can fool the boys but ye can't the old man.' "

At 3 o'clock came despatches from Puleston saying they would give a moderate but decided majority for the Administration & we w^d gain 4 or more Congressmen.

At eight o'clock the President went over to the War Department to watch for despatches. I went with him. We found the building in a state of preparation for siege. Stanton had locked the doors and taken the keys upstairs, so that it was impossible even to send a card to him. A shivering messenger was pacing to and fro in the moonlight over the withered leaves, who, catching sight of the President, took us around by the Navy Department & conducted us into the War Office by a side door.

The first despatch we received contained the welcome intelligence of the election of Eggleston and Hays in the Cincinati districts. This was from Stager, at Cleveland, who also promised considerable gains in Indiana, made good a few minutes after by a

---

[9] The name is omitted in the diary as though Hay had failed to remember it when he made the entry.

statement of 400 gain in Noble County. Then came in a despatch from Sandford stating we had 2,500 in the City of Philadelphia and that leading Democrats had given up the state. Then Shallabarger was seen to be crowding Sam Cox very hard in the Columbus district, in some places increasing Brough's colossal vote of last year.

The President in a lull of despatches took from his pocket the Nasby Papers and read several chapters of the experiences of the saint & martyr, Petroleum V. They were immensely amusing. Stanton and Dana enjoyed them scarcely less than the President, who read on, *con amore,* until 9 o'clock. At this time I went to Seward's to keep my engagement. I found there Banks and his wife, Cols. Clark & Wilson, Asta Burnaga and Madame, the New Orleans people, and a young Briton who was nephew to the Earl of Dorset, somebody said, & w^d like to enter our Army before we finish this thing up. Dennison was also there. We broke up very early. Dennison & I went back to the Department.

We found the good Indiana news had become better and the Pennsylvania had begun to be streaked with lean. Before long the despatches announced with some certainty of tone that Morton was elected by a safe working majority. The scattering reports from Pennsylvania showed about equal gains and losses. But the estimates and flyers all claimed gains on the Congressmen. A despatch from Puleston says, "We have gained 4 or five or even 6 Cong^m. I am going to New York to sleep a few days." Not a word came from any authorized source. Cameron and the State Committee silent as the grave. It was suggested that Cameron had gone home to Harrisburgh to vote. It looked a little ominous, his silence. The President telegraphed to him but got no answer.

Reports began to come in from the hospitals and camps in the vicinity, the Ohio troops about ten to one for Union and the Pennsylvanians less than three to one. Carver Hospital, by which Stanton & Lincoln pass every day on their way to the country, gave the heaviest opposition vote—about one out of three. Lincoln says, "That's hard on us, Stanton—they know us better than the others." Co. K, 150 P.V., the President's personal escort, voted 63 to 11 Union.

An enthusiastic despatch announcing 30,000 for Morton came

in, signed McKim. "Who is that?" "A quartermaster of mine,"
said Stanton. "He was sent there to announce that." "By the way,"
he added, "a very healthy sentiment is growing up among the
quartermasters. Allen is attending all the Republican meetings,
so is Myers. A nephew of Brough's that I placed at Louisville &
made a Colonel, I reduced to a Captain and ordered him South
the other day. He was caught betting against Morton." A murmur
of adhesion filled the apartment.

I suggested to the Secre   what Dorsheimer had told me about
Dandy's regiment being   McClellan. I added that Dandy
wanted promotion. "He will get it," said the Secretary, puffing a
long blue spiral wreath of smoke from his stern lips. Colonel
Dandy's dream of stars passed away in that smoke.

They spoke of McClernand's manifest, and seemed glad to be
rid of him. A vain, irritable, overbearing, exacting man who is
possessed of the monomania that it was a mere clerical error which
placed Grant's name and not his in the commission of the Lieutenant General.

Washburne read an amusing letter about Scates, saying that the
old fellow was declaring in favor of revolution in case McClellan
is elected. He has gone crazy in the fiery exuberance of his young
Republican zeal. These new converts put us old originals to the
blush.

I am deeply thankful for the result in Indiana. I believe it saves
Illinois in November. I believe it rescues Indiana from sedition &
civil war. A Copperhead Governor would have afforded a grand
central rallying point for that lurking treason whose existence
Carrington has already so clearly demonstrated, which growing
bolder by the popular seal and sanction w^d have dared to lift its
head from the dust and measure strength with the Government.
The defection of the Executive Governments of those two great
States, Illinois & Indiana, from the general administration would
have been disastrous and paralyzing. I should have been willing
to sacrifice something in Pennsylvania to avert that calamity. I
said as much to the President. He said he was anxious about Pennsylvania because of her enormous weight and influence which,
cast definitely into the scale, w^d close the campaign & leave the

people free to look again with their whole hearts to the cause of the country.

October 12, 1864. This morning made arrangements with Mr Harrington and Secretary Fessenden to have a revenue cutter send along the Blockading Squadron to pick up the boats.

A committee is on here bothering about the New York Navy Yard, saying it is used against us. The President told me to say to Fox that he (the Pres^t) must be relieved in this matter. Something must be done to satisfy these people. Fox says everything possible is done: that the dissatisfied cannot even agree among themselves & that if they can poll the Yard the Dep^t stands ready to turn out any man hostile to the Administration.

The indefinite claims of last night's Pennsylvania despatches are not borne out by this morning's details. The home vote will be very close & we may need the soldier vote after all to give us a clear majority.

TO J. G. NICOLAY

EXECUTIVE MANSION,
WASHINGTON, October 13, 1864

I suppose you are happy enough over the elections to do without letters. Here are two. I hope they are duns to remind you that you are mortal.

Indiana is simply glorious. The surprise of this good thing is its chief delight. Pennsylvania has done pretty well. We have a little majority on home vote as yet & will get a fair vote from the soldiers, and do better in November. The wild estimates of Forney & Cameron founded on no count or thorough canvass are of course not fulfilled, but we did not expect them to be.

Judge Taney died last night. I have not heard anything this morning about the succession. It is a matter of the greatest personal importance that Mr Lincoln has ever decided.

Winter Davis' clique was badly scooped out in the Mayoralty election in Baltimore yesterday. Chapman (regular Union) got nearly all the votes cast. I have nothing from you as yet.

CHAPTER XX

October 13—November 11, 1864

October 13, 1864. Last night Chief Justice Taney went home to his fathers. The elections carried him off, said Banks this morning. Already (before his poor old clay is cold) they are beginning to canvass vigorously for his successor. Chase men say the place is promised to their *magnifico,* as crazy old Gurowski styles him.[1]

I talked with the President one moment. He says he does not think he will make the appointment immediately. He will be, he says, rather "shut pan" in the matter at present.

October 14, 1864. Judge Lewis talked to me this morning earnestly against Chase for that place. He says he is not a man of enlarged legal or financial knowledge; that his supreme selfishness has gradually narrowed and contracted his views of things in general; that his ignorance of men, & many other things that I knew before, &c., &c.

He says he thinks Chase really desired, toward the end of his continuance in office, to injure and as far as possible destroy the influence and popularity of the Administration. By his constant denunciation of the extravagance of expenditure, his clamor against the inefficiency of other departments, his personal tone of slighting comment upon every act of the President, and more than all by his steady & persistent attempts to make the taxes more & more burdensome upon the people (having increased his demands from $150,000,000 to $300,000,000 in the face of Lewis' and Morrill's representations), he clearly indicated his desire to excite popular discontents and grumblings against the Government.

His selfishness, continued the Judge, blinded him utterly to

[1] Chase was nominated Chief Justice, Dec. 6.

the character of the flatterers who surrounded. (I gave him some
instances of this.) Lewis says that Field, for whom he gave up his
place, expressed himself as relieved by his absence.

Pennsylvanians returning from their voting furloughs almost
all accuse Cameron of having botched the canvass badly.

November 6, 1864. Marshal Murray came from New York today to get the release of a blockade runner, rec⁴ by Weed. Forney
writes to have a fellow released from Old Capitol.² The President
sent me to Stanton about it. I found him sick in bed. But he made
the necessary orders. We spoke of Jim Brady's recent foolish somer-
set back into the mud of Copperheadism. He ascribed it to Brady's
envy & jealousy of the recent magnificent movement of the War
Democrats.

He seemed thoroughly sick & tired of the constant jobs that
people were asking for, under pretense that they are to aid the
election; and heartily wished for Tuesday to come and go to end
the nuisance of this.

November 7, 1864. Talking with the President a day or two ago
about Sherman, he told me that Sherman was inclined to let Hood
run his gait for a while, while he overran the Gulf States in Hood's
rear. Grant seems rather inclined to have Sherman strike and destroy Hood now, before going South, but gives no orders in the
case.

Spent Sunday evening with the Lorings. They are bitterly despondent: and with a most wonderful assurance talk about *our*
frauds.

Bartlett writes to President that Mʳˢ J.G.B. has become an earnest Lincolnite. Poor Mᶜˢ visiting those people and compromising
himself to them has been of no avail and must be terribly humiliating to a man so well bred as McC. is.

Nov. 8. The house has been still and almost deserted today.
Everybody in Washington, not at home voting, seems ashamed

---

² The "Old Capitol," where Congress met after the burning of the original Capitol
in August, 1814, during the Civil War was used as a military prison.

of it and stays away from the President.

I was talking with him to-day. He said, "It is a little singular that I, who am not a vindictive man, should have always been before the people for election in canvasses marked for their bitterness: always but once; when I came to Congress it was a quiet time. But always besides that the contests in which I have been prominent have been marked with great rancor."

At noon Butler sent a despatch simply saying, "The quietest city ever seen."

Butler was sent to New York by Stanton. The President had nothing to do with it. Thurlow Weed was nervous about his coming, thought it would harm us and even as late as Sunday wrote saying that Butler's presence was on the whole injurious, in spite of his admirable General Order.

Hoffman sent a very cheering despatch giving a rose-coloured estimate of the forenoon's voting in Baltimore. "I shall be glad if that holds," said the President, "because I had rather feared that in the increased vote over that on the Constitution, the increase would rather be against us."

During the afternoon few despatches were received.

At night, at 7 o'clock we started over to the War Department to spend the evening. Just as we started we received the first gun from Indianapolis, showing a majority of 8,000 there, a gain of 1,500 over Morton's vote. The vote itself seemed an enormous one for a town of that size and can only be accounted for by considering the great influx since the war of voting men from the country into the State centres where a great deal of Army business is done. There was less significance in this vote on account of the October victory which had disheartened the enemy and destroyed their incentive to work.

The night was rainy, steamy and dark. We splashed through the grounds to the side door of the War Department where a soaked and smoking sentinel was standing in his own vapor with his huddled-up frame covered with a rubber cloak. Inside a half-dozen idle orderlies, up-stairs the clerks of the telegraph. As the President entered they handed him a despatch from Forney claiming ten thousand Union majority in Philadelphia. "Forney is a little excitable." Another comes from Felton, Baltimore, giving us "15,000 in the city, 5,000 in the state. All Hail, Free Maryland." That is superb. A message from Rice to Fox, followed instantly by one from Sumner to Lincoln, claiming Boston by 5,000, and Rice's & Hooper's elections by majorities of 4,000 apiece. A magnificent advance on the chilly dozens of 1862.

Eckert came in shaking the rain from his cloak, with trousers very disreputably muddy. We sternly demanded an explanation. He had slipped, he said, & tumbled prone, crossing the street. He had done it watching a fellow-being ahead and chuckling at his uncertain footing. Which reminded the Tycoon, of course. The President said, "For such an awkward fellow, I am pretty sure-footed. It used to take a pretty dextrous man to throw me. I remember, the evening of the day in 1858, that decided the contest for the Senate between Mr Douglas and myself, was something like this, dark, rainy & gloomy. I had been reading the returns, and had ascertained that we had lost the Legislature and started to go home. The path had been worn hog-back & was slippery. My foot slipped from under me, knocking the other one out of the way, but I recovered myself & lit square, and I said to myself, 'It's a slip and not a fall.' "

The President sent over the first fruits to Mrs. Lincoln. He said, "She is more anxious than I."

We went into the Secretary's room. Mr Wells and Fox soon came in. They were especially happy over the election of Rice, regarding it as a great triumph for the Navy Department. Says Fox, "There are two fellows that have been especially malignant to us, and retribution has come upon them both, Hale and Winter Davis." "You have more of that feeling of personal resentment than I," said Lincoln. "Perhaps I may have too little of it, but I never thought it paid. A man has not time to spend half his life in quarrels. If any man ceases to attack me, I never remember the past against him. It has seemed to me recently that Winter Davis was growing more sensible to his own true interests and has ceased wasting his time by attacking me. I hope for his own good he has. He has been very malicious against me but has only injured himself by it. His conduct has been very strange to me. I came here, his friend, wishing to continue so. I had heard nothing but good of him; he was the cousin of my intimate friend Judge Davis. But he had scarcely been elected when I began to learn of his attacking me on all possible occasions. It is very much the same with Hickman. I was much disappointed that he failed to be my friend. But my greatest disappointment of all has been with Grimes. Before I came here, I certainly expected to rely upon Grimes more than any other one man in the Senate. I like him very much. He is a great strong fellow. He is a valuable friend, a dangerous enemy. He carries too many guns not to be respected in any point of view. But he got wrong against me, I do not clearly know how, and has always been cool and almost hostile to me. I am glad he has always been the friend of the Navy and generally of the Administration."

Despatches kept coming in all the evening showing a splendid triumph in Indiana, showing steady, small gains all over Pennsylvania, enough to give a fair majority this time on the home vote. Guesses from New York and Albany which boiled down to about the estimated majority against us in the city, 35,000, and left the result in the State still doubtful.

A despatch from Butler was picked up & sent by Sanford, saying that the City had gone 35,000 McC. & the State 40,000. This looked impossible. The State had been carefully canvassed & such a result was impossible except in view of some monstrous and undreamed of frauds. After a while another came from Sanford correcting former one & giving us the 40,000 in the State.

Sanford's despatches all the evening continued most jubilant: especially when he announced that most startling majority of 80,-000 in Massachusetts.

General Eaton came in and waited for news with us. I had not before known he was with us. His denunciations of Seymour were especially hearty and vigorous.

Towards midnight we had supper, provided by Eckert. The President went awkwardly and hospitably to work shovelling out the fried oysters. He was most agreeable and genial all the evening in fact. Fox was abusing the coffee for being so hot—saying quaintly, it kept hot all the way down to the bottom of the cup as a piece of ice staid cold till you finished eating it.

We got later in the evening a scattering despatch from the West, giving us Michigan, one from Fox promising Missouri certainly, but a loss in the first district from that miserable split of Knox & Johnson, one promising Delaware, and one, too good for ready credence, saying Raymond & Dodge & Darling had been elected in New York City.

Capt Thomas came up with a band about half-past two, and made some music and a small hifalute.

The President answered from the window with rather unusual dignity and effect & we came home. [Added later: "I wrote the speech and sent it to Hanscum."]

W.H.L.[3] came to my room to talk over the Chief Justiceship; he goes in for Stanton & thinks, as I am inclined to think, that the President cannot afford to place an enemy in a position so momentous for good or evil.

He took a glass of whiskey and then, refusing my offer of a bed, went out &, rolling himself up in his cloak, lay down at the President's door; passing the night in that attitude of touching and dumb fidelity, with a small arsenal of pistols & bowie knives around him. In the morning he went away leaving my blankets at my door, before I or the President were awake.

November 9, 1864. Mr Dana came this morning to ask the President to come over to the War Department, Mr Stanton being unable to come to the Ex. Mansion. They are to consult in regard to some suggestions of Butler's who wants to grab & incarcerate some gold gamblers. The President doesn't like to sully victory by any harshness.

Montgomery Blair came in this morning. He returned from his Kentucky trip in time to vote at home. He is very bitter against the Davis clique (what's left of it), and foolishly, I think, confounds the War Department and the Treasury as parties to the Winter Davis conspiracy against the President. He spoke with pleasant sarcasm of the miscalculation which has left Reverdy

---

3 Lamon.

Johnson out in the cold, & gave an account of his "being taken by the insolent foe" in the Blue Grass Region. He says he stands as yet by what he has said, that Lincoln will get an unanimous electoral vote. The soldier vote in Kentucky will save the State if the guerrillas have allowed the country people peace enough to have an election.

2 o'clock: Hoffman just reports a splendid set of majorities in Maryland reaching an aggregate of 10,000.

Webster brings a despatch from Hastings (Albany Knickerbocker) saying we will have the state by 5,000.

Swett sends a desponding despatch in which he virtually gives up the State, charging it to frauds and the demoralizing influence of Seymour's military patronage.

November 11, 1864. This morning Nicolay sent a superb despatch from Illinois giving us 25,000 majority and 10 Congressmen, which we take to mean Wentworth, Farnsworth, Washburne, Cooke, Ingersoll, Harding, Cullom, Brownwell, Kuykendall, and Moulton at large, leaving the Copperheads Thornton, Morrison, Ross and Marshall.[4]

At the meeting of the Cabinet today, the President took out a paper from his desk and said, "Gentlemen, do you remember last summer I asked you all to sign your names to the back of a paper of which I did not show you the inside? This is it. Now, Mr Hay, see if you can get this open without tearing it?" He had pasted it up in so singular style that it required some cutting to get it open. He then read as follows:

EXECUTIVE MANSION
WASHINGTON, *Aug. 23, 1864*

This morning, as for some days past, it seems exceedingly probable that this Administration will not be reelected. Then it will be my duty to so cooperate with the President elect, as to save the

---

[4] In the final returns it appeared that McClellan had carried only New Jersey, Delaware and Kentucky. Lincoln had a popular majority of nearly half a million votes.

Union between the election and the inauguration; as he will have secured his election on such ground that he cannot possibly save it afterwards.

A LINCOLN

This was indorsed:

> William H. Seward
> W. P. Fessenden
> Edwin M. Stanton
> Gideon Welles
> Edwd Bates
> M. Blair
> J. P. Usher

August 23, 1864

The President said, "You will remember that this was written at a time (6 days before the Chicago nominating Convention) when as yet we had no adversary, and seemed to have no friends. I then solemnly resolved on the course of action indicated above. I resolved, in case of the election of General McClellan, being certain that he would be the candidate, that I would see him and talk matters over with him. I would say, "General, the election has demonstrated that you are stronger, have more influence with the American people than I. Now let us together, you with your influence and I with all the executive power of the Government, try to save the country. You raise as many troops as you possibly can for this final trial, and I will devote all my energies to assisting and finishing the war."

Seward said, "And the General would answer you 'Yes, Yes;' and the next day when you saw him again and pressed these views upon him, he would say, 'Yes, Yes;' & so on forever, and would have done nothing at all."

"At least," added Lincoln, "I should have done my duty and have stood clear before my own conscience."

Seward was abusing Forney today for a report of his (S.'s) remarks last night at the serenade, which appeared horribly butchered in the *Chronicle,* in which S.'s Biblical lore is sadly out at the elbows.

The speeches of the President at the two last serenades are very highly spoken of. The first I wrote after the fact, to prevent the "loyal Pennsylvanians" getting a swing at it themselves. The second one, last night, the President himself wrote late in the evening and read it from the window. "Not very graceful," he said, "but I am growing old enough not to care much for the manner of doing things."

To-day I got a letter from Raymond breathing fire and vengeance against the Custom House which came so near destroying him in his district. I read it to the President. He answered that it was the spirit of such letters as that that created the faction and malignity of which Raymond complained.

It seems utterly impossible for the President to conceive of the possibility of any good resulting from a rigorous and exemplary course of punishing political dereliction. His favorite expression is, "I am in favor of short statutes of limitations in politics."

CHAPTER XXI

December 1864

[*November 16, 1864?*] 12th November, 1864, I started for Grant's headquarters. We left the Navy Yard at 2 o'clock in the afternoon. The party consisted of Fox, Dyer, Wise, M. Blair, Pyne, Ives, Forbes Ives, Tom Welles, Foster, a Chinese-English merchant, and Reid of the *Gazette*. The day was sad, blowy, bleak, and a little wet.

We dined and some played cards and all went to bed. When we got up in the morning we were at Hampton Roads. We made no stay there but after communicating with the Admiral, D. D. Porter, we started up the James River, he following in his flagship, the *Malvern*. He overtook us about noon or a little after, & came on board, with Captain Steadman of the Navy. Porter is a good-looking, lively man, of a little less than medium height, a ready off-hand talker; a man not impressing me as of a high order of talent—like the McCooks rather; a hale-fellow; a slight dash of the rowdy.

In the afternoon, we passed by the island of Jamestown. On the low, flat, marshy island where our first colony landed, there now remains nothing but ruins. An old church has left a solitary tower as its representative. A group of chimneys mark the spot of another large building. On the other side of the river there is high, fine, rolling land. One cannot but wonder at the taste or judgment that selected that pestilential site in preference to those breezy hills. They probably wished to be nearer their boats & also thought a river was a handy thing to have between them and the gentle savages that infested the shores of the James.

Fort Powhatan we saw also—where a battalion of negroes flaxed out Fitzhugh's Command of F.F.V.'s.

We arrived at City Point at 3 o'clock. There are very few troops there but quite a large fleet lying in the river.

We went ashore; walked through the frame building standing in place of that blown up by the late fearful explosion. We climbed the steep hill whose difficulty is mainly removed by the neat stairs that Yankee care has built since our occupation of the Point. At the top of the hill we found a young sentry who halted us & would not let us go further; till Porter, throwing himself on his dignity, which he does not use often, said, "Let that General know that Admiral Porter & Mr Fox are here to see him." He evidently impressed the sentry for he said after an instant's hesitation,—"Go ahead. I reckon it's all right."

A common little wall-tent being indicated, we went up to beard the General. At our first knock, he came to the door. He looked neater & more careful in his dress than usual; his hair was combed, his coat on & his shirt clean, his long boots blackened till they shone. Everybody was presented.

After the conference was over, we went back to the boat: the General accompanied us. We started down the river and soon had dinner. During dinner Porter talked in very indecent terms of abuse of Banks, saying that the Fleet got ahead of the Army & stole the cotton which the Army intended to steal. He spoke of some articles which had appeared in the papers criticizing his action & said he could stand the criticism as long as he had his pockets full of prize money.

After dinner we all gathered around Grant who led the conversation for an hour or so. He thinks the rebels are about to the end of their tether & said, "I hope we will give them a blow this winter that will hasten their end."

He was down on the Massachusetts idea of buying out of the draft by filling their quota with recruits at $300, from among the contrabands in Sherman's army. "Sherman's head is level on that question," he said in reply to some strictures of Mr Forbes. "He knows he can get all these negroes that are worth having anyhow & he prefers to get them that way rather than to fill up the quota of a distant State and thus diminish the fruits of the draft." Sherman does not think so hopefully of negro troops as do many other Generals. Grant himself says they are admirable soldiers in many respects; quick and docile in instruction and very subordinate; good in a charge; excellent in fatigue duty. He says he does not think that an army of them could have stood the week's pounding at the Wilderness and Spotsylvania as our men did: "In fact no other troops in the world could have done it," he added.

Grant is strongly of the belief that the rebel army is making its last grand rally; that they have reinforced to the extent of about 30,000 men in Virginia, Lee getting 20,000 and Early getting 10,-000. He does not think they can sensibly increase their armies further. He says that he does not think they can recover from the blow he hopes to give them this winter.

He is deeply impressed with the vast importance and significance of the late Presidential election. The point which impressed him most powerfully was that which I regarded as the critical one —the pivotal centre of our history—the quiet and orderly character of the whole affair. No bloodshed or riot—few frauds, and those detected and punished in an exemplary manner. It proves our worthiness of free institutions, and our capability of preserving them without running into anarchy or despotism.

Grant remained with us until nearly one o'clock at night—Monday morning & then went to his own boat, the *Martin,* to sleep till day. Babcock, Dunn, and Badeau, of his staff, were with him.

In the morning we were at the Roads again. Breakfasted and went on shore. Ives and I visited Mrs Stackpole and Miss Motley.

Porter before leaving us for his flagship, the *Malvern,* off Newport News, Sunday night, invited us to luncheon at 12. We went. There was quite a large party. Mrs Porter was present.

Ives & I, wishing to see the *Florida,*[1] took one of the *Malvern's* boats and went on board. Com^r Beardsley, in command of the prize, showed her to us. She is a dirty looking beast: the worst-kept craft I ever saw.

---

[1] The Confederate raider *Florida* was captured in the harbor of Bahia, Brazil, Oct. 7, 1864. The *Florida* was brought to Hampton Roads, where she foundered Nov. 28.

Some of her officers were still on board; among them Emory's boy Tom. Some of our people had committed the folly of asking him to take the oath of allegiance: the privilege of refusing gave him a sense of importance to which he had no right. [Added later: "He afterwards took it before me in Paris."]

There was a very fine display made by the sailors and marines of the Fleet in a review and drill in landing. Some fifty boatscrews were going through their evolutions at once. The boats were gay with flags.

We left Fort Monroe at 3 & ½ and arrived at Washington Tuesday morning, the 15ᵗʰ, at 7 A.M.

November 17, 1864. Ives came in in the evening, and he and I went over to Wise's. I found there Benton of the Army ordnance, Wise, Aulick, and Jeffers of the Navy. They were discussing the project of which the President spoke to me some time ago, as having been suggested by Butler, that of exploding a great quantity of powder between the enemy's forts at the mouth of the Cape Fear River for the purpose of dismantling them. The late occurrences at Guth in England were discussed at length, together with all the few events in history bearing on the point. All seemed to think there was something in it but no one seemed to me to speak with conviction. This morning Gillmore was in my room for a while, & I spoke of the matter to him. He gave it no credit whatever; said Col. Tighlman had such fancies which came to nothing; that to produce any considerable wave a fabulous amount of powder would be required; but concluded by saying that the whole question was as yet unascertained and dependent upon experiment; that a shock *might* be produced which would unship all the guns and give the Fleet time to sail in.

Dana gave the President today a letter from General Dix.

December 18, 1864. This morning Blair came into the office and talked a good while about the President's singular policy of favoring his enemies and crushing out his friends. He says that although he has elected everybody in Maryland, his own people are getting disheartened and demoralized, fearing that they are not recognized as the friends of the Administration, and that Senator Hicks, who is to be appointed Collector of the Port to make room for Blair in the Senate, is finessing with the factious opposition lest he should be rejected when before the Senate for confirmation & it is suspected that he may throw himself into the hands of the anti-Lincoln Davis faction, as really the stronger party.

Blair denounces nearly everybody as Lincoln's malignant enemies. He says Chase is—which nobody doubts—that Seward and Stanton are in league against Lincoln. That Stanton went into the Cabinet to break down the Administration by thwarting McClellan & that Seward was in cahoot with him. That Seward was last fall coquetting with the Copperheads to run as their candidate for the Presidency against Lincoln on the platform of the Crittenden Resolutions. I asked him what gave him that idea. He said he was in correspondence with Barlow about McClellan: that he told Barlow that if McClellan would withdraw himself from politics & would make that sort of an announcement, he had no doubt the President would assign him to a command—which he could not do so long as McC. held so prominent a position of political antagonism to the Administration. Barlow answered that McC.'s position was identical with that of "the leading member of the Government" and quoted from a letter "lying before him" to that effect. Blair says this letter was Seward's. He claims to have *exposed* Seward in this way to the President & also to the Barlow crowd. He says he made known to them Seward's duplicity & treachery & this prevented them offering him the Democratic candidacy—which, he says, excited against him the bitter enmity of Seward & Weed and their party.

And much more of the same sort.

When the President came in, he called Blair and Banks into his office, meeting them in the hall.

They immediately began to talk about Ashley's Bill in regard to States in insurrection. The President had been reading it carefully & said that he liked it with the exception of one or two things which he thought rather calculated to conceal a feature which might be objectionable to some. The first was that under the provisions of that bill negroes would be made jurors & voters under the temporary governments. "Yes," said Banks, "that is to be stricken out and the qualification 'white mail citizens of the U.S.' is to be restored. What you refer to would be a fatal objection to the Bill. It would simply throw the Government into the hands of the blacks, as the white people under that arrangement would refuse to vote."

"The second," said the President, "is the declaration that all persons heretofore held in slavery are declared free. This is explained by some to be not a prohibition of slavery by Congress but a mere assurance of freedom to persons actually there in accordance with the Proclamation of Emancipation. In that point of view it is not objectionable, though I think it would have been preferable to so express it."

The President and General Banks spoke very favorably, with these qualifications, of Ashley's Bill.[2] Banks is especially anxious that the Bill may pass and receive the approval of the President. He regards it as merely concurring in the President's own action in the one important case of Louisiana and recommending an observance of the same policy in other cases. He does not regard it, nor does the President, as laying down any castiron policy in the matter. Louisiana being admitted & this bill passed, the President is not estopped by it from recognizing and urging Congress to recognize another State of the South, coming in with constitution and conditions entirely dissimilar. Banks thinks that the object of Congress in passing the Bill at all is merely to assert their conviction that they have a right to pass such a law, in concurrence with the executive action. They want a hand in the reconstruction. It is unquestionably the prerogative of Congress to decide as to qualifications of its own members; that branch of the subject is exclusively their own. It does not seem wise therefore to make a fight upon a question purely immaterial, that is, whether this bill is a necessary one or not, and thereby lose the positive gain of this endorsement of the President's policy in the admission of Louisi-

[2] Congressman J. M. Ashley of Ohio introduced, Dec. 14, 1863, a bill which with some changes became the joint resolution submitting to the States the 13th Amendment. The resolution passed Jan. 31, 1865.

ana, and the assistance of that State in carrying the constitutional amendment prohibiting slavery.

Blair talked more than both Lincoln and Banks, and somewhat vehemently attacked the radicals in the House and Senate who are at work upon this measure, accusing them of interested motives and hostility to Lincoln. The President said, "It is much better not to be led from the region of reason into that of hot blood, by imputing to public men motives which they do not avow."

CHAPTER XXII

March 31, 1865—[January, 1867]

TO CHARLES E. HAY [1]

EXECUTIVE MANSION,
WASHINGTON, *31 March, 1865.*

MY DEAR C[HARLIE]:

I have been a little neglectful of my duties to you lately. I have written almost no letters except on business for some time.

I am getting very hurried as the time approaches for me to give my place in the Executive Office to some new man. The arrears of so long a time cannot be settled in a day.

You have probably seen from the papers that I am to go to Paris as Secretary of Legation.[2] It is a pleasant and honorable way of leaving my present post which I should have left in any event very soon. I am thoroughly sick of certain aspects of life here, which you will understand without my putting them on paper, and I was almost ready, after taking a few months' active service in the field, to go back to Warsaw and try to give the vineyard experiment a fair trial, when the Secretary of State sent for me and offered me this position abroad. It was entirely unsolicited and unexpected. I had no more idea of it than you have. But I took a day or two to think it over, the matter being a little pressing—as the Secretary wanted to let Mr. Bigelow know what he was to expect—and at last concluded that I would accept. The President requested me to stay with him a month or so longer to get him started with the

---

[1] Text from Mrs. Hay's privately printed volumes, I, 253.

[2] John Hay, March 22, 1865, accepted an appointment as Secretary of Legation in Paris where John Bigelow, since 1861, had represented the United States, first as Consul for four years and, since Dec. 1, 1864, as Charge d'Affaires and Minister. Hay returned to New York in January, 1867, shortly after the presentation of John A. Dix, who succeeded Bigelow. Either the diary was kept very irregularly or else portions of it have been lost. There are only a few letters.

247

reorganised office, which I shall do, and shall sail probably in June.

Meanwhile Nicolay, whose health is really in a very bad state, has gone off down the coast on a voyage to Havana, and will be gone the "heft" of the month of April, and I am fastened here, very busy. I don't like to admit and will not yet give up that I can't come on to your "happiest-day-of-your-life," but I must tell you that it looks uncommonly like it just now. But whether I come or not, I will be with you that day in my love and my prayers that God will bless you and yours forever.

I very much fear that all my friends will disapprove this step of mine, but if they knew all that induced me to it they would coincide.

TO JOHN BIGELOW [3]

LEGATION DES ETATS UNIS
November 11, 1865. PARIS

MY DEAR SIR

I have just received your note of yesterday.

I went yesterday to the Spanish Embassy: looking fine enough to have passed for a footman of a successful brewer. I made my speech to the Hidalgo—at least so much of it as I could remember under the appalling consciousness of good clothes: expressing your desolation at being unable to degrade yourself in that way in person: to which his Excellency replied, giving utterance to the highly commendable aspiration that he might have the pleasure of cultivating your acquaintance on your return. I then backed out of the presence of the affable grandee profoundly penetrated with the importance of maintaining amicable relations with the great powers. The sword has its uses; the pen is mightier (*teste* Sir E. L. B. Lytton) but your true civilizer and peacemaker is the gold-laced coat and the chapeau that won't stay on.

General Webb is here. So is General Sanford. So are the Générales S. & W. General King's suite still linger at the Hotel Empire. We have a large pile of letters for General Pruyn. Hence, expect him soon. It is, as Loubat says in one of his best bad things (did you

[3] Clark letter.

ever hear it?) an *inondation Générale*. Dr Henry asks me to say to you that he has gone to Heidelberg where his address is Hotel de Bade. He has probably gone there to meet his son who is also going to the Bad.

The weather has been as gloomy as—as an Illinoisan in Paris. I was searching for a strong metaphor. But the sun is shining today and the world is cheerful.

M[r] Beckwith is giving himself to his work and giving M[r] Derby a realizing sense of his lost and ruined condition. He sent him nearly his weight in instructions a day or two ago. All your appurtenances are well. The youngest hope, I found in the Legation a day or two ago exercising with your dumb-bells. She was posing for an Infant Hercules.

TO MRS. JOHN BIGELOW [4]

[Paris, September, 1865]

MY DEAR MADAME BIGELOW:

I am very much obliged for the letter of Miss Shaw.

I will pay you by a great bit of news.

Charles Sumner the hitherto invincible is engaged. He is to settle at last & cultivate in future only tame oats. The most characteristic point of the matter is that he wrote a long letter full of joy and happiness to Mrs. Adams, announcing his engagement without even mentioning the lady. He will forget he is married more than half the time. He has not written to me, so I know who the lady is—the daughter-in-law of M[r] Sam Hooper the widow of Captain Sturgis Hooper—young and pretty and Bostonian. What more can human ambition desire? I am very busy calling on all my Boston friends to announce the event. It makes me rather poor in spirit however, as you know M[r] Sumner and I are the only two remaining bachelors of the grand abolitionist Army of 20 years ago. And now he leaves me and I linger.

> Like some red leaf the last of its clan
> That dances as often as dance it can

4 Clark letter; undated but evidently of about this period.

As our mutual friend Mr Coleridge expressed it.

Mr Welling has passed through begging to be recalled to your remembrance.

Father Smith of the Propaganda at Rome also.

And Griswold Gray.

And Major Wurtz.

An elderly person called yesterday to see Mr Pomeroy. She looked as if her affections had been trifled with. She was in a hurry—had a great many letters to write—wanted to know Gen. Scott's address. I informed her of the General's change of planet. She said "How dreadful. I was like a daughter to him. Dear! Dear! Well—" after a pause "there's one letter less to write, I'm glad of that."

There is cheerful philosophy for you.

J. H.

DIARY

September 25, 1866. W[ickham] tells me that once while Sumner was sick, he said to him, "Sumner you ought to marry & have a woman to take care of you." Sumner answered, "Don't talk of that W.! I am left behind." W. tells me another very good thing on Sumner. When the question of the admission of Louisiana & Arkansas in President Lincoln's time was before the Committee, Buckalew opposed it giving his reasons. Sumner agreed with him & urged him to make a speech to that effect in the Senate. "No," said Buckalew, "I am what you call a copperhead & a speech from me to that effect will do the question more harm than good. You make the speech." "I can't," said Sumner, "have got too many irons in the fire now." "If you will deliver a speech *I* will write it," says Buckalew. "Agreed," said Sumner. Buckalew wrote the speech & Sumner, after putting a quotation from Milton in, delivered it. While he was giving it to the Senate in that high-priced style of his, old Collamer, the Nestor and pride of the Senate, suddenly pricked up his ears & began to listen, a thing he seldom did when the great Bostonian had the floor. His seat was near Buckalew's toward whom he leaned & nudging him said, "Buckalew, listen! Hanged if the fellow isn't arguing!"

I believe this to be a Copperhead fiction, but it is very good, "all same so," as Japanese Tommy used to say.

Townsend tells me that Dr Johnson is abusing Bigelow, in echo of John Jay, for being subservient to the Court. That is too silly for anger.

Just before going to Biarritz, Beckwith says, the Emperor went to see the Palais de l'Exposition. He seemed to be very bilious. On coming in sight of the Champ de Mars he said, "Call that a palace! Looks like a gasometer!" When he came to the high closed fence surrounding the park, he said "What does this mean? Tear it down! The people have a right to see the building." They explained & he compromised by tearing holes in the fence at intervals. On each side of the North Entrance were neat brick structures for the officers of the Exhibition. Here his bile biled over. "Otez-moi ça. What the Devil do you spoil the view so for? Tear them down!" and this week you see workmen demolishing with pick and shovel what they built laboriously last week with chisel and trowel.

The Emperor never was the meekest of men, but his temper is sour this autumn as the disappointed vintage of Burgundy.

September 27. Yesterday Mr Bigelow was one of the party that accompanied L.L. M.M. on the visit to the iron-clad fleet at Biarritz. I wish Fox had been there.

Loubat gives an odd reverse to the brilliant account of the Russo-American festivities of this summer. He says the persons in charge of it swindled the Government infamously. That the appropriations were most munificent but that the arrangements made were paltry and shabby.

September 30. This morning I found at the Legation a despatch from Mr Seward (sent through the French Ministère de l'Intérieur) saying "Resignation accepted—General Dix appointed successor—leaves here 28 October," dated Washington, 29th September, 12.45 at night. I sent copy to Biarritz.

The morning papers contained the bare announcement. The *Patrie* in the afternoon contained an attack on Mr Bigelow for his ultra-American stiffness in the Mexican question.

The *Constitutionnel* this morning shows by its announcement that it has been made acquainted with Seward's despatch.

[TO J. G. NICOLAY?]

[*Dec. 1866*]

Read about "Mr Gibb" & let your soul have rest. Read about the President's household & howl over the paradise you are excluded from. Read (& send back) (keeping the rest) my Herndon. "The only biographer of Lincoln in wh. the Future will take any stock." & send back my "Anna Rutledge" before you forget it.

DIARY

[*December, 1866.*] The General [Dix] immediately after his arrival was presented by Mr Bigelow to the Marquis de Moustier, and a few days afterwards received from the Grand Master of Ceremonies a letter informing him that he would be received by the Emperor on Sunday the 23^d [December] at two o'clock. He afterwards received a note from the Duke de Fasches la Pagerie, informing him that the Empress would receive him immediately after his audience with the Emperor.

I hired a carriage & two servants in the Rue Boissy d'Anglais for Hoffman and myself. It was a highly respectable looking affair, not fresh enough to look hired, with a couple of solemn flunkies that seemed to have been in the family for at least a generation. We went to the General's and in a few moments came in the Baron de la Jus. He said he was very much crowded today with besoigne that he had five Ministers to bring to the Palace and that therefore we would please excuse his hurry. Upon which we all rose & went to the door, where we found a court carriage, the Imperial arms blazing on the panels & the harness, drawn by 4 horses & accompanied by two mounted outriders. Everything covered with tawdry tarnished gold lace. It seemed like the Triumphal Car in a flourishing circus. Into this vehicle mounted the General & the Chamberlain, Hoffman & I following in our sham-private remise and we had the

honors of a stare from the *badauds* on the asphalt of the Champs
Elysées as the party lumbered down to the Tuileries. We were all
in our Army Uniform.

Arrived there we were shown to a warm cheery anteroom, with
a superb wood fire and a fine view of the Tuileries gardens, the
river & the Arch of Triumph. The Colombian Minister had already
arrived. He and his Secretary stood conversing with one of the fine
violet-colored chamberlains. Another received us and we talked of
nothing in particular—the weather which was sharp for Paris,
skating, monuments, acquaintances. One torment of diplomatic
life is that you never know the names of these agreeable fellows.
They lose all identity in their violet coats and Imperial moustaches.
You do not hear their names when you are presented to them and
if you look upon the official list of the officers of the Emperor's
household you only find that you may take your choice of a dozen
names for the man you are looking after.

Fane, the British Minister *ad interim* came in. I presented him
to Gen¹ Dix. They talked Alabama, Fenians & stuff. Then a long
gaunt Bavarian, Pergler de Perglas, & his Secretary who seemed
moved by rusty springs—in military uniform; a thin, wiry, blue-
blooded Brazilian, a Peruvian, and some more. Bigelow at least a
half head taller than anybody but Fane, who is not tall by the way
— only long.

There came some more violet people and moved us into a larger
salon. There we were presented to the Duc de Cambacérès—a
jaunty old gentleman lean and shaven & wigged—long also. He
bowed lavishly & seemed distressed that nobody would sit down.
Bigelow in a few moments was called for. He entered the next room
where the blaze of the Imperial presence dazzled us through the
opening door. His audience of leave was soon over. General Dix
followed by me and Hoffman was then ushered into The Presence.
The General looked anxiously around for the Emperor, advancing
undecidedly until a little man who was standing in front of the
Throne stepped forward to meet him. Everybody bowed profoundly as the Duc de Cambacérès gave the name and title of the
General. The little man bowed and the General beginning to
recognize in him a dim likeness to the Emperor's portrait made his

speech to him. I looked around the room for a moment admiring as I always do on ceremonial occasions in France the rich and tasteful masses of color which the various groups of Great Officers of the Crown so artistically present. Not a man's place is left to accident. A cardinal dashes in a great splash of scarlet. A *cent-garde* supplies an exquisite blue and gold. The yellows and the greens are furnished by the representatives of Law & Legislation, and the Masters of Ceremonies fill up with an unobtrusive violet. Yet these rich lights and soft shadows are accessory to the central point of the picture—the little man who is listening or seeming to listen to the General's address. If our Republican eyes can stand such a dazzling show, let us look at him.

Short and stocky; he moves with a queer sidelong gait like a gouty crab: a man so wooden looking that you would expect his voice to come rasping out like a watchman's rattle. A complexion like crude tallow—marked for Death, whenever Death wants him —to be taken sometime in half an hour, or left, neglected by the skeleton king, for years perhaps, if properly coddled. The moustache and imperial which the world knows, but ragged and bristly, concealing the mouth entirely, moving a little nervously as the lips twitch. Eyes sleepily watchful—furtive, stealthy, rather ignoble: like servants looking out of dirty windows & saying "nobody at home" and lying, as they say it. And withal a wonderful phlegm. He stands there as still and impassive as if carved in oak for a ship's figurehead. He looks not unlike one of those rude inartistic statues. His legs are too short—his body too long. He never looks well but on a throne or on a horse, as kings ought.

But the General, who has raised his voice and grown a little oratorical as he closes his speech by recalling the bonds of union which ally America to France, hands the Emperor his sealed letter of credence. He receives it & gives it to the Duc de Bassano who stands at his right. His face breaks up with ungainly movements of the moustache & the eyelids. You can imagine it a sort of wooden clock preparing to strike. When he speaks you are sure of your theory. The voice is wooden; it is not so strong & full as a year ago. He speaks rather rapidly & not distinctly. He slurs half his words, as rapid writers do half their letters. He makes his set speech, which, with the General's, will appear tomorrow in the *Moniteur* & then comes sidling up and says (smilingly, he evidently thinks, but the machinery of smiles at the corners of his mouth is apparently out of repair), "You expect many of your countrymen in Paris this year?"

"A great many doubtless."

"There will be a regiment of your *milice?*"

"There has been some talk of it," &c., &c., "but your Majesty will not expect them to compare with your veterans."

"But you have shown that it does not take long to make good troops."

When I & Hoffman (that is awkward but I preserve the order) were presented, he, clearly wishing to be very civil, as it is most rare that a monarch addresses a Secretary of Legation, said, "But you are very young to be Col-o-nel. Did you make the war in America?"

I wanted to insist that older & wickeder men than I were responsible for that crime but I thought best to answer the intention rather than the grammar & said I had had an humble part in the war.

"*Infanterie* or *cavalerie?*"

"The general staff."

"And you?" he said, turning to Hoffman, and received the same answer.

We bowed and backed out of the presence.

We were then taken to the apartments of the Empress. She was charmingly dressed in a lilac walking dress with an almost invisible bonnet. She had doubtless been to church like a good pious lady as she is and received afterwards in her promenade costume. Time has dealt very gently with her. She is still full of those sweet winning fascinations that won her a crown. There are few partisans so bitter as not to be moved by her exquisite manner. Even the little stories at which men smile, her subjection to priests, her hanging up over old Baciocchi's deathbed the holy rag from the baby linen of John Baptist which extorted from the tormented old sinner his last grim smile, her vestal lamp in the Church of our Lady of Victories, and all that mummery is not unfeminine & people do not care to be bitter about it. To the General she was charming. She talked about the President & his trip to Chicago (which the Gen¹ explained was purely a personal visit of friendship to the tomb of a friend!!!).[5] When we were presented she made the identical remark made by the Emperor: "You are young to be colonel?" People after a dozen years of intercourse get the same ideas & ways of looking at things. She asked if the grade of colonel was the same in our army as in the French. She spoke English with a charming Castilian accent, which is infinitely prettier than the French.

She is so winning and so lovely that one feels a little guilty in not being able in conscience to wish her eternal power for herself, her heirs and assigns.

So we left the gracious blonde Spaniard & passed down through avenues of flunkeys to the door where our own sham flunkies received us and drove us to the Rue de Presbourg.

The ceremony is concluded by giving to the Chief Piqueur a present of 250 fr.

[*January, 1867.*] The last time I saw the Emperor was on the 1st of January 1867, at the Diplomatic reception. Instead of admitting the Diplomats by a door nearest the Salle du Trône, they always manage to drag them through a long series of salons crowded with footmen of portentous calf development and chamberlains in purple: to strike the imaginations of outside barbarians. We were passed on as usual through these blazing hedges of tinsel to the Reception Room. It was pretty well filled when we entered and we passed a pleasant half hour talking to our acquaintances in the Corps. A good deal of interest was taken in the General, who was one of the newest arrivals and whose venerable and gentlemanlike appearance produced a most favorable impression. At the order of the bustling chamberlain we took our places, the United States by a queer chance finding itself between the two American Empires, Mexico & Brazil, Almonte having been presented just before & the Brazilian just after Gen[l] Dix. The Brazilian Minister presented Dix to Almonte, the Gen[l] thinking that much could be

---

[5] In August, 1866, President Johnson set out upon what became a famous journey, ostensibly to visit the tomb of Stephen A. Douglas in Chicago. Actually the trip was to provide an opportunity to appeal to the country for support against Congress. The opposition represented the tour as being little less than a drunken orgie, which was a political libel.

sacrificed to courtesy, & they began to recall an old Washington acquaintance, when the door opened and the usher shouted "*L'Empereur.*" Everyone bowed with various degrees of abject servility. The Emperor came woodenly in. He was dressed in his usual uniform of General of Division. The Prince Imperial, a nice slender child with pleasant sad eyes like his mother, came in with his august sire for the first time. The Emperor only begins to associate him with great public ceremonies. He was dressed in black velvet coat & short full breeches with red stockings—the broad cordon of the Legion of Honor over his shoulder and across his little chest. He walked beside his father, bowing when he bowed, & stopping, a little fidgetty, while the Sphynx talked with the wise men of the world.

But on entering the Emperor paused, bowed & took position—the Pope's nuncio—Mgr Chigi—made the usual formal speech of congratulation, to which the Emperor replied with his best wishes for the perpetuity of thrones and the prosperity of peoples and his hopes that the Exposition would bring the millennium this year. He evidently has his brain full of the vast results that are to accrue to him from that unsightly structure in the Champ de Mars. He then went around the circle, speaking a word to most of the Ministers. I stood next to Almonte and waited with great interest to see how they met.

The Emperor came rolling up to the Mexican & stopped. Both bowed. Almonte seemed rather ill at ease. The Emperor held him a moment with his dead eyes half shut. He then said in a manner which was carefully cold and insolent, "Les choses sont bien compliquées là bas." The poor devil, who doubtless feels himself lost by his advocacy of the Imperial cause in Mexico, had no reply ready to this insolent remark from his angry and ungrateful tempter. The Emperor bowed, the Prince Imperial bowed & Almonte bowed. I did not dare to look at him.

I looked at the Emperor instead, who came to General Dix, & was very gracious—speaking French this time—asked the General where he lived & said it was a *beau quartier*—the Genl said yes, thanks to His Majesty—and His Majesty pulled the corners of his mouth into a sort of smile & bowed to the General and bowed to me

& passed to Brazil—and put a malicious little question to Brazil about its war & then walked almost hastily past the smaller powers —pausing an instant with Fane (who was below us, having been presented five minutes later the day we were)—then passed out and we loafed down to the door and waited in the uncomfortable entry for our carriages till we were blue & ill-natured. Then made calls on the necessary nobs by writing our names in a book at their door and at last went home and took off our livery & were glad it was over.

CHAPTER XXIII

February 2—March 5, 1867

DIARY

[*February 2, 1867.*] On arriving in New York [from Paris] on the
1st February 1867 I went as usual to 17 Wall Street. I found Carver
and one or two others in the back room. They had nothing special
to say. Vanny [Vanderhoof] came in. He talked a little more but in
a chastened and subdued tone as if at a funeral. I thought it a glum
company and rose to go. Van followed me. "Haven't you heard?"
"No! What?" "The boys are bust up & gone to hell again." We
walked down to Delmonico's for bitters & he told me of Billy's
colossal campaign & its utter collapse. He had himself been swamped
with the rest & for that reason had hung up on his matrimonial in-
tents. Later I saw Billy [Marston] &c. They were not so cast down
as Van. "Ups & downs," they said, cheerfully enough.

Charlie Chase told me I had a balance of about $500. [Footnote
added later: Of which I have never since heard. The boys are too
hard up to be interpellated about it.]

I spent the evening with Charlie and got off in the owl train.
Met on the cars a lame darkey in trouble & paid his fare to Washington.

The day was drizzling and damp—Saturday, 2nd February—when
I arrived in Washington. I drove to Willard's, saw the same
dead-beats hanging around the office, the same long-haired listless
loafers moving gloomily up and down, pensively expectorating.
Several shook hands with me cordially. The Radical fellows wanting to sympathize with me as a martyr and a little disappointed
when they found I was none. Lamon picked me up & I went to his
office, saw Judge Black and talked politics for a while. The terrible
defeats of the past year have sobered & toned down the conserva-

tives. They talk very quietly and sensibly.

I drove out to the State Department after lunch. Mr Hunter received me and after a little delay ushered me into the reception room to await Mr Seward. He came swinging in saying, "Well, John Hay, so you got tired of it and came home." "Yes," I said, "it was time. I had enough of the place and the place had enough of me."

He then went into a long and very clever disquisition on the danger of a man holding office—the desiccation and fossilizing process—illustrating it by Mr Hunter and saying he feared Nicolay was getting into that way. I assured him Nic. was not: that he was singleheartedly pursuing 10,000 dollars & that when he got it he would come home & go to his ranch. He was glad to hear that, he said.

He talked of the Motley business, which was new.[1] He explained his letter to M., wh. to me needed no explanation, being the same as he sent to Nicolay & wh. Nicolay & I thought was meant to call out a denial simply of the charges made against him. The Copperhead Democrats who now form almost the entire support of the President, are continually boring him for offices and accusing Mr Seward of wickedly keeping in their places the old Radical Lincoln appointees. They make charges against these and Mr Seward sends them notifications thereof. Everybody but Motley has considered them as kindly intended & answered them in that sense.

He told me Fred^k Seward had gone to St Domingo to buy a harbor and bay for a naval station for the United States. Not having heard a word since they sailed, Admiral Porter & he, he was a little anxious about him.

He talked a great deal of the present position of politics, and of his own attitude. He never seemed to me to better advantage. His utter calmness and cheerfulness, whether natural or assumed, is most admirable. He seems not only free from any political wish or aspiration, but says distinctly that he cares nothing for the judg-

[1] Early in the Johnson Administration many American diplomatic representatives in Europe were charged with disloyalty to the President, and with conduct unbecoming plain Americans. Seward reported the charges to the accused men and invited explanations. Motley was incensed and resigned. Seward would have asked Motley to withdraw his resignation, but the President, desiring to show his dislike of Sumner, Motley's sponsor, insisted on its acceptance, April 18, 1867.

ment of history, so that he does his work well here.

He speaks utterly without bitterness of the opposition to him & the President. He thinks the issue before the country was not fairly put, but seems rather to admire the cleverness with wh. the Radical leaders obscured and misstated the question to carry the elections. He says the elections in short amount to this:

Congress to the North. Do you want rebels to rule the Government?—No. Do you want more representation than the South?— Yes. Do you want negroes to vote in the South and not in the North? —Yes. Do you want to give up the fruits of victory to the South?— No.

Congress to the South. Do you want your negroes to vote—and not Northern negroes?—No. Do you want to lose fifty members of Congress?—No. Do you want to be deprived of a vote yourselves?— Not by a damned sight.

And so the issue is clearly presented in such a style as to decide the question beforehand.

He asked me if I wanted anything—if I would like to go back to Europe. I said I w^d like anything worth having, if it could be given to me without any embarrassment to him or the President at the present time.

He asked me to dine with him the next day, Sunday, & go to church in the morning.

I spent the rest of the afternoon at Mrs. Sprague's & Mrs. Wallach's receptions, and saw many people I knew. The evening I passed with Harry Wise and Charlie Keep. Wise is disgusted with Johnson. His first words to me were, "Everything is changed—you find us all Copperheads." Painter said, "You will find the home of virtue has become the haunt of vice." Adams said, "A man asked me the other day if I had been at the White House lately & I told him no. I want to remember that house as Lincoln left it." Every one I met used some such expression. It is startling to see how utterly without friends the President is.

3^d Feb. I went in the morning to my rendezvous with Mr Seward. He had gone to Phil. Johnson's funeral. I went to church alone;

walked home with Miss Loring & listened a half hour to her clever Washington gossip, the most spiritual in the world, then made several visits; saw Hooper and Agassiz.

Dined with Mr Seward at 4. No one but myself & his son Augustus. Doolittle came in while we were dining; then Thurlow Weed. They talked mostly about subjects not political: of Paris; of the great accretions of populations in ancient and in modern times. Weed talked most of Rome & Italy; Seward of the East, Babylon & Palestine. His pictures of the desolation of those countries which once nourished its millions & where now a rat w^d starve, were very graphic.

He suddenly said to me, "And now, John Hay, if it were not that Weed is continually in the way I would make you a Minister. But it seems Mr Harris is a very good man & has been defeated and the President is fond of him and so a mission must be kept for him. There is a vacancy in Sweden & I suppose Weed will insist on Harris having it."

"Would Harris take such small change?" I asked.

Here Weed, who had not much relished Seward's badinage, broke out, "It is too good for him. He would take anything. He deserves nothing."

This led to some conversation on Cowan's chances. They all thought them rather slim. Seward said it ought to be known in justice to Cowan that he had asked for nothing and knew nothing of the appointment until it came to the Senate. Doolittle said he w^d try to persuade Sumner to report upon the nomination without a recommendation & let the Senate act upon it in that way.

Seward asked Doolittle if he had any influence left in the Committee on Foreign Relations. "Scarcely any," said Doolittle. "If there were anybody there you could depend on," said Seward, "I w^d like to have mischievous and annoying questions about our foreign policy prevented. When a private negotiation is begun, & not finished, a blast of publicity destroys it: there is nothing more to be done. The attention and jealousy of the world outside is attracted to us & obstacles spring up in an hour. I have an understanding with Banks & have always had such a one with Sumner until he has of late become hopelessly alienated. Conness is especially troublesome. I could manage him by giving him all the offices in the Department, but he is so greedy & unreasonable that one can not talk sensibly with him."

Weed went off to New York in the evening, just after dinner. Doolittle stayed a little while longer. He and Seward talked of the situation. Doolittle thought the public temper was calming a little. Seward agreed with him—thought every day was a day gained for the cause of reason. Doolittle said Wade was very ambitious for the place of President of the Senate, that he had great strength, but that Fessenden was beginning to be spoken of; that Fessenden evidently desired to be elected, which was a little unexpected as Fessenden had never for a moment occupied the chair, but had always avoided taking it. The same is true of Wade.

Seward said that Morgan had called upon him that afternoon & had said the same thing of Fessenden. Seward told him that he was for Fessenden, though that w^d probably injure Fessenden's chances if it were known. That Fessenden was by nature & habit of mind a safe & reasonable man, "though he has more temper than I, for I have none; he would bend and make concessions for the sake of retaining his power to do good, which I never could do. I am satisfied that Fessenden wants that place for the good he can do & the harm he can prevent."

The whipped-out stunned way of talking that I have seen in all the Conservatives is very remarkable. No bitterness, no energetic denunciation, no threats; but a bewildered sort of incapacity to comprehend the earnest deviltry of the other side, characterizes them all but Seward, who is the same placid philosophic optimist that he always was, the truest and most single-hearted Republican alive.

Doolittle went away. As he arose to go, Seward said, "You must somehow help me to do something for John Hay." I was touched & astonished at this kind persistence of the Secretary in my favor.

I staid an hour or so. He told me that it seemed as if they would prove General Dix to have been in the receipt of the two salaries of the Minister & Naval Officer. He seemed much disgusted at this. He said, "It almost makes me determined never to give up a prejudice again." He ran over Genl Dix's history, showing how consistently the Genl had always pursued his bread and butter in every conjunction, always getting on pretty well, but always losing the great prizes of his ambition by an unlucky lack of political principle and an overgreed of office, in every period of party crisis. He had always been opposed to him but had taken him up & stood by him since the beginning of the war in spite of the General's attempt to "cut under" from time to time. Seward got him into Buchanan's Cabinet through Stanton. When Bigelow's place fell vacant by his resignation last July, Seward kept it for Dix. And now it seems he is to fall by this ignoble charge of avarice.[2]

We had some comforting optimist talk. I believe so utterly in Republicanism that I am never troubled long about the future.

Baron Gerolt came in and we talked Napoleon & Bismarck and *fusil à aiguille.*

I went to see Charles Eames—found there Ashton & Chandler. Eames was unusually sesquipedalian over the Motley correspondence—denounced Seward's letter as one "from which every element of tolerableness had been carefully eliminated," & the Treasury men came in with the same style of thing till I got loud & oratorical also & Mrs. Eames came in & sent her husband to bed for getting excited.

Found a card from Sumner at the Hotel when I came in asking me to tea six hours before.

4th Feb. Monday was one of God's own days. I went to shake hands with the Interior & P.O. Departments & saw, between the two, Mrs Sprague & Miss Hoyt doing a constitutional. Walked with them in the blessed sunshine & shopped & rode in street cars (they paying for I found the Fenians at Willard's had stolen all my money wh. like an idiot I had left lying on my table. The curse of Donneraile be on them!)

They took me in the afternoon to the President's to make a bow to Mrs. Patterson & Mrs. Stover.[3] The House is much more richly & carefully furnished than in my time. But the visitors were not quite up to the old mark, which itself was not hard to reach.

[2] Dix, although already at his post, had an *ad interim* appointment subject to confirmation by the Senate. If the Senate had failed to confirm, Dix's appointment would have expired at the end of the current session of Congress.

[3] Mrs. Patterson and Mrs. Stover, the President's daughters.

Dined with Wise—Alden & Ammen were there. Ammen told a neat story illustrating the difference of point of view. He went at the beginning of the war to report to Admiral Stringham. The old sea dog did not know him till he mentioned his name & told him he had made one of his earliest cruises with [him]. "Oh yes," said Stringham, "now I recollect you perfectly, but you boys grow so there is no keeping track of you." He called upon Miss Chase soon afterwards and she was as pretty & gracious as usual & said, "Well, Captain Ammen, I suppose you consider y^r seagoing days as about over!" The veteran called him a boy & the girl a veteran. Tuesday morning I went to Congress: sent my name in to Cullom who brought me in on the floor & there I staid an hour or two and shook many hands. Everybody said something about the better days gone & nobody spoke of the better days coming. Yet in those better days they mourned, a million fine fellows were slaying each other with swords and guns and the widows and the orphans were increasing faster than the babies.

I spent the evening at Mr Sumner's. I was astonished to find that he attributed the half advocacy by the French liberals of the President to Bigelow's influence. I told him it was as unjust as to ascribe to Bigelow the attacks wh. these same men are now making upon the Presidential policy.

I am inclined to think since I returned that Bigelow could not have retained his place very much longer. He did not suspect this when he resigned, though you cannot make any one believe that. His talents and his services are not held at their true value.

I went to a ball at John Potts' & staid only a few moments, leaving before the cotillion.

6th Feb.—Wednesday morning. Called to see Mr Seward: found M^r & Mrs Frederick [Seward] had returned. The Secretary told me I had been appointed temporary employé in the Department of State, that for the present I was to take the place of his private secretary. I made no reply in the presence of Mrs Seward but went later to the Department and saw the Secretary and said that if he wished my personal services in the Department that of course they were entirely at his service; but that if he had done this out of his usual

kindness for me that I thought best to decline, that I had better
go home & see my parents for the present. He agreed with me & left
me perfectly free to do as I liked, saying the place in the Department was open whenever I wanted it. He said he had proposed my
name to the President the day before as Minister to Sweden. The
President said he had another man for it, Gen¹ Bartlett of N. Y. We
are doing all we can for the soldiers you know, &c. He said the matter
was strictly confidential as yet. I told him I had business proposals
under consideration—they were not what I wanted but would
probably support me & give me in time a competence. He said he
had no doubt that a good position in business was worth very much
more to me than any appointment I could hold under the Gov^t. I
agreed but said that after being Minister I could make better arrangements. He said he w^d not forget me. I thanked him for all his
goodness & took leave.

Now the real reason I declined this thing was, I believe, a motive
I did not suspect or acknowledge to myself—the note & telegram I
had received the night before.

I went to Mrs. Sprague's & she had slept on it & said no. So I determined to stay here till after Monday anyhow.

I made calls on Mrs Stanton, Mrs Welles, & Mrs Randall: would
have gone to Browning's but got stuck in the red mud of Georgetown.

I dined with Sumner. The party was M^r & Mrs Sumner, who looks
very sweet & matronly in her secondes noces, Miss Clover Hooper,
Mr Field of Philad^a & George Wm. Curtis & myself. I like Sumner
better since his marriage. He should have been married long ago.
Every man should who can afford it. His ready-made family is very
taking. Little Bel Hooper came running in for dessert & rated Curtis
soundly for not giving her the largest bonbon. It was quite startling
to see Sumner in the bosom of his family.

The conversation was entirely political. The debate of the day
in the Senate, Sherman's speech against including Cabinet Ministers
in the Tenure of Office bill,[4] was rather severely criticised by Sumner
who thought he had been too magnanimous in allowing it to pass

---

[4] The Tenure of Office Bill, passed Mar. 2, 1867, denied the President the right
to remove civil officials without the consent of the Senate.

unanswered. Sumner thought the power of appointing & removing members of the Cabinet more properly belonged to the Senate as a permanent body than to the President. He said the Senate was less liable to become depraved and bad than the Pres^t. He said "for instance I can scarcely imagine a Senate that would now confirm Mr Seward."

As to the argument in favor of harmony in the Cabinet he scouted that altogether. He said that in every constitutional government in the world the head of the Gov^t was frequently obliged to accept ministers that were personally and politically obnoxious. That it was the duty often of a patriotic Minister to remain in the counsels of a perverted administration as a "privileged spy." He referred to Stanton and said it should be made impossible for Johnson to remove him.

In all this ingenious and really clever and learned talk of Sumner's I could but remark the blindness of an honest earnest man who is so intent upon what he thinks right and necessary that he closes his eyes to the fatal consequences of such a course in different circumstances and different times. The Senate is now a bulwark against the evil schemes of the President: therefore he would give the Senate a power which might make it the most detestable engine of anarchy or oppression. Had this law that he now demands existed in 1861 the rebellion would have had its seat and center in Washington and loyalty would have been the bloody color of revolution. I told him so, but he would not see it, saying if the South had taken that course they would by that act have abnegated their rebellion—which to me seems absurd.

Genl Dix was discussed. Curtis favored letting him slide for his two years. Field thought the "hoary old place-hunter should be marked and punished." Sumner treated with contempt the charge of cumulation against Genl Dix. His crime of presiding at the Philadelphia convention is capital.[5] How can the Senate reject the small fry of renegade Unionists and permit to go unscathed the man who gave to that wicked scheme all its momentary respectability?

Sumner's account of the rejection of McGinnis was very amusing.

[5] The National Union Convention met in Philadelphia Aug. 14, 1866. It enthusiastically endorsed President Johnson.

"The Senate's answer to Master Seward." He said Bartlett's name had come in in McGinnis' place. "He is an old-fashioned Copperhead—did good service in the war, they say, but that won't save him." ["Bartlett was at last confirmed."—Marginal note added later.]

After dinner we were talking about Jay. Sumner gave me the account of Jay's estrangement from him on the Vienna mission business.

7th Thursday. Called at the State Department and talked a good while with Fred^k Seward. He is very well & jolly. I have never seen him appear to such advantage. His pictures of the *dolce far niente* of the Indies are very amusing. They almost make you yawn with languid enjoyment.

Went to the House. The bill for the Military Gov^t of the rebel states was up. Brandegee made a little flourish of the eagle with a long Latin quotation that made the Western members grin.

Banks I talked with some time. He was really despondent about the course things were taking—deprecating most earnestly this abdication of the civil power in favor of the irresponsible military. I thought the case was not hopeless—bad as it was, as Congress could at any time resume the powers it now delegates for a temporary purpose. He said the people would more likely acquiesce in a bad thing done than work for its repeal. I talked with Boutwell five minutes afterwards. He was confident that the measure was a good one and that the army could be trusted. I think there never was an army that could be trusted, as an army. It is un-Anglo-Saxon to perpetuate this state of things. I recognize the miserable situation of the South & perhaps this bill is necessary—but it is a bad thing to do for all that. Woe be to him by whom this offense cometh!

Genl Harding, the member from my district, is for the bill of course—he takes it from his caucus as he would a dose of salts from his doctor without questions. A hard, dry, practical blasé old fellow —rude and vulgar, but with a dull slow sagacity of his own.

I dined with Lamon. After dinner dressed for the President's reception—found the crowd too great at the door and went over to Seward's. The Secretary, Banks & Fred^k were together in the salon. I asked for Mrs Seward. Fred took me into an adjoining room. A servant told us Mrs S. had gone to bed. It was after 10. I rose to go. Frederick took me by the shoulders & pushed me into a fauteuil. We talked of indifferent things, seasickness & St Domingo, half an hour. I took leave & was passing down stairs when Banks came out. While he & I were putting on our coats, the Secretary shouted for me to come up again. He wanted to show me a superb set of Chinese chessmen which he had recently received. They were by far the finest and most elaborate I had ever seen. I asked him about the propriety or expediency of calling on Browning. He advised me to do it.

I told him Bartlett would probably be rejected. He said, "That is part of the general system of pyrotechnics. They will fire them all off in their turn."

I then went over to the Executive Mansion & got in, the crowd being much thinned. The President was very cordial to me: said I must come and see him. Mrs Johnson received for the first time: a quiet, invalid old lady. The crowd not choice but as good an average as ever: scarcely any distinguished people and none squalid. We used to have plenty of both.

Friday, 8. Went to see Browning: he was very cordial & promised at once. He feels very gloomy. Thinks we are going to the devil. He is a brighter man and an older man than I, but I know we are not.

Wrote all day. Rainy & muggy.

Dined with the Hoopers. There heard of Banks' unexpected and dramatic heading off of Overseer Thad. in the House. Enormously clever man is Banks. Too moderate and wise just now—a doomed Girondin, I am afraid. Raymond is as clever, but not as good and strong.

Doolittle said the other night to Seward that Banks had told him a few days before that he saw no earthly power that could prevent the impeachment of the President. This impressed Doolittle very much, as he said, Banks being himself against impeachment. Seward said it w^d impress him more if it were not that he remembered that Banks had thought there was no salvation out of knownothingism —when in fact there was none in it.

Went to Secretary Welles' reception. Sheridan was the lion, looking, as Miss Hooper says, as if he would blow up on short provocation. A mounted torpedo, somebody once called him—inflammable little Jack of Clubs—to whom be all praise!

Then a German cotillon at Reverdy Johnson's, very ill-led by a booby son of his—who danced in a straddling sort of way, "wide between the legs as if he had gyves on."

Saturday. [*Feb. 9.*] Went up to the House again. Talked with C. about the affair of the day before. Saw another instance of the curious intolerance of the majority and the feebleness of individual judgment when opposed to the decisions of the caucus. C. was heartily for Banks & his motion & was full of delighted admiration of the way he carried it against Stevens—but acknowledged that he had voted the other way. He says Boutwell is jealous of Banks and anxious to discredit him before the people of Massachusetts.

I got the end of Boutwell's speech which was very fine and nervous. Boutwell always shows to good advantage when thoroughly roused and excited.

Raymond talked a little—clever and fluent as ever, and impressing nobody.

In the evening there was a German cotillon at Baron Gerolt's. Kasseroud led, and very well. I danced with Miss Haggerty. Invitations were for 6 1/2, being Saturday. People accepted and went early. We dispersed to bed at midnight with a queer sense of its being the next morning.

Sunday. [*Feb. 10.*] At breakfast Drake DeKay handed me Nasby's last letter about the legal lynching of a negro preacher in Kentucky. The wit and satire of Locke are growing so earnest and savage that it is painful to read him. This article is as pathetic as it is grotesque.

Wandered out to the Department & found nobody: coming back saw the Sprague-Hoyt party in a street car & went home with them. Dined with Lamon. He thinks I can make something out of the swamp-land claims. I will try it if I get off in time.

Spent the early part of the evening with [erased] and the latter at Sumner's. Discussed with him the subject of the rejection of Mc-Ginnis & the prospective bilking of Bartlett; told him something of my prospects: he said there would be no question whatever of my confirmation if it were not for the question of what was due to Campbell. It seems Campbell [6] is squirming and does not want to go out: has written to Senators to stand by him and protect him. So that they may reject every one who is nominated to the place. Of course that will not save Campbell but the Senate is a little *toqué* and does not seem to see that. Seward says there is a vacancy though the Senate does not know it.

I told Sumner what I conscientiously believe, that Seward has done all in his power to save Mr Lincoln's appointees from being displaced by the Copperhead pressure, that he had spoken of giving a place to me without demanding or suggesting any adhesion to the present administration as the condition of the appointment.

I asked Sumner if he did not intend to write a history of these times. He answered in a way to convince me that he had thought a great deal of the matter. He greatly regretted the absence of jottings to fix in his mind the incidents of his daily intercourse with the President, the Ministers of Gov^t & the leading Congressmen. He considers himself the most highly qualified man in America to write an exhaustive political history of this great period, on account of his great & unusual facilities of intercourse with every branch of government & opinion. He said it was impossible to do anything of the kind so long as he remained in the Senate. I suggested that he might find the necessary leisure in the representation of the country for a few years in Europe. This suggestion was by no means novel to him. —— —— He told me that several months ago when he spoke to Seward about the Harvey matter, Seward had said that every minister in Europe was with the President as against Congress. He said he did not answer, as he might have done that he had at that moment in his pocket a letter from Motley and one from Hale, disproving that assertion. —— Sumner has grown very arrogant with success. He feels keenly the satisfaction of being able to bind and loose at his free will and pleasure. There is no selfish exaltation in it, or too little for him to recognize—it is rather the fierce joy of a prophet over the destruction of the enemies of his Lord. He speaks

[6] John Wilson Campbell of Ohio had been appointed Minister to Mexico May 4, 1866; he resigned June 16, 1867.

with hearty enjoyment of what is to happen to Cowan—referred to Doolittle's "sleek, purring attempt" to soften him in that matter so far as to have Cowan's name referred to the Senate without recommendation—and his snort of rejection.

Met the Vicomte de Chabool at Willard's: he rather deprecates our violence—thinks the rejection of Dix would make all Paris Copperhead.

Monday. February 11. Went to the Department; got my letter from [erased]. Told Mr Hunter that Hoffman was not yet nominated to the Senate; called up Bartle who says he was. The conclusion is that the nominations are sticking in the Executive Mansion. Spoke to Fred^k Seward, who thought it was perhaps as well to wait now till Dix's case is decided, that I may be Chargé in case of his rejection: in the meantime I am still Secretary of Legation on leave.

* * * *

Mrs. Sprague gave a beautiful ball. The ladies who danced the cotillon & many who did not, had their hair powdered *à la marquise*. I have never seen so beautiful and picturesque a roomful. Some of the most striking were the hostess herself (with whom I danced), the Hoyts, Miss Romaine Goddard, Miss Haggerty, & Mrs. Banks, who was very correctly dressed, even to the extent of the blue ribbon around the neck, a little refinement in which she was alone, Miss Kinzie, a fresh western beauty and a superb danseuse. Mrs. Sumner & Miss Hooper, though not powdered, were beautifully dressed.

The Chief Justice showed me Carpenter's engraving of the Reading of the Proclamation. He objects to the whole picture being made subsidiary to Seward who is talking while every one else either listens or stares into vacancy. He thinks it would have been infinitely better to have taken the 22nd of September when the Proclamation was really read to the Cabinet.

I referred to Seward's criticism that the subject was not well chosen—that the really decisive Cabinet meeting was that at which it was decided to provision & reinforce Fort Sumter.

He said there was no such meeting—that Mr Lincoln asked the opinion of the Cabinet in writing—that there were but two of the Cabinet who favored the reinforcement, himself and Blair—that Blair was more decided than he in favor of reinforcing the fort— that *he* (C.) thought some strong and decided assertion or proclamation of the intentions of the Gov^t should have been made at that time.

Chase was always a little addicted to coups de theatre.

I said I thought an exaggerated importance was often ascribed to the manner in which events were accomplished, that in great revolutionary times events accomplished themselves not by means of, but in spite of, the well-meant efforts of the best and wisest men. The Girondins nearly monopolized the brains of France: yet they were crushed out as it was probably necessary they should be—that the destiny of the people should be accomplished through their fever and their struggles.

He quite agreed with this, insisting however upon the individual responsibility of each one to do what seems best in his sight for the Commonwealth.

Of course this was also my view. I am obstinately optimist but not fatalist. Every man should do what he thinks is right but he should know also that what the Republic does is right—in the largest sense.

Someone was expressing his surprise to Sumner that he should base his opposition to Dix on his Presidency of the Philadelphia Convention, instead of the charge of cumulation of offices. He said, "It is the only ground I can stand on. I once reported against a man because he had delirium tremens. Saulsbury & McDougall denounced me as a water-drinking fanatic. I once objected to a candidate that he could not read. I was accused of searching an impossible Boston ideal of scholarship for public service. So now, if I say of a man that he supports the policy of the President, and that I will not send him abroad to misrepresent me and the Senate, that is intelligible and satisfactory "

Wednesday, 13. Went to see Father Newton: he launched off in his buzzing way about Mrs. Lincoln how imprudent she was—how he protected & watched over her & prevented dreadful disclosures;

how at one time when Watt had entered into a conspiracy to extort 20,000 from the President by using three letters of Mrs Lincoln, he sent for Sim. Draper who went to Watt in his greenhouse on 14th Street & told him he was come to take him to Fort Lafayette, with much bluster & great oaths as Simeon's wont; how Watt fell on his literal marrow bones & begged, & gave up the letters & the conspiracy got demoralized & came down, down, to 1500 dollars which was paid, and the whole thing settled.

"Oh," said the old fellow, "that lady has set here on this here sofy & shed tears by the pint a begging me to pay her debts which was unbeknown to the President. There was one big bill for furs which give her a sight of trouble—she got it paid at last by some of her friends—I don't know who for certain—not Sim Draper for he promised to pay it afore Cuthbert but after Lincoln's death he wouldn't do it," & other horrors like that for half an hour.

He told me of a "singlar dream" he had had. He saw Lincoln in the room: he said, "Friend Newton, there is great deal better place up there than down here." "I was a getting around behind him to see where Booth's bullet had hit when he said, pinting to the White House, 'Things is as wrong as they kin be. I must go up there tomorrow & try to fix 'em right.' When he said that I knowed he was going to stay all night & as I see the bed in that room wasn't long enough for his legs I went to call my wife & ask if there wasn't a bed long enough in the house, & when I come back he was gone."

He told me what I had not known before that the Jay Cooke fund was never given to Mrs L., but on the scandals of her last days at the White House becoming known was quietly restored to the donors, most of whom were Quakers.

I received today from Alsop my Florida papers & left them with Com^{d} Willson for adjustment.

Oil Co. stock gone to China or elsewhere. Dined with Philp. Delposse, the Belgian Minister, was there, a very agreeable fellow who plays the piano very well.

After dinner went in to say goodnight to the Chief Justice. His guests had just gone: it was eleven o'clock. I walked up and down the deserted salon with him a few moments. He said there had been a good many southern people there that evening: that he made it a point to treat them always with especial courtesy. I agreed that this was a good thing to do even where they abused you for it and called it Yankee subserviency & charged mean motives for it. They know it is not true: they feel their inferiority & their bluster is the protest of wounded pride.

Chase said he felt kindly towards the people of the South. He only demanded that no man of any color should suffer for having been loyal during the war—which is little enough to ask & which must be insisted on, *ruat cælum.*

Walked home with Bing & Drake DeKay.

Thursday. [*Feb. 14.*] Went to the State Dep^t. Seward refused to hold any conversation as to what sh^d be done in the contingency of Dix's rejection—says it is not loyal to Dix for him to foresee such a thing. He said his intention was to promote Campbell in sending him to Bogota, where there was work to do & he could have won reputation.

I saw Harris at Wallach's. He says Dix will be confirmed: that he has behaved rather badly and that the long delay has been simply to give him a lesson.

Spent the evening with M.

* * * *

TO J. G. NICOLAY

WASHINGTON, D. C. *February 14, 1867*

MY DEAR NICOLAY

Your letter enclosing Mrs A.'s greeted me as I entered the State Department on the 2nd Inst. having beaten me across the Atlantic. We had rather a rough passage. I was in the condition of every man, *qui se respecte,* on such occasions, the first day or two, but afterwards experienced a salutary shock by falling in love with the prettiest woman you ever clapped eyes on, which kept me on my sea-legs the rest of the voyage.

At New York after abluting at the Astor House I went to see Marston—found a glum set of fellows sitting by the fire glowering at the coals—couldn't get a word out of anybody—Carver, Stimson

&c. Billy was out—Vanderhoof got up & followed me out—"You haven't heard?" "No." "The boys are gone to hell again. Lost 2 million dollars last week—every man you saw in there is ruined. Cleaned me out too." Which was a cheerful reception.

Later in the day I saw Billy & Charlie. They were not so gloomy as Van—talked about making everything good—asked me to go home with them & stay & altogether seemed plucky enough to make another million. Think of that, you purblind mortal, peacefully pursuing your little 10,000 through the narrow path of frugality & toil —think of those two young fellows who have lost in one week $1,700,-000 & propose to go in & make it over again. It makes my head swim.

I found Mr Seward as admirable as ever—calm, philosophical, optimist as ever. Not a word against his enemies and slanderers, a little astonishment at the completeness of the defeat, but a perfect comprehension of it. He treats me with the most distinguished kindness: offered me any mission that was falling in—proposed my name to the President for the reversion of Sweden, McGinnis having fallen a victim to the celestial wrath of the gods senatorial. But the President wanted the place for a dead-beat copper soldier named Bartlett of New York, a gambler & of ungrammatical disposition. Sumner says the Senate will reject him. Campbell squirms—don't want to be turned out—begs the Senate not to allow it & the Senate seem inclined to protect the poor devil by rejecting everybody who is nominated to succeed him. I am inclined to decline a nomination in that state of affairs—though Sumner thinks I would be confirmed. I will wait a day or two to see what becomes of Gen. Dix. The Senate is very ugly—will certainly reject Cowan for Austria & talk of rejecting Ewing for the Hague. Dix's chances are growing every day darker. Foster & Harris both want his place. Sumner has blood in his eye. He is splendid in his present temper—arrogant, insolent, implacable—thoroughly in earnest—honest as the day.

He seems very happily married. I see a good deal of his wife & like her more than ever.

You are all right everywhere. That push against you came from Cops who want your place. Seward wrote you that letter simply to give you an opportunity to say the charges were lies. He was rather amused at the completeness of your defense—"Ten times over justified," he said. Letters like that were written to nearly everyone in the service—nobody grew furious & resigned but Motley. He becomes a high-priced martyr and has the sure thing on a first-class mission two years hence. I can't find out the person who made these charges against you. It is hard for Seward to save Lincoln's friends from being pushed off their stools by hungry Copperheads—he defends them whenever he can.

I have seen your nephew John. He is well—is a little surprised to find his head still on his shoulders. Says all the clerks are Rads.

It is all one way here. Nobody dares for an instant oppose the current. The thing must work itself clear. I have faith in the end.

* * * *

Yours

J.H.

[P.S.] The town is gayer than you ever saw it. Balls nearly every night—receptions without number. Everyone asks after you.

CHAPTER XXIV

<hr>

March 5—June 28, 1867

<hr>

ASTOR HOUSE. [NEW YORK]
March 5. 1867

I start West today. Dix is confirmed & I bid farewell to diplomacy. I have received three fair offers in business. I shall not decide for a month. I am going to stay a few weeks at Warsaw, to restore my moral tone.

I think matters are growing a little quieter in politics.

Nobody talks turkey as distinctly as we could wish in relation to the Lincoln book. They say the market is glutted &c. That will be after all, I fear, a labor of love that we will do when we get rich and idle.

Arnold is to publish the works of Lincoln—at least so Colfax tells me—at the request of the family. That dishes our chances at the papers. I will see Bob at Chicago.

Everything is frightfully dull in the way of business.

* * * *

TO J. G. NICOLAY

WARSAW ILLINOIS. *March 18. 1867*

I am safely lodged at last among my Lares and Penates. I find my parents as well as ever; my mother better than usual and full of her old good spirits, my father at 66 with not a gray hair, with the ruddy cheek and ravenous appetite of a growing boy. He is of course an uncompromising Rad: wrote Randall a most plucky and impudent letter, full of sound doctrine and classical rhetoric, in which he compared the Johnsonian policy to the Trojan horse & himself to the sagacious Laocoon. I have great good times, spinning yarns with the Old Boy.

There is little comfort in the country now. The weather is hideous, i.e., what people insanely call "beautiful fresh cold weather." A cloudless sky, white shining distances, and a thermometer ten degrees below 0, according to Meinherr Fahrenheit. I have escaped six winters and my good nature has been nipped and frozen in this absurd springtime.

So much for nature. Society much worse. Poverty everywhere. In the East it is still tempered by the fever of speculation. But in the West everything & everybody is flat as a buckwheat cake, *de la veille.* There is no money and no business. One endless Sunday seems to gloom over all the little towns you pass. A man can live for *almost* nothing here. But he just misses that, and he makes nothing. For instance, a very decent fellow came to Warsaw some time ago to start a newspaper. He had a little money, within $200 of the amount. He could not raise in the town the other 200. Again: a church here gave a fair and a supper. They spent $50. They received $40. These trivial figures give you some idea of the strength of the thumb and finger with which Hard-times is pinching.

Moral: You stay where you are for the present. In the East if you are lucky, these things would work to your benefit. There are some men who are growing rich. Lamon is making a fortune, practising law in Washington. Barney has a princely income from his profession. I am afraid to say how much; probably $50,000 clear, from his law business. You will have to remodel y^r opinion of Barney. A man don't make so much money by mere luck and respectability—and keep on making it. In the West you would not make y^r Kanawha salt. (That h has given me a world of trouble.) Nobody is keen for our book. We will have to write it and publish it on our own hook some day, when we can afford. You had better not come home till you are kicked out, and our crazy friends in the Senate have legislated all the dead-beats now in office, into an eternity of bread and butter. Newspapers are all running down. The *Evening Post,* the *Journal of Commerce* & a few others are doing well. The Washington papers *nil.*

*　　*　　*　　*

Arnold is making a collection of Lincoln's letters & speeches &c, but on his own hook. Bob encourages it but will not give him the key to the boxes. He will keep them for the present & still hopes for our assistance in classifying them. He has commenced practice in partnership with Scammon's son—with brilliant prospects. Mrs. Lincoln was well—was extremely kind—insisted on my moving my traps to her house: I could not as I only remained one day. She is living in a pretty house of her own.

My regards to Mrs. & Miss Nicolay

J.H.

June 11, 1867. The newspapers a week or so ago announced my appointment to Austria—all, so far as I know taking their cue from the New York *Times,* which ought to be good enough authority on that matter. Bigelow & Pomeroy write me very hearty letters of congratulation. I write to Bigelow:

My Dear Mr. Bigelow, If nothing more comes of it, I am grateful to the *quid nunc* who first sent the news of my appointment on its travels, some weeks ago, since it has procured me so kind and cordial a letter from you. And another from Pomeroy to the same tenor. I am without any further intimation of the truth or falsehood of the report—and indeed do vehemently doubt it. If it comes I may not go to Austria, but I will try to borrow money enough on my crop to go to Washington & see what it means. If it means a scandal & row about the place, i.e., if Motley insists on being kicked out, another boot than mine must do it. Not that I object to the kicking out *per se,* but I don't think the fun of doing it and then parting my own coat tails for the heavy-shod Senate will pay for a month of sea-sickness.

The Senate is of late gone clean daft in its Presidentophobia. It slaughtered a dozen brave fellows because they were nominated & then confirmed another dozen vile Cops for no better reason. They threw over McGinnis because they thought he might be a Copperhead & confirmed Bartlett who was a blatant one of the 5-Points race—a gambler of highly ungrammatical habits. They confirmed Dix, who was the Philadelphia Convention incarnate, obstinate & unrepentant, and smothered Raymond who did more than any mother's son of them to defeat the nominee of that movement and elect Fenton. They refuse to be comforted because of Motley and there are not half a dozen Senators who would not have said of him just what that shabby blackguard McCracken said, after a week in Vienna. So though my record is of the straightest radicalism—abolitionist when many of them were doughy of face, and ever since —they w^d fling mud upon me if my appointment were attended with any squeak of martyrdom. As to all that, I am ignorant. I do not know where Mr Motley is—where the Legation is—who is running it—what has become of Lippitt. All this, if I shd. be appointed I w^d go to Wash^n to inquire about & decide according to my best lights & the state of my liver.

I make you a thousand impressive compliments in recognition of your kindness in asking me to your estates. It w^d be the greatest pleasure incident to this probationary state of existence—but it does not look probable. If I can, I will, gladly & gratefully. Make Miladi remember me & recall me to the young people whose memories have doubtless cicatrized the impression I made in past pleasant days. Your friend & Servt. J.H. Until this thing is developed you had better write to me, Care State Dep^t. Mr Chew always knows my address & is good enough to send me my letter.

TO MISS ELIZABETH HAY [1]

WARSAW, ILL. *June 12, 1867*

DEAR AUNT:

I have a presentiment that a weary and wayworn pilgrim will knock at your door between dusk and midnight of Monday evening next, craving shelter from the warm blast of summer and the fierce rays of the moon. Deny him not—for he will bring you tidings of your brethren and friends in this country. You can recognize him by his answer to the name of John, and by a broad accent derived from a prospective residence in the city of Vienna! He is unable to go to a tavern, having expended his last kreutzer in the purchase of this half sheet of paper. You will do well to lock up your spoons, as I fear that a sojourn of several years in Washington has not had a beneficial effect on his morals. Don't set any wine before him, as he has sunk his entire fortune in an unprofitable vineyard, and bursts

[1] Text from Mrs. Hay's privately printed volumes, I, 288–9.

into tears whenever grape-juice is mentioned. Treat him kindly, for, though feeble-minded and erring, he is still a fellow-worm. But be careful about the spoons.

DIARY

[*Undated*] Monday, June 17, 1867. I started from home to Washington. On the train to Hamilton met Col. Cahill with his dog, a singularly intelligent pointer which he had captured during the war as a pup. Met at Hamilton, where we waited 2 hours for the train, Pros. Atty. Peterson. Told me of the decay of the Archy Williams family. "When a young man gits bloated—with a crick in his neck you know—he's about a gone coon."

Rode to Carthage in the same seat with Robert Lincoln, a second cousin of the late President. He is 41 years old, looks much older. The same eyes & hair the president had—the same tall stature & shambling gait, less exaggerated: a rather rough farmer-looking man. Drinks hard, chews ravenously. He says the family is about run out. "We are not a very marrying set." He is dying of consumption he said very coolly. There was something startling in the resemblance of the straight thicket of hair, and the grey cavernous eyes framed in black brows & lashes, to the features of the great dead man. He was a pioneer of our county. Knew my father since long years. Brought a load of wheat to Gould & Miller in 1842 with ox teams; got $90 in gold for it. Told me that in 1860 he had talked to "Abe" about assassination. Abe said "I never injured anybody. No one is going to hurt me." He says he was invited by Abe to go on to Washington at the time of the inauguration but declined thinking it dangerous—a naïveté of statement I thought w^d have been impossible out of the West.

Spent Tuesday the 18th at Springfield. Talked with Cullom at length. He was rather disgusted with the extra session but could not think of disregarding the summons. He promised to talk to Trumbull and Yates about my confirmation. Thought there was no doubt about it.

When I left Springfield Charlie came with me to New York. I went there, instead of directly to Washington, because I saw in the papers that the President and the Secretary of State w^d be there on Friday on their way to Boston. They passed up Broadway in the evening. I was on the balcony of the Metropolitan. Two or three men beside me made criticisms on the President, not kindly, but when the Common Council came by, they looked at each other & said, "Don't say anything abt. them or they'll get out & bust your snoot."

I went late in the evening to the 5th Avenue Hotel & saw a good many people, but not the President nor the Secretary. Most of the men I saw were balmily tight & insisted on my drinking with them. I found Mr Seward afterwards at Thurlow Weed's. He explained the vacancy in the Austrian mission—asked me when I could go. "At once." He told me to go down to Washington & get my papers & start by the first steamer. I would do so. I spoke of the Senate's possibly throwing me out, but he said that was not probable & there was no use anticipating it. He had told Morgan that evening that the moderate men who did not want an extra session & who compromised on this provisional arrangement, now found themselves like a man whose reprieve had run out & who had gained nothing by the delay. He thought nothing w^d come by the extra session. Congress were called together on false issues & they will see when they get here, that the President instead of being reckless and factious is carrying out their own law in good faith.

This is all true but I think as Weed said to me in the morning, it is regrettable that the President & Stanbery sh^d have given room to these false issues by stirring up this row before the 4th July.

The next day, Saturday, George Denison brought me a kind invitation fr. Leonard Jerome to go to the races at Jerome Park in his drag. The day was exquisite—the crowd brilliant—the morning very fair. I became acquainted with Sam Barlow a very agreeable fellow, spite of his politics. Marble was there and as I had outgrown my animosity we were friendly enough. Raymond was on hand. He has a great talent for talking to women. Sir Fred^k Bruce was also on hand—& was civil enough to say that he hoped they w^d not get a minister to Vienna till they took me. John Magruder was strutting about, less important than of yore, waxed & dyed & holystoned, like the battered old buck he is. I met the Vanderbilts, Stoughtons,

Cravens & many more. Was delighted to have one more hour with
Mrs. Bigelow who was as lively as ever. As old Plon said, "Mon Dieu!
qu'elle est vive, qu'elle est vive!"

Went to see the Keeps, & the Stimsons & more ladies. Saw a good
many men who were all cordial. Everybody thinks my appointment
is a good thing & does not for a moment conceive that I can refuse it.

Went to Washington in the Owl train Sunday night. Alighted at
the Owen House Monday morning.

I made my first visit to the State Department: got my papers
started & was told to come back for them next morning. Fred^k Seward asked me to dine *en famille.* He had just received a business
despatch from his father in Boston, saying among other things,
"Send John Hay to Vienna." He told me the Secretary had been a
little puzzled and impatient at my delay in acknowledging the appointment, saying, "Why, even if in no other way he must have
seen it in the newspapers," whereupon Fred^k laughingly suggested
that my experience had not been such as to lead to implicit trust in
journalistic intelligence.

*   *   *   *

At the War Department I saw Mr Stanton: spoke of the rumors
of his resignation. He said the newspapers must have their little item
now and then. I don't think he is going just yet. He was quite cordial
to me, said he hoped I would be made Minister; as many do. I
rather like to hear it though of course the supposition is almost absurd. I am not sure I w^d wish to be minister. The added responsibility is not desirable & Motley has spent so much more than the
salary that any poor successor would be ruined in trying to vie with
him. As Chargé I can get on more modestly and easily. And I don't
care to stay away more than a year.

*   *   *   *

Afterwards went to see Mrs Lamon—then the Y—g. Found there
a negro funeral. A servant had died and there was great pomp and
brass band and ululation. Went to Sewards to dinner. No one but
me. It was very talkative and agreeable. Drove out around Wash-

ington till eight or so. Passed the evening at Wise's, Knap's &
Johnnie Clark's.

*   *   *   *

[Tuesday morning] I called on Judd at Willard's and had a long-
ish & pleasant talk with him. He thinks there will be no opposition
to my confirmation. He is still in full glee over his defeat of Long
John.[2] Accounts for the *Republican's* hostility to him and its frantic
8 hours ravings by its perennial desire to be opposed in everything
to the *Tribune*. He gave me a whimsical idea of his little early em-
barrassments in running the machine in Berlin without speaking
any German or French. I can scarcely imagine a more painful position, at dinner, for instance.

Found a note from Bob Lincoln but could not find him.

Left at 7 o'clock and arrived in New York Wednesday morning,
the 26th June 1867. Made a good many visits. Reade, Morton, Max-
well, Stedman, Alsop (with whom or at whose office I left all my
Florida papers except the orange grove papers, to do what he pleases
with—& so dismiss the thing from my mind). Saw Guernsey who
gave me back "Kain and Abel" thinking it a little too audacious.
Could not find Young. Missed also Halpine & Bigelow, who were
seeking and sought all day. As I came home to dinner an old Spaniard whom I had made chaplain, came & wanted to borrow money.
The old home spirit of mendicant flunkeyism. The next day I found
Young & had quite a talk with him. He said he had written to Wendell Phillips, the other day, that we must fight fire with fire, soldier
with soldier. If we beat Grant we must do it with Sheridan. He
thinks Grant will not do, from a Radical standpoint. I defended
Grant as opposed to Sheridan, regarding him as a cooler man, one
more likely to reverence and obey the law as such than Sheridan wᵈ
be. I also said I hoped we wᵈ some day have a President in harmony
with the people if for no other purpose than to rebuke, and with
popular approval, such insufferable impertinence as Sheridan has
been lately guilty of.

He says naïvely enough that his recent Radical articles on Stan-

---

[2] Norman B. Judd, after serving, 1861–65, as Minister in Berlin, returned to Chicago
and, 1866, was elected to Congress; reelected two years later.

bery's decisions, have been the result of a hedging policy which he has thought necessary to counteract Greeley's visit to Richmond & other recent follies.

He spoke with great freedom of these things. Feels himself rather strong in his position: expects to remain there, though he says the power he wields is anything but pleasant. He especially hates to make appointments.

He seemed a little surprised & hurt that Seward should treat him coolly; says his kindness & admiration for Seward have undergone no change, but he is not the *Tribune*. The *Tribune* is a Republic, where no one will is conclusive.

I breakfasted with Roosevelt at Halpine's on Friday, and came down with them. Halpine was never more cynical or witty. He said he had the Irish vote in his belly & both parties were plying him with emetics for it. He was equally unblushing in regard to public and private matters.

Saw Walter Noyes & had a long walk & talk with him. He is as fanatical as Peter the Hermit in this new Ritualistic war, but the same good jolly fellow as of old—fond of his pipe, of the girls, and I doubt not of a good stoup of wine. Spent a couple of evenings with the Keeps.

CHAPTER XXV

April 18—October 14, 1868

[*Vienna.*] *April 18, 1868.* Post spent the evening with me. We had a long talk about old-fashioned politics. I told him of my chance shot at the Methodist preachers who wanted a Brigadier General, and of the young Kansian who thought the Government should have a better system of police.

He told me many picturesque incidents in the history of Lane. At a time when Lane's fortunes were most desperate, Robinson committed the fatal error of trying to conciliate the Jayhawkers by appointing Jennison & other ring-leaders to offices in the militia. Jim Lane saw his opportunity and instantly made a stumping tour through the southern tier of counties, denouncing with the greatest audacity and bitterness his former friends and comrades, and holding up the bargain between them & the Governor to the indignation of the people. In Jennison's own town, a most dramatic scene took place. Lane was savagely denouncing some lawless act of Jennison, when the astonished Jayhawker rose in the audience & shouted, "Jim Lane, I done that by your order."

"You lie," roared Jim.

"By your written order, I say."

"You lie!" Lane repeated, with a most brazen confidence, which was not altogether unreasonable as he had managed to secure and destroy all his correspondence of that period.

He continued, "You, —— Jennison, are a murderer!"

"By God, I never murdered Jenkins," said Jennison, and the apt retort tickled the Kansas fancy.

Lane's audacious campaign was a great success. A legislature was returned friendly to him. His connexion with the Methodist

[Church] was a very singular passage in his history.

Redpath, after having been his intimate friend & adherent, one day turned upon him. His paper had been publishing Lane's autobiography by instalments. Now, however, the autobiography disappeared from its columns & instead, an exposé of the crimes of the Danite Band, of which Lane was chief, appeared in the *Journal*. It had a tremendous effect. The *contre-coup* against Redpath himself was so great that he was compelled to leave the State. But the exposé remained & Lane suffered vastly in public estimation. He resolved on a bold stroke. He "got religion" in Western phrase & joined the Methodist Church. He was at once rehabilitated in the opinions of many. He fell from grace before very long. One day a man who heard him cursing furiously said, "Take care, Lane, you'll be kicked out of the Church."

"They may kick me out, but damned if they can keep me out," said the meek Methodist.

After he murdered Jenkins, he suffered another great eclipse of popularity. Kansas never minded killing a man in fair fight, but this was a decidedly irregular proceeding. Jenkins went to draw water from a well which Lane claimed as his own property. Lane shot him, coolly, brutally, cynically. Kansas looked upon the deed as "awfully low form" and rather snubbed Lane. He never could stand the frown of his world. Something must be done "to get up his rep." He joined the Methodist Church again.

Post told me an amusing incident of Lane's second conversion. He had been making a rambling exhortation one night in church before a great audience, & perorated by referring to the bloody scenes he had passed through in the Mexican war, & how he had been spared to testify, etc.—as they all say. A drunken young editor, who was also a member of the Convention, then rose in the body of the house & proceeded boozily to the pulpit, followed by friends anxious to prevent a scandal. He anathematized them for interfering with him and began his remarks. "Feller citizens, General Lane has told you how he fought, bled, & died in Mexico. Feller citizens *I* have fought, bled, & died in Mexico, nary time." Here his friends seized him, took him in their arms, & carried him down the long aisle to the door. He lay back, much at his ease, gravely repeating, in all the tones of the musical scale, "Nary time—nary time," till his voice died away out of doors.

Post thinks Lane had a power over men little short of magnetic. Many of his opponents feared to become acquainted with him, lest they should become his friends. I have often heard this before, and always with great surprise. To me (and I knew him well) the man had no charm. He seemed coarse, mean, and ignoble. His craft was too rude and bungling to deceive any one apparently. He had the sad, dim-eyed, bad-toothed face of a harlot. Yet he had a certain easy bonhommie that made him at home everywhere.

They say in Kansas that his suicide was occasioned by the fear of detection in a corrupt contract bargain with Fuller & McDonald, which he had solemnly denied in the Senate, but the proof of which had subsequently come to the War Office.

April 19. Finished today Badeau's life of Grant & sent him a note of thanks. I have read it with more interest than I read novels. It is very successfully written as a popular work. I am glad Badeau has made a strike.

Some good things in it. I think there are few things in history so ludicrous & touching at once, as Bragg riding up & down his lines waving his sword & announcing a victory to his troops, when they were really beaten & the invincible West was swarming over Missionary Ridge.

April 26. A letter from Mr Motley asking if I will stay as Secretary in case he is Minister. Answered that I could not.

27. Letter from Mrs Bigelow which I answered & then wrote another to J.B. "Dear Mr B. I have rec^d & ans^d a letter from Mrs B. this evening & I don't yet feel inclined to leave your company. So I will say a word or two to you—lingering with my hand on the doorknob.

"I had no idea when I came abroad last summer that I should be here so long. I thought they w^d fill up the vacuum (abhorred of nature & office seekers) in a few months—so I came for a flyer, principally because I was a little ashamed of having been in Europe nearly two years & having seen nothing. I have had a pleasant year of it.

There is very little work to do at the Legation. I have sinned griev-
ously against certain ten-day regulations that I have heard of. I have
seen all I care to of Prussia, Poland, Turkey, & Italy. I have drawn
my salary with startling punctuality. I have not wearied the home
office with much despatches. My sleep is infantine & my appetite
wolfish. I am satisfied with my administration of this 'arduous &
delicate post.' I believe that is the regular shriek of the Radical
press in alluding to the Vienna Mission. You and Mr Adams worked
while you were in harness. I am not sure but that a serious man
could always find work in those two missions. But equally sure am
I that no two other American diplomats can catch each other's eyes
without mutual guffaws unless they have a power of facial muscle
that w^d put the Roman Augurs to shame. Just let me get into Congress once, and take one shy at the Diplomatic appropriation bill.

"I am very glad I came. Vienna is worth while for a year. It is
curious & instructive to see this people starting off in the awkward
walk of political babyhood. They know what they want & I believe
they will get it. The Aristocracy are furious and the Kaiser a little
bewildered at every new triumph of the Democratic & Liberal
principle. But I don't think they can stop the machine now—though
they may get their fingers mashed in the cogs. I don't think the world
ever seemed getting ahead so positively & quietly [?] before. Two
years ago—it was another Europe. England has come abreast of
Bright. Austria is governed by Forty-Eighters. Bismarck is becoming
appalled by the spirit of Freedom that he suckled with the blood
of Sadowa. France still lies in her comatose slumber—but she talks
in her sleep & murmurs the 'Marseillaise.' And God has made her
ruler blind drunk, that his Helot antics may disgust the world with
despotism.

"If ever in my green & salad days, I sometimes vaguely doubted,
I am safe now. I am a Republican till I die. When we get to Heaven,
we can try a monarchy perhaps.

"I suppose Mr Motley will be restored as soon as Mr Meade gets
in the White House. I will resign at once thereafter & come home—
after a few weeks Switzerland & England. This is confidential as
yet. I do not want to set a swarm of amiable noodles upon the State
Dep^t.

"You once spoke of the correspondence between S[eward] & M[otley] about the Paris Legation [?] in the Mexican business. There is none on the books here but what is published. He may have written private letters also.

"If you take the trouble to answer this, please tell me what you have been doing. I have heard a work on Franklin mentioned, but have not seen it advertised. Why don't you write a history of American Diplomacy?"

May 26. This evening in the Volksgarten there were a good many Americans. I said, in answer to some questions, I thought conviction extremely doubtful.[1] I found myself almost entirely alone in this opinion.

27th. Finley Anderson sent me a despatch announcing the acquittal of the President.

While discussing this subject with Lippitt in Venice, two months ago, I said I thought impeachment w^d fail, because from the way the trial had begun, I was convinced it w^d be a purely legal one, and that, on a strictly legal basis, there was no case against the President. He must be turned out, if at all, on political grounds, as an obstacle to peace and union—this could be well done in twenty-four hours —and this in my opinion was the only way to do it. These were my first strong impressions. They rather gave way when I saw the apparent unity of the Republican party in the pressure of the case. But when the news of the first adjournment [2] came—not knowing it was for Howard's sickness—I took it that the majority was stampeded, & have had no confidence in impeachment since.

June 3. It is very curious to see how the Senators that saved the President have changed their tone. They are gradually becoming the apologists & defenders of H[is] E[xcellency]. Forsaking the safe ground of "incompatibility of temper," on which it was certainly agreed the President was to be ousted, they have narrowed their

[1] The impeachment proceedings against President Johnson began March 13. The vote was taken May 26.
[2] May 11.

minds to the purely legal aspect of the matter, and having cast loose from party dictation, seem already drifting out of the party jurisdiction. It would not surprise me much to see some of these men zealous Johnson men before the year is out—not corrupted or seduced, but merely fighting themselves off their own lines into the enemies; while the stupid devils who never had an idea in their lives get honor and credit from their party for voting solid with the general ruck.

A most interesting letter from Bob Lincoln in Washington.

On the whole, analyzing my own sentiments, I am not very sorry —not at all sorry at the result. I think Johnson will put some water in his whiskey now. I don't think he can do much more harm. We are still in opposition, where a party always works best. Impeachment is demonstrated not to be an easy thing. The lesson may be a good one some day if we have a Republican President & a Copperhead Senate. The Tenure of Office law [3]—a fruit of haste & folly— is knocked to pieces. A two-thirds majority in both houses is anomalous.

Pratt, of the Department, has been here for the last ten days. He made some capital puns. Two Germans at Dornbach were guilty of some little hoggishness. Post called them sardines. Pratt said, "No, they are Herren."

TO J. G. NICOLAY

ST. MORITZ. CHUR. SCHWEIZ.
July 13. 1868

Surrounded by the fragments of my broken fetters, I read your blessing backwards like a witch's prayer, and *am* of good cheer. If now Mr Watts-his-name [4] will only hurry up his cakes and let me off in time to vote, I will ask no more of the fates this year of grace.

One knows so little of one's self; I was not sure whether I wanted

[3] The Tenure of Office Act was passed over the President's veto in February. It was not repealed until the advent of the Cleveland administration in 1885.

[4] Hay, as Chargé d'Affaires, was succeeded by Watts.

to go back or not till I read the announcement of Watts' confirmation. I sincerely hope he may have a pleasant winter of it, and rattle
around in the hole Motley left until that injured patriot comes back
next March.

I have had a day with Clarence Seward in Vienna. He is "neutral
in politics and religion" as you know, but an awful smart fellow
withal. He is not a Grant man but he says the General has no fight
to make—will walk over the course. So says everyone I have seen.
I have a line from Colfax in which he anticipates a sharp fight but
a sure victory.

*   *   *   *

If anything of interest comes in your way let me have part of it.

P.S. While I was writing the *Tribune* came in, which says Watts
is a Republican, & *as sich,* confirmed. That looks badly for Motley
next spring.

TO J. G. NICOLAY

ST. MORITZ. CHUR. SCHWEIZ.

August 16. 1868

*   *   *   *

I hope to be out and a-rambling by the 1st October. I will spend
a day or two with you in Parigi O! Cara then make a strait *Hemden-
schweif* for sunset.

It seems a thousand years till I start.

I call my year a very fruitful one. I don't want to spoil it by hanging around too long.

I have a modest letter from the Congressional Committee asking
for war-sinews. Concussional Committee! I will send them something according to my poverty of resources. General McClellan is
here. He sails for home on the 19th September. He "don't take no
sort of interest."

I have sucked that Austrian orange dry. I don't want to keep
wasting good wind on the peel.

TO J. G. NICOLAY

LIVERPOOL, *October 14, 1868.*

(alludes to the Inmanner)	My boat is on the shore
(alludes to J. H. Horticulturalist)	My bark is on my tree
(announces a fact in fysic)	Seasickness is a bore
(gives financial counsel)	You bet your pile it be.

I had a rapid and prosperous voyage from Paris here. I found George Sand's "Cadio" at the station. It *is* dedicated to Harrisse.

The channel was like a duck-pond. For these mercies, *laus Deo ventorum.*

I passed through London with contemptuous speed. Spent 15 minutes in the Metropolis. Was afraid, if Reverdy [5] saw me, he would make too fierce a Radical of me.

I ran head-first into a piece of luck that you, of all men, will envy me. That true-hearted American and profound statesman, C. Dickens, Esq., read last night here, and I contributed 6 shillings to alleviate the sufferings of his honest poverty. Murdoch can knock the spots out of him, reading, but whether it was what he read, or what he is, I don't know—he kept that houseful of placid Britons chained tight for two mortal hours as I never saw a house held.

I got the worth of my "6 bob." (The pens here require mending every five minutes.)

Liverpool town is a good town to pass through in a hurry. The sun takes till noon to struggle through the fog. The muffins are good.

Dudley is out of town. I am gradually lowering the tone of my spirits to suit sea-life. I shall have attained the proper indifference to life in about an hour.

My tug is by the shore
My ship is on the sea.
As I cannot write no more

---

[5] Reverdy Johnson was Minister to England, 1868–69.

Here's a treble health to thee,
To Madame and *the* Babee.

Yours

J.H.

Hurrah for the elections! [6]

[6] The October state elections indicated very clearly that Grant would be elected in November.

CHAPTER XXVI

December 8, 1868—July 10, 1869

TO J. G. NICOLAY

WASHINGTON. *Dec. 8. 1868*

As my mother has been occupying the last week in moving into her new house, and as she told me my absence would be of more value than my assistance in this moment of crisis, I seized the occasion by the forelock and came to Washington in the peaceful pursuit of a fat office. But there is nothing just now available. I go back tonight to the West a broken-down politician. The Secretary says he will keep a weather eye open for me, and "wrastle" with Andy for anything that turns up.

Your sixty days I fixed all right & you doubtless have it before this. I would advise you to stick it out at Paris as late as possible. Send Madame & Mamzel to Nice or elsewhere, if the chill blast is too much for them. But don't you come home before the 1st of March or so. It takes a month to do anything here and you can't afford to get stale before the inauguration. Grant is as close-mouthed as ever. It is confidently asserted by our folks that neither Schofield nor Washburne [1] yet know what they are going to get, if anything.

I saw Painter yesterday. He spoke of you—said you could get anything you wanted, if Wade got into the Presidency.[2] Says he hasn't given up all hope yet. Andy may die of "snakes" before March.

Before I forget it please send by the Legation bag Doré's *La Fontaine* and *Juif Errant* to Mrs Fred. W. Seward, and charge to

---

[1] Washburne was made Secretary of State under Grant, to be replaced very shortly by Hamilton Fish.

[2] If Andrew Johnson had been successfully impeached or had died, there being no Vice President, Senator Wade, president *pro tem* of the Senate, could have become President until Mar. 4, 1869.

me—writing on the outside "Compliments of John Hay."

There is nothing worth telling. Grant's reticence is maddening to the newsmongers. There will be a quiet session, everybody thinks. Mr Seward is not to be married. Is not to remain in the Cabinet. Is not going to Europe—all of which has been reported.

Charlie Chase & Marston have been badly smashed again. They are thoroughly good fellows & I am very sorry for them. They seem to keep up a good heart & are pegging away again. Stoddard is rather seedy—still curbstoning in New York. Whitelaw Reid is on the Editorial Staff of the *Tribune*. He says Mrs Sprague managed the whole New York Convention in July until the fatal moment when the devil broke loose and Seymour was nominated [3]—that then she bore her defeat like a major. She has retired to her estates & will not come to Washington this year. Miss Janet is keeping house for the C[hief] J[ustice]. She is a splendidly accomplished girl with more heart and culture than the *ainée*. She is large and blonde and, barring the irregular profile, like a Flemish Venus.

Walker made a splendid pun the other night. Being asked to drink and offered whiskey and Sauterne he said "Paradoxical as it may seem, I prefer whiskey to Sauterne and so turn to whiskey!"

Our club has gone where the Washington clubs go. Another has been founded by the Diplomats.

Ed. Stanton is practicing law by himself. Ed. Welles is Chief Clerk of the Navy Dep^t. Dahlgren is back in his old Bureau. His wife is rejuvenated with her three new babies. . . .

Hattie Loring is wittier than ever—flings vitriol in the neatest way on all subjects mentioned.

Sumner has built a handsome house on Lafayette Square, north side. Trumbull has a fine house on Capitol Hill on the site of the old Capitol Prison. Ellen Jayne & Lucy Starne are keeping house for him this winter.

I have confided the fact of your visit home this winter to no one but George T. Brown & he will not blab.

Before this reaches you I will be again in Warsaw, and—to the extent of my Hancock County influence—entirely at your service.

My regards to Mrs Nicolay & Miss Butterfly.

[3] Democratic candidate running against Grant.

28. Dined last night with Mr John Ganson. He told a good story on Butler. Ben F. B. had a scheme at Charleston for harmonizing the party by a compromise between the two wings: laid it before Richmond & asked him, "Isn't that an honest & fair proposition?"

Richmond said, "Butler, you know what I think of a man with a cast in his eye. I never saw but three that were thoroughly fair & trustworthy & they are You, Buchanan & Bennett (of the *Herald*).

TO J. G. NICOLAY

WASHINGTON. May 14. 1869

I was in New York & thought I would go through here on my way home. I find the town dismally dull. The newspaper men are growling rather savagely. But on the whole the Administration—though not strong nor original in any respect—seems to be running on decently enough. The appointments and removals are its weakest feature.

Boutwell [4] is thinking about Gibbs. I think Montgomery's days are numbered. I went myself to the Treasury Dep^t & told the Secretary what I thought of him. If you have anything to say about him, say it distinctly. He slanders you in the most infamous and atrocious terms. He has set Washburne & Morrill of Vermont against you. No man has lost prestige so terribly in three months as Washburne. He might have stood at the head of the party in the House, but his visit to the State Department & ransacking it like a burglar in his fumbling haste has disgusted many who like myself had a great esteem for him.

I dined with Sumner last night. He is a good enough Grant man but sees the very inadequate character of the new diplomatic appointments. Grant, as yet, is on trial. His cabinet is of no use to him with the exception of Boutwell & Cresswell.[5] Rawlings [6] is a good and able man as far as his ill health & political inexperience allow.

I start West today. The *Journal* men in Springfield have offered

---

4 George S. Boutwell was Secretary of the Treasury.

5 J. A. J. Cresswell, Postmaster General.

6 J. A. Rawlings, Secretary of War.

me the editorship. I will make a stagger at it this summer and see
what I can make at it. I assume the scissors on Monday morning next.
I wish I had you here to give me some words of wisdom.

I have sold a few sketches recently. "Down the Danube" to Putnam's, "The Foster Brothers" to Harper's, and "Kain & Abel" to
Frank Leslie. I have also written a somewhat full sketch of the death
of Joe Smith—not yet published.

I wish you would write to me at Springfield and let me know
when you think of coming over. Do you remember Read? You met
him at Mrs. Bridge's. He is a nephew of hers and a classmate of mine
at Brown. A dilettante man of letters. Gibbs was Washburne's man.
Grant & Fish got disgusted with his ill-savor, and Fish rushed his
friend Read through before Washburne could interfere. John Cook
was beaten by Gibbs. Cook says he will go to Europe still if he can
sell his house in Springfield—the fourth he has built there.

You will find Washington intolerable. I have been here one day.
I am quite sure that by hanging around and eating dirt, I could
get some office. But my stomach revolts. It is almost too great a
strain of a man's self-respect to ask for an office: still worse to beg
for it.

I thank God today that I am independent in my poverty and
capacity of content with little.

Write to me soon telling me when we may see you in this country.
My compliments to Mesdames.

TO E. C. STEDMAN [7]

ST. JAMES HOTEL, NEW YORK
July 10, 1869

MY DEAR MR. STEDMAN:

I tried to find you yesterday but failed. I sail to-day.

Might I venture to ask you to withdraw that poem of mine from
the G[*alaxy?*] I do not suppose it is in print—if it is, never mind—
only suppress the name. I have resumed the padlocked mouth.

I wanted to tell you how much genuine enjoyment I and some
other western people have had in your "Blameless Prince." I con-

[7] Text from Mrs. Hay's privately printed volume, I, 375.

fess when I heard the subject announced, I was a little afraid of a certain foreign flavor—but there is not a trace of it. Familiarity with all that has been done before—assimilation of the best fruits of others—all this is there, of course; but the poem in manner and sentiment and progress is thoroughly new, and, it seems to me, American. How you can keep your spirit so green and fresh in Wall Street is a marvel to me. I think a month or so of this town would drive me melancholy mad.

Can you use me in any way, in Madrid? [8] I will not be gone long.

[8] In June, 1869 Hay was appointed Secretary of Legation at Madrid.

CHAPTER XXVII

August 19, 1869—March 30, 1870

TO JOHN BIGELOW

MADRID, *August 19. 1869*

DEAR MR. BIGELOW

It comes from so many sources that I can no longer disbelieve the good news that you have taken the *Times*. The right man sometimes strays, even in this ricketty world, into the right place. I congratulate you and the *Times* and journalism generally. I am fallen so into the habit of believing evil of persons & corporations who make appointments that I had almost given up the idea of seeing you where you ought to be. But it is perhaps on the whole to a newspaper's interest that it should be conducted by a man of brains, and that doubtless determined your selection. In the civil service, it makes no difference to anybody who holds the offices. *Hinc* the deaf and dumb tenants of our Legations. With the exception of Madrid—'pon my modesty, there is not a house on the vast continental sea-line from Lisbon to Petersburg over which streams the national buzzard, tenanted by a man who can speak French, or write English without rolling out his tongue. Cheerful despatches Messrs. Fish & Bancroft [1] must read—confined exclusively to discussions of Alabama politics and the Contingent Fund.

As for me, I am the right man in a tight place. We have a great deal of work to do here. But it is interesting and instructive. The Government at home expects brutalities and impossibilities. As *you know* it always does. But our relations with the people in the Spanish Government are very cordial and everything is as pleasant as the state of the case will permit. There is up to date nothing decided, often an ocean of talk, but there is no question of principle

---

[1] J. Bancroft Davis, Assistant Secretary of State.

at stake. The whole game is in the hands of Fish & Grant, if they know what to do with it. But I am not a hero worshipper any more, & if I were, where is the Hero?

You are too busy to write to me now, but tell Miss Annie to exercise her infant faculties on an epistle to her elderly friend, to let me know you are all well and happy.

Convey my best compliments to Mrs Bigelow. I dined, my one day in Paris, with Mrs Richards who spoke affectionately of both of you, & hoped to see you this summer. I hinted at a possibility of your being detained longer at home.

I had a long good talk with Huntington too. The Tribune has turned him off—like idiots. He has written better letters this year than ever. Don't you think so? I wish you could use his talents some way. He really regrets his removal—though manly & philosophical about it.

Good Bye. If I ever get time I will write you a less scrambling letter.

Your true vassal J. H.

TO J. G. NICOLAY

MADRID. October 7, 1869

*   *   *   *

I still hold to my original plan of coming home next spring. I am glad I committed the folly of coming. I have seen a great deal and learned something. I speak the language—well enough to be understood & not well enough to be taken for a D.D. Spaniard—*à Dieu ne plaise.*

The amount of talk we have done since we came here is something portentous. I have been always on hand, as a medium of communication, and so have seen more of the *gros bonnets* than usually falls to the lot of Secretaries. We have had a good enough time of it, have done nothing but show our amiable intentions. The Government here is crazy to accept our offered mediation, but does not dare. The cession of Cuba to the Cubans—which was our little game—would be a measure too frightfully unpopular for the Government to face in its present uncertain tenure. Still, if it continues to grow stronger, as now seems probable, it may take the bit in its teeth and do something after a while.

Our State Department is a failure *selon moi*. Vacillation and fuzziness seems to trail over everything it does. Sickles is a pretty good fellow and a man of much more ability than I had ever given him credit for. He is fearfully deliberate and cautious.

He has been very well received. The newspapers have blackguarded him a little, but he has been very civilly treated by everybody in the Government.

Some of the Spaniards are men of sense—all of them have an astounding facility of expression which is simply incomprehensible to one of our stammering Teutonic race. Castelar, for instance, is an orator, such as you read of & never see. His action is as violent as Forrest. His style as florid as Gibbon. His imagination & his memory equally ready & powerful. He never writes a speech. Yet every sentence, even in a running debate, when all the Government hounds are yelping at him at once, is as finished & as elegantly balanced as if he had pondered all a rainy Sunday over it. I am afraid he will cease to be the Republican idol before long. He has too much sense and integrity to follow the lead of the socialist fanatics.

We are a little blue, just now—we Republicans.[2] The Republican insurrection in Barcelona was premature and silly and has injured the cause, which looked most promising a month ago. It is by no means hopeless yet—though the propaganda is checked for the moment.

I wish you would write me as long a letter as your eyes will permit and tell me your condition and your plans.

B. L. M. de Madame et Mademoiselle.

Write to me that you have burned this indiscreet letter, or McHay will sleep no more.

[2] In 1868 the government of Isabella II collapsed and the Queen was expelled. The republican movement was feeble. Spain was under the government of a military dictatorship with Gen. Serrano as regent, and Marshal Prim as president of the council.

TO JESSIE L. BROSS

MADRID. *Christmas Eve. 1869.*

MY DEAR MISS JESSIE

There are two days in the year in which my vagabond habit of life is powerless to protect me against a feeling of hopeless loneliness and homesickness. One is my birthday and the other is this blessed Advent Evening. Since I was thirteen years of age I have not spent a birthday nor a Christmas Eve in the house of my mother. I have my share of friends wherever I go—and perhaps need as few of them as most people, but on days like this I appreciate how much solitude there is in a crowd. All this day my thoughts have followed the sun in his westward journey, and now when the quick night has gathered over this mountain capital, I prefer to think of the bluffs of the Mississippi and the shores of Lake Michigan where the sunlight still lingers.

I am going to close my night here with a visit to San Lorenzo where the midnight Mass is celebrated. I am waiting for my good-natured Spanish friend who is to take me there and who has considerately warned me to leave my purse and watch at home. "I know my people," he says, injuriously. I had hoped that the honesty which has fled finally from official Spaniards had taken refuge in the lower classes, but I fear I must abandon that flattering theory. The thieves are as bad as the Ministers. Looking back over three months of constant communication with leading men of Spain, I do not recall a single instance where one of them has committed the indiscretion of telling the truth. Yet they are pleasant fellows and gay companions, charming at the dinner table and amiable at home. They only suffer from that utter elimination of the moral principle from their natures. So, as we western people prefer men somewhat flavored with honesty, I must say I do not wholly approve of the official Spaniard. His wife and daughter, however, meet with my hearty approval. I do not object to his cousin—I mean his *cousine*. They are as frank and genuine as he is sinister and false. I think I would be in love with them, but I don't like the idea of the consequent brothers-in-law. Did you see that bad joke that somebody made about Gen. Grant, saying that when he took the oath to support the law, he meant his brother-in-law. I don't think it is at all witty, and besides has no foundation in fact.

I have passed this afternoon gloomily wandering about Madrid. I spent one odd hour in the Plaza Mayor where the Holy Office used to burn heretics, but which is now sacred to turkey merchants and fruit hucksters. I wish I could show you that wonderful spectacle of tropical luxuriance under this wintry sky. Mountains of oranges plucked yesterday—acres of apple stalls—the air of December fragrant with nutty and fruity odors. And over all the haunting memory of the just that went to heaven from that old pavement in their chariots of fire.

I ought to have waited for you to write to me, but perhaps my letter went down on the way, and is now flashing with fins through the waters of the Gulf. Anyhow I write, to spend some minutes in good and improving company, and to wish you with all my heart, the richest blessings of this Holy Christmastide.

J.H.

TO MRS. H. A. WISE

MADRID. *January 9. 1870*

MY DEAR MRS. WISE

Your kind letter has just reached me, having been sent to London and forwarded here. I am at present Secretary of Legation at this capital.

I also received, a few days ago, a letter more than a year old which you had written from Dresden and which had gone all over the world after me. It was a most melancholy and touching reflection to contrast the different appearance life had to many hearts, the day that letter was sealed, and the day it was opened. Nothing new—nothing worth while, I am sure, can be said to you. It was in the backwoods of Iowa that I read the telegram announcing your terrible bereavement.[3] My own grief gave me some faint idea of yours. It was a day of sorrow in my father's house when they heard of it. Everyone of my name had learned of me to love him. I think of him often with tears. There are few incidents of my life for which I am

3 The death of her husband, Henry Augustus Wise.

so grateful as that it was given me to know him well. His was so bright, vivid and alert an intelligence that it seems as if many friends passed away in him. There was something peculiarly affecting in the last year or two—the heroic struggle of his unconquerable spirit and goodness against constant suffering, until compassion was lost in admiration. There are none like him remaining. I remember well one day; he and Leutze and Aulick and I dined together, and were very gay. He had the faculty of making even dull people witty for the time. I, the least valuable, am the only one left of that pleasant party.

I thank you a thousand times for your kind letter and will gladly avail myself of your permission to write when I have anything that you might care to hear.

With my regards to the young ladies.

I am very faithfully yours

JOHN HAY

TO DR. CHARLES HAY

January 28. 1870

MY DEAR FATHER

It has been several weeks since I have received a letter from you but I never allow myself to fret much about the silence of my correspondents. No news I always take to be good news & so escape a great deal of worry.

We are in a little uncertainty here about the General's confirmation.[4] I suppose by the time you read this, some definite action will have been taken by Congress. The General is what we call in the West a "cool hand" and takes everything in the most matter-of-fact manner. But of course he would not relish being rejected.

If he is rejected, it will be for no fault of his own, but because he has discreetly and silently done his duty here, and used his best discretion to accomplish the object of his mission. I am convinced that the effort to obtain justice for Cuba, or a peaceable cession of the

---

[4] Gen. Sickles, like Gen. Dix in 1866, had received an *ad interim* appointment as Minister to Spain, subject to confirmation by the Senate at its next session.

Island, is impossible.[5] The Spanish people are too ignorant to see that the Empire in America is really at an end, and the Spanish volunteers are utterly unmanageable by the Government. So that the Ministry of Prim and Serrano here could not cede the Island without incurring fatal unpopularity in Spain, and they cannot introduce the necessary reforms in Cuba without inflaming the cruel and bloodthirsty Spaniards in the Island to absolute mutiny. So my opinion is, that Sickles' mission will accomplish nothing important, and, as a personal point of view, the sooner I am honorably relieved of my part in it, the better I will be satisfied. I am very glad I came, as I told you once before. I have learned to speak the language with some facility. I have gained some insight into the ways and customs of a people who have always been very interesting to me. I have passed a most agreeable fall and winter.

I only wish I could have been at home when our dear A.L. was with you. I am expecting a letter from him every day.

My love to my mother & sister.

Yours affectionately

J.H.

TO J. G. NICOLAY

MADRID. January 30. 1870

*   *   *   *

I have no news for you. This Legation has absolutely nothing of importance now on its hands. There is a great deal of tiresome routine work which employs the fingers more than the brain, and by way of keeping the circulation regular there is dancing enough to keep the feet from rusting. I am getting rather tired of it and shall

---

[5] The Ten Years War in Cuba began in 1868. The reforms demanded included correction of administrative abuses, gradual emancipation of slaves, equality with Spaniards for the civil service and universal suffrage. There was also a separatist party. The revolution was accompanied by horrible abuses. The American government was involved because of popular sympathy with the revolution, the interference by the Spanish naval vessels with commercial intercourse, the arrest of American citizens, and filibustering. Annexation would have been welcomed by many American imperialists. Indeed the conditions in 1868–69 were very comparable to those which preceded the Spanish American War in 1898.

begin to plume my wings for flight sometime in the spring. I am sorry Sickles has not had a better chance; but nothing was possible with Fish's system of platonic bullying. I am afraid Cuba is gone. This government wants to sell but dares not, and has no power to put a stop to the atrocities on the Island. The only thing left to our Government is to do nothing and keep its mouth shut, or interfere to stop the horrors in Cuba on the ground of humanity, or the damage resulting to American interests.

Write to me when you can and tell me of your welfare and your plans.

My regards to Mrs Nicolay and Mademoiselle de Papillon.

[P.S.] I have heard nothing about my confirmation and have ceased to care, as I shall stay anyhow as long as I want to.

TO WILLIAM L. STONE

January 31. 1870

My Dear Old Boy

I send you a little letter on Spanish politics. I am forbidden by law to do this, so that you must publish it, if you think it worth publishing, without my name.

I am sorry about the ode. I am sure you would laugh if you knew how often I have tried, without making a rhyme. I have treated the muse so shabbily that she stopped visiting me years ago, and I never expect to meet her again.

I like the *Review* very much. I wish you abundant and merited success.

Yours affectionately

J.H.

TO MRS. JOHN BIGELOW

Madrid. *February 20. 1870*

My Dear Mrs Bigelow

I was delighted with your letter for many reasons. It informed me that you were not in Europe, which I thought was the case. Some idiot told me so, and Madrid is so far out of civilization that a con-

tradiction of a false report never reaches us. Then I was glad to
hear that the Marquise de Canigy was in the enjoyment of robust
health—though who the Marquise is I have not the faintest idea. The
well-being of Schnoodle was also a source of devout thanksgiving.
But the news for which I thank you most cordially, is of my marriage. Now I beg you will make my joy perfect by telling me whom
I have made miserable for life. Be sure and tell me when you write.

* * * *

I was never so thoroughly out of the world before. There is never
a wandering Yankee rests the sole of his square-toed boot in Madrid.
I have seen one American family this whole winter; Mrs Gilbert
of Milwaukee and her nieces of Otsego county—winsome damsels.
It was so new and strange to see pretty girls who could talk, that I
felt quite young again, and went around doing the sights with them
just as I used to in the early part of this century. And last night after
they were gone, I watched the moon rise in a very youthful and
spoonful manner.

The winter has been rather a gay one, in spite of the owlish
prophecies of the reaction. The Countess Montijo, mother of our
Mootooal friend Mrs Bonaparte, has the pleasantest house in town,
where one dances all the Sundays—except when somebody dies, or
bad boys like Harry Rochefort frighten the Empress into hysterics.
On the account of the bad boy and the hysterics there was no dancing there last Sunday nor tomorrow—which gives the beautiful
world an opportunity to go to the Palace or to the War Department
to make its bow to the lovely and unamiable Duchesse de la Torre,
or the plain and most amiable Countess of Reus. I shall always remember Mrs Prim with affectionate gratitude for the number of
stout girls and monumental ladies to whom she has presented me
this winter. I like the Spanish ladies. They are very deficient in
education and so are not always mortifying me by questions I cannot
answer and allusions I do not comprehend. In Boston an acquaintance with the Saurian period is of more value socially than the German cotillon; and in Vienna I never could admire anything without some blonde *fraülein* asking me whether my remark was to be
taken in an objective or subjective sense.

It is the deadest of secrets, but I shall not stay here very much longer. If you do not write pretty soon and tell me who the Marquise de Carnigy and Mrs Hay were, I shall never know.

My regards to Mr Bigelow, whose article in Putnam's I received with gratitude & read with delight. My love to all your young people and kiss for me *la petite* Flora, who, as she has never seen me [two words undecipherable].

TO WILLIAM DEAN HOWELLS

Feb. 26. 1807

MY DEAR HOWELLS

I have this moment received your letter of Feb. 11 and hasten to say that I hope you will take no trouble about the matter. It will do no damage whatever. My writing is simply irregular—not criminal. No harm can possibly result. I only requested the suppression of my name so as to be entirely *au règle*. I am more a Republican than a diplomat anyhow and I would much sooner give up the latter position than the former.

Don't think of the matter at all. It is only too flattering to me to see my name mentioned in such fine company.

I cannot afford to remain much longer here. If you have any orders for me to execute I should be happy to be of any use. I cannot say at this moment when I will sail for home, but I think not later than June.

With my kindest regards to Mr Field, I am,

TO WILLIAM DEAN HOWELLS

March 3. 1870

MY DEAR HOWELLS

I have another letter from you about that article of mine. I am really sorry you are so annoyed about it. I repeat, it is not of the slightest practical importance, if it were known. I only asked that my name be *withheld*—not concealed.

So far am I from wishing to avoid the responsibility of the ex-pressions that I have used—that I ask as a favor that you will print my name in your usual index at the end of the volume as the author of the article. I am not capricious in the matter, you understand. There is a certain propriety in reserving the name of an office-holder who writes on politics—but this is only for the time being. I am afraid I must have expressed myself imperfectly in my first letter.

TO DAVID GRAY

March 9. 1870

MY DEAR DAVID

There is a Jesuit in the Cortes here who is my joy. Whenever he is hit hard in a debate, he rises and in a tone of angelic spitefulness threatens to intercede for the aggressor before the throne of Grace. It is that mixture of love and resentment which stirs my heart whenever I think of you and the way you have handled me.

But I pour on your hard head the live coals of forgiveness, and wonder I cannot hate you more. I even descend into the valley of humiliation and thank you some myriads of time for the *Courier & Express* I have received today. Oh, David of my pride and my hopes!

Read the article I wrote in the *Atlantic Monthly* for March on Spanish politics. Howells was unnecessarily nervous about protecting me & so calls the author "James West," I believe in delicate compliment to my birthplace.

Good-bye. Don't write unless you feel like it. I shall see you some day.

My affection for you is decaying under your evil behaviour but my pride in you waxes day by day.

TO CHARLES E. HAY

March 10. 1870

MY DEAR CHARLIE

Although I wrote to you not long ago I take advantage of your letter to write again. You wrote to me just one month ago. I think mail communication in Spain is more uncertain than anywhere else.

Very few of my letters get actually lost but a good many are greatly delayed. The good steamer *City of Boston* in which I made two voyages has not been heard from for 7 weeks and is given up for lost [page from the copybook is missing].

Sickles and I made a long call today on the Duke of Montpensier who is trying hard to be King. He expressed himself, with caution, but still decidedly, in favor of the emancipation of Cuba from Spanish rule. Whether he would change his tune when he got on the throne is another question. He is a very sensible, respectable man. If the Spaniards must have a King, they would do infinitely better to take him than any of the half-baked boys they have been talking about.

How does this rapid fall in gold affect you? I am afraid it will damage you somewhat, as it must result in a corresponding fall in coffees and sugars. But you have always spoken as if you foresaw it —and I hope you were prepared for it.

My love to Mary & the boys.

[P.S.] This letter is rather confidential. You can show it to Uncle Milton, however, if you happen to see him.

TO P. SIDNEY POST

March 30. 1870

MY DEAR GENERAL

As a writist I believe you can beat any living letter writer, but I must acknowledge that your letter is always a good one when it comes. Your last, especially, has been my delight for a week. But you are wrong, as well as injurious, in your supposition that I pay for my puffs. The *Times* pays me double for them not only on account of the interest of the news, but of their accuracy also. When a man talks about himself, he has the sure thing on the item. Seymour is here. I delivered your message and he heaved a sigh of regret for the Kaiserstadt. Madrid is now at its dullest—the wind which for a week or two has been very pretty behaved, is now uproarious. (Excuse the sudden change in the ink—my Spanish Joseph has just carried my green inkstand to Daniel of Gettysburg.)

I wish I could take you once more by the hand of Western fellow-ship. But I fear I must adjourn that pleasure to the Greek Kalends. I have been hoping all along to visit Vienna before going home, but the prospect is now a dissolving view. The most prosaic of all reasons prevents. I shall have money enough next June to buy a ticket to Warsaw—only this and nothing more—Republics is un-grateful. They give their servants board wages, but they won't let them steal unless they are sharp. And we can't all be fisks and but[lers].

*   *   *   *

You ask what will I do for the summer! I will go home. Do not talk about it—or Grant will appoint his cook or his stable boy in my place. I would like to have a gentleman succeed me, if only for the variety.

My best regards to M^{rs} & Miss Post.

CHAPTER XXVIII

April 2, 1870—December 12, 1870

TO JOHN JAY

April 2. 1870

MY DEAR SIR

The accompanying letter has been sent to me from Vienna, but is intended for you. The writer is a year or two behind the times and has not heard how much the United States have lately improved their representation in Austria.

It refers to the establishment of a Consulate at Pest. I see paragraphs from time to time in the American journals which lead me to believe that Dr Czapkay is now in Washington, working for that appointment. If you should be consulted in the matter, I can assure you that Czapkay is a most improper person to fill such a place. He was for a while Consul at Bucharest and a thorn in the side of all honest men. General Post will inform you fully in regard to him. I have no motive in writing except to prevent serious annoyance to you and discredit to the service.

*   *   *   *

TO MRS. JOHN BIGELOW [1]

This letter is dreadful. You must not read it but once. Then burn & forget it.

April 4. 1870

DEAR Mrs BIGELOW

I thank you very heartily for your letter and the definite and satisfactory information it contained about the Marquise and my

---

[1] Clark letter.

fiancée. You did not remember her name, but that is not important
—Nous allons changer tout cela.

I am awaiting a great pleasure. Mrs. Sam. Hooper of Boston will
be here in a day or two. The first friend I have seen for a year. She
will tell me great heaps of gossip and I will repay her by repeating
verbatim your last letter, and we will be merry over our tea cups as
in old times at Washington. Did you ever know Mrs Hooper? She
is very well worth while. I like her better than any of my aunts. "If
this be treason make the most of it." Do you remember (Of course
you don't) a young lady named Wilson from Indiana who came
to Paris to study art, during your reign? She is here now, with Mrs.
Butterfield (sister-in law to ours) and a Miss Dart. They are devoted to art and the Protestant propaganda.

What is the matter in America? A half dozen Major Generals
have recently died. A young lady in Boston went to a party with
His Satanic Majesty and coming back, suicided herself with a
brand-new pearl handled pen knife. George Wilkes has received
personal correction on the street from Bill Leland—the first debt
William ever paid. And to add a new element of disorder Prince
Pierre Bonaparte has sailed for New York. He is greatly disgusted
with France—says he is going to the only country in the world where
a gentleman can enjoy himself with a revolver. You know the Jury
found him innocent and fined him 25,000 francs & costs, to teach him
not to be so innocent the next time he kills a man. Who will give
him the first dinner and the first ball? He makes rather a better
figure dining than dancing. His appetite is sprightly, but his feet
are gouty.

Ogden Haggerty passed through here a few days ago. His daughter
Mrs Crafts is in Paris. The climate of Ithaca is bad for her health.
So the Professor stays and Madame Clementine pines in necessary
exile in Paris.

I hear Mr Washburne is suffering from a severe attack of con-
scientiousness. Mr Fish ordered all the Ministers to dismiss their
attachés and Washburne was forced to cast off Wurtz, which he did
with cracking heart strings. But Jay and *We* &c., who are older and
wiser have as many as we can cram into the Chancellerie, and cheerful youngsters they are. One is a blooming young Knickerbocker of

military antecedents—who on great occasions wears so many corps
badges that he looks as if he had been insured against Fire in several
expensive Companies—and another who is our Bard [2]—a young poet
who goes to the English Chapel for the sins of all of us and attracts
eyes of favor from the pious and gigantic Mrs Layard. And another,
our fast man, who is the greatest authority in Spain on sky blue
cravats.

The General's daughter is greatly admired by the downy hidalgos.
They call her Meess Seekless—and ask me in strict confidence, what
is the state of the General's bank account. These idiots in Europe
will never learn what Américaines are. They are received civilly
and they think in five minutes that the fair Yankee is in love with
them. They carry this pleasing delusion about for a day or two—
until led by a feeling of compassion, they propose and are declined
with thanks. Then they are savage, and la belle Américaine is denounced as a heartless flirt. I have seen this a hundred times in the
last few years.

Good night. My regards to Mr Bigelow and the young people.
Please write once more and when I answer I will say—Au revoir.

TO MRS. S. HOOPER

April 4. 1870

This will be given you by Genaro Soubrie whom I have sent to
you upon probation. He is a very civil and intelligent young man
and I think will answer your purpose. You asked for some one speaking French, but I interpreted this, somewhat liberally, to mean
some civilized language. Genaro speaks English perfectly well.

There can be no objection to him except his limited experience
as courier. But you do not need, as many travellers do, a "guide"
who shall be at the same time "philosopher and friend." Genaro's
father has been a courier for several centuries, I believe. He is mentioned in the Gospel, according to Murray.

However, he will do perfectly well for Burgos and Madrid and
if you want an older and more rascally courier for the South we will
find one after you arrive here.

2 Alvey A. Adee.

While you remain here I shall beg the privilege of usurping the position of your most devoted servant. Madrid is at best a dreary place, and now with Lent and a Revolution both on its hands, it is as still as Salem and much more dusty. But its pictures are a wellspring of pleasure and its skies are as blue as its prospects. But I will be reconciled to it while you are here and after you go I shall not have long to stay.

In the hope of soon seeing you I am with the deepest respect and regard.

TO O. M. HATCH

Confidential

SPAIN. *April 12. 1870*

I intend to come home as early this summer as I possibly can and am as yet a little uncertain whether I shall hang out a shingle somewhere or go again into journalism. I have a sort of good offer in New York, but I do not want to live in the East.

I write now to ask whether there would be any chance of getting some work on the *Republican*. I do not mean the chief place, but some subordinate position which would pay for my board and clothes.

Please answer immediately so that if there is anything going, I may know it before landing at New York.

I have only received one letter from George Nicolay since I came here and that was in Major Bates' handwriting. I am very much afraid that he is growing worse instead of better. If you have any news of him, I should be glad to hear them.

As to Spain, there has been positively no progress made in a year towards the definite settlement of the question of the Crown. They have now stopped looking for a King and pretend to be giving their minds entirely up to the organic laws. They had a draft last week for 40,000 men, and grave disorders broke out in several provinces. It is a curious fact that the old moderate parties are losing ground every day and the only two live and vigorous organizations that now exist and flourish are the two extremes—Republicanism, and Carlism—the rule of the priesthood. I do not hope for any immediate final solution. It will take several years to undo the work of centuries of misgovernment and superstition.

Don't bankrupt yourself in postage. Six cents will carry your letter to Europe and it will come the rest of the way by itself. Letters have more sense than any other class of travellers.

My compliments to Mrs Hatch.

TO MRS. S. HOOPER

April 13. 1870

I inquired of Mr. Adee about the Washington Irving House at Granada, and he, as I was sure he would, dazzled me with light. Its advantages are:

1. It is the best house in Granada.
2. It is not in Granada, but is at the Alhambra and saves you a mile or so of wretched cab every time you visit the Palace.
3. It has all the comforts of a home.
4. The proprietor is bland, passionate and deeply religious.
5. The cook is an Italian and eschews the use of saffron and garlic in the cuisine.
6. There is nothing American about it but the name.

This last remark would certainly decide me. I have suffered all my life from the tyranny and contumely of hotel clerks. They have a proud consciousness of malice and impunity that reminds me of Shelley's description of Jove— "Strong— As one that does, not suffers, wrong." Sometimes I have tried to gain their favor by shameful subservience and have even had the meanness to ask one of them to give me a letter to another—which would get me some breakfast and a bed by paying a little more than the price. One of these introductions ran, with a marvelous confusion of architecture and ornithology, thus: "My Dear Jim— Take care of this bird. He is a brick. Yrs. muchly, Tom."

When I think how meekly we groan under this galling tyranny, I wonder the man on horseback delays.

I am awaiting with spasmodic interest some intimation of how the venerable Mʳ Soubrie fulfills his functions. I have learned this morning that he was, towards the close of the last century, the favorite servant of Joseph Bonaparte—but that the story of his having assassinated a sacristan and robbed a church has never been clearly proven. I am glad to hear this. He informed you, I suppose, that he has spent the last few years in a hospital for the feeble-minded.

Pray do not let the care of him occupy all your time—but visit my Lord of Montpensier at San Selmo and tell him that America is the only country in the world where a gentleman can amuse himself with a pistol without impertinent criticism. But he must take care to be insane when he uses his revolver.

I wish you pleasant moons and balmy airs through Andalucia and Granada and a happy return to Madrid.

P.S. Be sure to bring G.S. back with you. I should never smile again if you should lose him.

TO. CHARLES E. HAY

May 6. 1870

MY DEAR CHARLIE

* * * *

Several times recently, it has seemed possible that the whole Legation might move away from Madrid at short notice. The outrages in Cuba against American citizens and the American flag still continue and we have had some very sharp talk here. The Dons bluster a good deal, but generally manage to do what we ask, unless it involves the payment of money. Here they make a stand—and will lie till doomsday to keep from paying a dollar. We have just finished the first act of a disagreeable quarrel about the *Lloyd Aspinwall*.[3] They have given her up, with a very ill grace, but we shall have trouble about getting the indemnity. Their tactics are, first deny everything—then justify everything—and third, delay.

[3] The *Aspinwall* case was soon after this referred to arbitration and the owners awarded indemnity.

Give my love to Doña Maria Ridgely de Hay and to the Señoritos D. Arturo and D. Juanito de Hay y Ridgely and remember me kindly to all our people. If you write again I will get your letter.

Yours affectionately
JUAN DE HAY Y LEONARD

TO ORVILLE D. BAKER

Confidential

May 6. 1870

I thank you for the breeze of Italy that blows through your last letter. I got only enough of that haunted air to tantalize me.

I am afraid that thing at the Hague is gone up. Root is a clerk of Senator Pomeroy! To preserve anything like homogeneity the Secretary should be a bootblack. I will bet two to one against any gentleman.

You can do much better at home. It was only for the benefit of the service that I should have been glad to see you in. I may meet you in Paris: on my way home.

TO ROBERT T. LINCOLN

May 7. 1870

MY DEAR BOB

I have such a good letter from you yesterday that I will answer it today in the hope of provoking another from you before I leave Madrid. I find my hope of getting home in the spring a dissolving view—a horizon that recedes as I advance. I had thought I would be off next week, but my resignation lies untouched on Daniel's table and I have not the heart to leave him until he has made some sort of arrangement for my successor. Sickles is a better man to deal with than I had imagined. Our relations have been very pleasant and confidential.

Everything about this Legation is so uncertain that it is troublesome for Sickles to make up his mind what to do. In any 48 hours he may be ordered to pack up and start. The Spaniards treat us with great civility personally, but every day brings its new outrage upon the flag or upon citizens, which are never redressed. Plenty of fine words, but arguments without and against all claims & when they are beaten in argument they take refuge in delay. They have no money—their bonds sell at 23 cents—and all they take in they want to steal themselves. They have not paid & will not pay a cent of our claims without a fight.

They have a facility of lying which I thought had died out of the diplomatic service. They are unabashed when caught in a lie.

But all this is business. I have had a pleasant visit and shall go home, a little poorer, but not sorry for my misspent year. I have almost ceased to look forward to having a dollar in bank. Why should I? I have no chicks to feed. My wife has married another man. I will "loaf and invite my soul."

Do you remember Billy Lawrence of Boston? He has been here a week or two. Mrs. Sam. Hooper is coming to spend this month here. She brings a wholesome Washington atmosphere with her. She and I have great larks wandering about the old rookery, seeing where they roasted the heretics, and looking at the pictures. They all made kind inquiries for you. I got a letter from Dick Derby the other day. He has been in Berlin for a year—grubbing away at eyes. Miss Smythe says he is engaged to a nice Western girl named Gordon from Ohio. He says nothing of it.

I think this letter will never be finished. Just now a trio of beauties swarmed in upon me—Laura Sickles with two of the prettiest girls in Spain—dragged me up to Madorazo's studio, which is above my apartment, to see a portrait of one of them. Their pleasant voices and fine eyes have disturbed the current of my thoughts. After parting with them and saying, "May your Graces go with God!" I have come back to my den and I find lying on this letter a fan and a rosebud. So I must put the rosebud in my buttonhole and take the fan home. I have almost lost the habit of society. I go out so little that the young ladies ask me whether my complaint is love or the *espleen*. (The Spaniards cannot pronounce the *S* before a consonant. They called the Smythes *Esmity*.) I shall be sorry for it perhaps when I am gone for the Spanish women are the most cordial, frank and winning creatures in the world. They are also prettier than is necessary

Give my best love to Miss Lincoln & tell me next time what her name is, and to Mrs. Lincoln convey expressions of homage from your uncompromising adherent.

J.H.

TO CHARLES SUMNER

May 9. 1870

I must beg your pardon in advance for the impropriety of this note. I write to you, because I think you have more conscience about the service than any one else.

I see in some late papers the name of a Mr Jourdan mentioned as nominated for Consul at Seville. Mr. Jourdan could not have known what he wanted. The Consulate has no salary and does not pay anything. Mr. Cunningham, the present incumbent, is a gentleman residing in Seville, of great wealth and high position, who confers upon the post more honor than he receives. I do not know him personally but every one speaks of him in the highest terms. The Duke of Montpensier mentioned his name to me in the most flattering way. If he has not resigned, it would be a serious and unmerited affront to dismiss him without cause—and any one going there in his place and expecting to live upon the scanty fees, would be in a most painful position. It would be a kindness to Mr Jourdan to reject him. But perhaps he is already confirmed—if so, he has my profound commiseration.

This is an official impropriety—but I think, in my place, you would have done something like it.

I must express my cordial thanks for your profound and eloquent discourse on "Caste." I read it with great delight and then gave it to my friend Emilio Castelar. You are very well known in Spain, even. I have been much encouraged and fortified in my Republicanism here. Such men as Castelar, Figueras, Pi y Margall, and nearly all the representatives of the Republican press are as sound and conservative on all social and political questions as the thoughtful Democrats of our own race. The theory that the Latin races are incapable of self-government is a very convenient one for Latin aristocrats, but I expect before I die to see it practically contradicted.

I cannot afford to remain here much longer. If you have any commands I should be glad to execute them, before I go.

I had the pleasure of meeting Mrs. Hooper and her daughter recently, on their way to Granada. Miss Hooper seems much improved by her journey. Miss Sedgwick accompanies them.

TO JOHN BIGELOW

May 9. 1870

MY DEAR Mr BIGELOW

I am coming home as soon as I can decently get away. It will be I fear one or two months at least before I can be relieved. I gave warning early this spring and expected to be gone by this time. But the General has not exhibited much energy in filling the place and I am afraid to leave it exclusively to the supreme Washington wisdom for fear they should appoint a bootblack or tanner's apprentice out of the family. Starring would be the most likely man but as there is nothing to steal he would scorn the place. I was deeply disgusted at his silly drivel. He wrote it, I am sure, with no malice towards you or Nicolay, but simply to be pleasant in his flunkey way to Mr Read and Mr Fish, whence he expects loaves. He will hang around Washington and fawn and crawl until he gets another place—and I will bet two to one he will get something worth while. Have you noticed some of the recent appointments? Root to the Hague, e.g., is a clerk to Pomeroy of Kansas—parasite of a parasite—his master a nonentity, and he a millionth dilution. We are getting into full Bas-Empire. Along the whole vast European sea line from Lisbon to Petersburg inclusive there is not one Embassador who knows French—not one except Sickles who owes his nomination to anything but the personal fancy of Grant or a Congressman. You remember how all the flunkeys said when Seward went out and Fish in, that politics had left the State Department and respectability and culture were to have a chance. Look at the herd of swine Fish has commissioned—

besides the dozen or so whom Sumner has trained in committee. In the last papers I have seen, appears the name of one Jourdan of Washington for Consul at Seville. This must be some pestilent and ill-smelling hanger-on of the White House who likes oranges and wants to go where they are cheap. Seville pays nothing—and the gentleman who has done us the honor to act as Consul for the last dozen years is a man of great wealth and high position who used to make every American feel proud of his country in Seville. To think that such a man should be insulted and discredited in the eyes of his neighbors to make a place for some shabby bummer too ignorant to know what to ask for.

*   *   *   *

I have had a good year. It is a luxury I can't afford but I can scarcely say I regret it. My relations with the General have been very pleasant. He has done as well here as anybody could, I think. He has been greatly embarrassed and hampered by confused and contradictory instructions, which he has followed perhaps rather too strictly. But I do not see how any different result could have been reached. Cuba is lost to Spain, and I hope, lost to us. The Volunteers openly defy the Spanish authorities. They hope to kill or exile all the natives and then set up for themselves. Both sides lie so, that news are worth nothing. But the Spaniards are the best liars after all. If we want the Island we must go there and take it. If we bought it from Spain tomorrow she could not deliver. We would have a war with the hyena population of the Island before we could take possession—and many years of military government afterward with its inevitable corruptions and shames. The only grounds on which we can do anything are the daily outrages upon our citizens and our flag, and the crimes against humanity continually perpetrated by the Volunteers. These cannot be exaggerated—and they will never be redressed. For two very good reasons: the Spanish government has no money to pay indemnities, and they fear the Cuban Volunteers more than any nation in the world.

With my respectful homage to Mrs Bigelow, I remain very faithfully yours

JOHN HAY

June 18, 1870

*   *   *   *

I see the Evil One has broke loose in Washington. The President is instructed to protest against the fiendish atrocities of the Spanish Volunteers, and to ask for the help of other powers. Spain will laugh at the protest. Other powers will probably not join, and if they did, our good old Monroe doctrine goes to the demnition bow-wows. We have always held desperately to the position that the intervention of European nations in American affairs could not be favored by the United States. This was Seward's morning & evening song. The whole world knew the sound of it, while the grand old fellow sat, for our honor, in the State Department. But the lively lads of the House think they can do it better. They felt that something must be done or the Democrats would go one better & get all their seats. There is a heavy sea on. The only thing to do was to sit still and keep our mouths shut, till the infamy grew too intolerable and then right it, in the name of God and Humanity. We must have some day serious trouble with Spain. They need a licking. We will have to give it them. But I would like to see it done decently and in order.

Nothing new here. The Cortes are chattering away the last hours of the session. There will be a practical Prim Dictatorship all summer. To my sorrow and puzzlement the Republicans are apparently losing ground—and the Carlists gaining. Can it be they need their little '93?

June 22. 1870

MY DEAR Mʳ CASTELAR

I cannot refrain from expressing my admiration and delight at your magnificent discourse of Monday. You gave me one of the highest enjoyments of my life. I think rarely since men began to talk has so much beauty been united with so much strength in the same oration. I count as the most precious advantage of my visit to Spain, the privilege of having listened to the greatest orator of our time. Your glorious tribute to Lincoln I shall send to his family as the grandest anthem in his praise which has ever been sung.

Mr Moret, in his reply, made, unintentionally of course, a great error in what he said of John Brown. Brown received a regular legal trial, by the ordinary tribunals; was defended by distinguished advocates, and condemned to death for insurrection and homicide according to the laws of the State of Virginia: after his execution his body was delivered to his friends and buried with his family at his home in the forest of Adirondack. The charge which Mr Moret makes, that his remains were thrown into the sea, is absurd to any one acquainted with the manners and character of the American people. Brown died a victim of his own uncalculating and heroic love of freedom, and of the American regard for law. And although I revere and honor his memory and abhor the infamous cause and the cruel laws that slew him, I cannot say that his sentence was illegal. Where slavery is tolerated, the law is always cruel.

I am very faithfully

TO WICKHAM HOFFMAN

July 17. 1870

*   *   *   *

I gave young Santos-Suarez a line to you. If you see him you will like him. His family are most estimable people, a little too rich to get to heaven, but very good company up to that fork in the road called death, where the bloated aristocrats like you and Moore go for your singeing, and the trusting saints like me who have been kept on low fare all our lives, go straight to glory and music.

Receive assurances, more sincere than usual, from your friend and serving man

J.H.

TO JOHN BIGELOW [4]

July 21. 1870

DEAR Mr BIGELOW

The situation has greatly changed even since your letter of the 15th, which I have just received. You see that this government has swallowed without a whimper the insult of France, and positively seemed rather tickled that Prussia has to fight the matter out alone. Please never use the word "decency" in speaking of the contemporary breed of Spanish politicians. They retain the speech of Don Quixote, but the heart and stomach are Sancho's. The Emperor, with a shameless cynicism has given Olózaga the Grand Cordon. The old dotard is the tool of his pretty country woman, the Empress. She has a wonderful power over senile envoys. She kept Dix and keeps Washburne in a chronic priapism. It is as settled as anything can be here for 24 hours that Prussia is to fight Spain's battle with no help from Spain.

The Cuban question is not so simple as it seems. The Spanish government has no authority whatever in the Island. The old story of the loss of the Americas is repeating itself there. Caballero preserves a semblance of power by doing everything the Volunteers demand. Yet they despise him for his rare relapses into civilization, and adore Valmaseda who is a brute pure and simple. If Spain sold to us, or liberated the Island she could not deliver; she fears the Volunteers more than the rebels. I believe the thing wont wash. This is my individual opinion—not the General's. He preserves an attitude of vigilant observation.

What looks most discouraging to me is the attitude of the Senate. They threw overboard the vast advantages of the St Domingo treaty,[5] to prevent the White House boys from getting their little commish: which is what I call small. Is it likely they would accept a Cuban treaty, that no power human or divine could keep from dripping all over with the grease of the lobby?

I have a letter from Nicolay telling me he is in treaty for a Chicago paper. If he gets it, I will go home and help him. I would like to

[4] Clark letter.
[5] The annexation treaty, bitterly opposed by Sumner, was rejected by the Senate June 30.

stay here a while but I cant afford it from the moment I see a living possible at home.

TO J. G. NICOLAY

NEW YORK, Dec. 12. 1870

MY DEAR NICOLAY

I have delayed writing for a few days knowing you had seen Reid and that he had told you I was alive. I am living at the Astor House, which is now run on the European plan, and gives me a room on rather reasonable terms. I am working daily on the *Tribune,* writing Editorial—or as it is here technically called *brevier.* I get salary enough to pay my board and washing.

I cannot regard it as a successful experiment as yet, though Reid & the rest seem satisfied. I do not find myself up to the work of writing so much every day on a given theme. But the *Tribune* force is sufficient to allow a good deal of subdivision and so far I have written just what I please.

That ridiculous rhyme of mine has had a ridiculous run.[6] It has been published in nearly the whole country press from here to the Rocky Mountains. As my initials are not known, and they generally get worn off on the second reprint, I have not been disgraced by it.

*   *   *   *

Reid talks of sending me to Washington—not as a reporter—but as a sort of heavy swell correspondent; whereat I rather reluct. I do not like to blame and I mortally hate to praise. Which somewhat narrows a letter-writer's field.

Have you seen the first of my "Castilian Days"—which by a Hibernicism of Fields, is a night? He seems greatly pleased with the stuff I have given him & proposes to make a book of it next year. I went on there & spent a day or two very pleasantly among the *geistreich* of Cambridge & the Hub.

*   *   *   *

J.H.

---

[6] "Little Breeches" was published in the *Weekly Tribune,* Dec. 2, 1870. In Thayer's "John Hay," I, 356, where this paragraph is quoted, the title of the poem is interpolated in the text; it does not appear in the original letter.

Index of Persons

Adee, Alvey A. (1842–1924), private secretary to Gen. Sickles, 1869–77, and then in the Dept. of State until his death. (316, 318)

Ashmun, George (1804–70), representative from Mass., 1845–51; chmn. of the Chicago convention, 1860. (196, 198, 202)

Babcock, Orville E. (1835–84), aide to Grant; later his private secretary. (174, 242)

Badeau, Adam (1831–95), aide to Grant. (242, 289)

Baker, Edward D. (1811–61), Springfield, Ill. lawyer; friend of Lincoln; member of Congress, who went to the Coast and became senator from Oregon, 1860; entered the army and fell dramatically at Ball's Bluff. (30, 182)

Banks, Nathaniel P. (1816–94), after many years in Mass. politics during which he had been both congressman and governor, Banks moved to Chicago in 1861, whence he returned to Washington as major general of volunteers; had a distinguished military career and after the war reentered Mass. politics. (29, 36, 43, 47, 48, 67, 75, 124, 125n., 140–143, 157, 179, 183, 223–224, 228, 231, 241, 244, 245, 246, 262, 268, 269, 270)

Barlow, Samuel L. M. (1826–89), N. Y. lawyer; Democrat; Unionist in 1861; supported McClellan, 1864. (244, 283)

Bartlett, William Francis (1840–76), brigadier general, 1862. (185n., 232, 266, 268, 269, 270, 276, 280)

Bates, Edward (1793–1869), attorney general, 1861–64; he had been a candidate for the nomination in 1860. (50, 119, 134, 137, 207, 221, 222)

Bennett, James Gordon (1795–1872), owner and editor of *N. Y. Herald.* (168n., 178, 215, 298)

Blair, Francis Preston (1791–1876), journalist and politician; member of Andrew Jackson's "kitchen cabinet." (15n., 38, 94, 95, 133, 227)

Blair, Francis P., Jr., (1821–75), representative from Mo., 1857–62, 1863–64; organized regiment and became brigadier general, 1862; strong Unionist but opposed by radicals. (15n., 23, 38, 79, 87, 94, 95, 113, 114, 123, 133, 134)

Blair, Montgomery (1813–83), postmaster general, 1861–64; son of F. P. Blair, and brother of F. P. Blair, Jr., of St. Louis (15n., 16, 38, 47,

50, 69, 105, 112, 113, 119, 120, 122, 123, 129, 130, 132, 133, 134, 137, 143, 167, 208, 216, 219–220, 227, 236, 240, 243, 244, 246, 273, 298)

Boker, G. H., secretary of Union League of Philadelphia. (108)

Booth, John Wilkes (1838–65), actor whose career as a star began in 1860. (118, 274)

Botts, John Minor (1802–69), representative from Va., 1839–43, 1847–49; although joining in the Secession, he was opposed to the Confederate govt., was arrested in 1862 and confined in a negro jail; offered nomination for senator by "restored government" in 1864, but declined. (113)

Boutwell, George Sewall (1818–1905), commissioner of internal revenue, 1862–63 and then representative from Mass. (44, 75, 132, 201, 204, 268, 270, 298

Bradford, A. W. (1806–81), governor of Md., 1862–66. (114, 115, 119, 123)

Bramlette, Thomas E. (1817–75), U. S. District Attorney in Ky., 1862; governor, 1864–67. (125, 192)

Brooks, Noah (1830–1903), journalist; friend of Lincoln; subsequently on staff N. Y. Tribune. (195, 196)

Brough, John (1811–65), governor of Ohio, 1864–65. (98, 99n., 192, 193, 228)

Brown, Benjamin Gratz (1826–85), leader of the Mo. radicals; cousin of Frank P. Blair, Jr.; senator, 1863–67; one of the signers of the call for the Cleveland convention, 1864. (136, 137–138, 140, 167)

Browning, Orville H. (1806–81), intimate of Lincoln and one of the organizers of the Republican party; senator from Ill., 1861–63. (19, 266, 269)

Bruce, Sir Frederick, succeeded Lord Lyons as British Minister. (181, 283)

Bullitt, Cuthbert, collector of customs, New Orleans. (75, 185)

Burnside, Andrew E. (1821–81), rising from colonel of Rhode Island regiment to command of Army of Potomac; in 1863 in command, Department of Ohio. (78, 86, 92, 102, 111n., 114, 125, 127, 128, 172, 173, 218)

Butler, Benjamin F. (1818–93), entered army as brigadier general in command of the 8th Mass.; became major general. (6n., 11–12, 18, 19, 34, 37n., 42n., 72, 91, 92, 98, 100, 101n., 114, 115, 116, 148–152, 173, 174, 178, 179–180, 183, 184, 195, 197, 198, 221, 243, 298)

Butterfield, Daniel (1831–1901), major general of volunteers. (84, 85, 86, 87)

Butterfield, Justin, commissioner of the general land office. (80)

Caldwell, G. W., member of a commission to ask Congress to recognize West Virginia and admit it to the Union. (16)

Cameron, Simon (1799–1889), secretary of war until Jan. 11, 1862; had been candidate for presidency in the Chicago Convention, 1860; senator from Penn., 1867–77. (5, 7, 9, 80, 92, 98, 119, 120, 121, 130, 152, 153, 177, 184, 185, 221, 224, 226, 228, 230, 232)

Carpenter, Francis B. (1830–1900), portrait painter. (197, 272)

Cartter, David Kellogg (1812–87), Ohio delegate to Chicago convention; minister to Bolivia, 1861–62; chief justice Supreme Court of the Dist. of Col. in 1863. (53, 95, 115)

Castelar y Ripoll, Emilio (1832–99), Spanish republican; delegate to the Cortes from Saragossa. (303, 322, 325)

Chandler, Zachariah (1813–79), senator from Mich., 1857–75; bitterly opposed to McClellan. (31, 32, 122, 131, 204, 205, 264)

Channing, William E. (1818–1901), poet; son of famous Unitarian minister of Boston. (12)

Chase, Salmon P. (1808–73), secretary of treasury, 1861–July, 64, when he resigned; in Dec., 1864 he was appointed chief justice of Supreme Court. (7, 38, 50n., 54, 69, 70, 95, 99, 110, 111n., 119, 129, 134, 137, 143, 167, 198, 199–200, 201, 202, 203, 207–208, 220, 231, 244, 272–273, 274–275)

Chittenden, Lucius E. (1824–1902), registrar of the treas., 1861–65. (198)

Cisco, John J., asst. treas. of the United States. (145, 198, 199)

Clay, Cassius Marcellus (1810–1903), of Ky.; mentioned for vice president in 1860; appointed minister to Russia; eccentric, fanatical and probably more or less insane. (3, 8, 50, 124, 139, 170)

Cochrane, John (1813–98), lawyer; congressman from N. Y., 1857–61; raised regiment of Union troops, 1862; attorney general of N. Y., 1863–65. (184)

Colfax, Schuyler (1823–85), representative from Ind., 1855–69; speaker, 1863–69. (38, 114, 123, 130, 131, 137, 278, 293)

Conkling, Roscoe (1829–88), congressman from N. Y., 1859–67, except for 1863–65. (82)

Conness, John (1821–1909), senator from Calif., 1863–69. (80, 199, 262)

Covode, John (1808–71), congressman from Penn., 1855–63 when he was defeated; reelected for two terms, 1867–71. (102)

Cowan, Edgar (1815–85), senator from Penn., 1861–67. (199, 262, 271, 276)

Cox, Samuel S. (1824–89), representative from Ohio, 1857–65; from N. Y., 1869–85, 1886–89. (130, 131, 137, 143, 204, 228)

Cresswell, John A. J. (1828–91), Md. politician; representative, 1863–65; senator, 1865–67; postmaster general, 1869–74. (105, 118, 298)

Crisfield, John W. (1806–97), representative from Md., 1861–63; failed reelection; he had been a member of the "peace conference" of

1861. (113)

Cullom, Shelby Moore (1829–1914), Springfield, Ill. lawyer who formed law partnership with Milton Hay; in politics; he was a member of state legislature, 1856, 1860–61; representative 1865–71; subsequently for many years senator. (99, 237, 265, 282)

Curtin, Andrew G. (1817–94), governor of Penn., 1861–67. (80, 92, 99n., 107, 120, 129)

Curtis, George William (1824–92), after 1863 political editor, *Harper's Weekly;* also *Harper's Monthly.* (266, 267)

Dahlgren, John A., rear admiral; command of Wash. Navy Yard, 1861; of naval forces, Charleston, 1863. (11, 22, 44, 68n., 103–104, 107, 108, 111, 156, 198, 297

Dana, Charles A. (1819–97), correspondent for *N. Y. Tribune;* resigned, March, 1862, to enter War Department where he became asst. sec.; largely responsible for Rosecrans' removal. (106, 128, 184, 228, 236, 243)

Davis, Henry Winter (1817–65), Md. emancipationist elected to Congress, 1855; defeated, 1861; elected, 1863; joined opposition to Lincoln. (105, 118, 184, 204, 216, 227, 230, 234, 236)

Davis, Jefferson (1808–89), president of C.S.A., Feb. 9, 1861. (10, 21, 25, 77, 113, 172)

De Joinville, Count, accompanied the Orleans princes to the U. S. (33n., 84)

Delahay, Mark W., appointed to judgeship in Kas.; described by Beveredge, II, 47, as "dissolute Illinois attorney"; married to 5th cousin of Lincoln's mother. (99, 138, 153)

Dennison, William (1815–82), governor of Ohio, 1859–61; chairman of Baltimore convention, 1864; appointed postmaster general, 1865. (99, 100, 111, 216, 223, 228)

Dix, Dorothea Lynde (1802–87), appointed "Supt. of Women Nurses," June 10, 1861. (4)

Dix, John Adams (1798–1879), of N. Y.; major general in command of the Dept. of the East, stationed in New York in 1863; appointed minister to France, Sept. 24, 1866. (81, 243, 247n., 251–258 *passim,* 263–264, 267, 272, 273, 275, 276, 280, 306n., 327)

Doolittle, James Rood (1815–69), senator from Wis., 1857–69. (19, 140, 183, 262, 263, 269, 271)

Douglass, Frederick (1817?–95), escaped slave; settled in New Bedford, Mass.; became famous abolition orator; assisted in recruiting Mass. negro regiment. (19)

Eames, Charles (1812–67), Washington lawyer; frequently counsel for Navy and for Treasury Depts. (21, 182, 186, 264)

Eckert, Thomas T. (1825–1910), superintendent of military telegraph, War Dept., 1862–65, rising to rank of brigadier general. (66, 234, 235)

Edward, doorkeeper at White House since days of President Taylor. (2)

Ellsworth, Elmer Ephraim (1837–61), protégé and favorite of Lincoln; organized regiment of New York City firemen dressed in the style of French Zouaves; killed May 24, 1861; funeral from White House. (16, 17, 19, 20–21, 23)

Etheridge, Emerson, one of the clerks of the House, 1861–65. (114, 130, 131)

Evarts, William M. (1818–1901), N. Y. lawyer, born in Vermont; attorney general in Johnson cabinet. (100)

Everett, Edward (1794–1865), orator and statesman who in a normal lifetime was governor of Mass., president of Harvard, member of Congress, minister to England, secretary of state, and candidate for vice president on the Constitutional-Union ticket. (121, 122, 128)

Fessenden, William P. (1806–69), senator from Me., 1854–64, 65–69; chairman senate finance committee; secretary of treasury, 1864–65. (79, 199, 201, 202, 205, 230, 263)

Field, Maunsell B. (1822–75), assistant secretary of treasury, 1861–65. (171, 198, 199, 232)

Fish, Hamilton (1808–93), secretary of state, March 11, 1869–Mar. 12, 1877. (296n., 299, 301, 302, 308, 315, 323)

Forney, John W. (1817–81), Philadelphia journalist; established *Philadelphia Press*, 1857; supported Buchanan; became Republican in 1860; became clerk of the House, 1861–68; founded *Daily Morning Chronicle* in Washington, 1862. (74, 80, 98, 119–120, 121, 131, 136, 146, 153, 169, 170, 215, 220, 230, 232, 238)

Forrest, Edwin (1806–72), actor. (42, 169, 170, 303)

Fox, Gustavus Vasa (1821–83), chief clerk of the Navy Dept. and subsequently assistant secretary. (15, 28, 84, 85, 87, 88, 89, 103, 104, 108, 113, 116, 172–173, 174, 195, 198, 200, 208, 219, 230, 234, 235–236, 240, 241)

Frémont, John Charles (1813–90), major general in Dept. of West; removed by the President, Nov., 1861; subsequently served in Va.; nominated for presidency by Cleveland convention, 1864. (26, 32n., 37n., 38, 47, 100, 126, 133, 134, 153, 180, 183, 184, 213, 216n., 219)

Fry, James B. (1827–94), of Ill.; graduate of West Point; assistant adjutant general and brevet-captain in 1861; later lieutenant colonel and in 1863 provost marshal general to check desertion, reorganize recruiting and enforce conscription. (6, 81, 104, 177–178)

INDEX OF PERSONS

337

Leutze, Emanuel (1816–68), painter. (44, 226, 306)

Lincoln, Abraham. (4, 6, 11, 14, 16, 19–20, 25–33 *passim*, 36, 37, 42–47 *passim*, 50, 66–80 *passim*, 83, 87, 89, 90, 91, 95, 99, 100, 104–105, 108–122 *passim*, 126, 127, 128, 131, 132–146 *passim*, 165–168 *passim*, 171, 176–181 *passim*, 186, 187, 192–193, 195, 198–209 *passim*, 213, 216–221 *passim*, 225–230 *passim*, 234–238 *passim*, 243–246 *passim*, 250, 271–274 *passim*, 278, 280, 282)

Lincoln, Mrs. Mary Todd. (3, 40, 41, 75–76, 171, 234, 273–274, 280)

Lincoln, Robert Todd (1843–1926), son of President Lincoln; Harvard, 1864; served as captain on Grant's staff, 1865; lawyer in Chicago after 1867. (26, 67, 72, 75–76, 206, 208, 209, 278, 280, 285, 292, 320)

Lincoln, Thomas ("Tad"), younger son of the President, who died in 1864. (172)

Locke, David Ross (1833–88), *pseud.*, Petroleum V. Nasby; the first of his famous letters satirizing Democrats and Copperheads was in Mar. 1861; Nasby Papers published, 1864. (228, 270)

Logan, John A. (1826–86), representative from Ill., 1857–62, when he resigned to enter army; he had been a Democrat, and Douglas supporter. (82)

Logan, Stephen T., senior partner with Milton Hay. (99, 212)

Loring, Harriet B. (262, 297)

Lovejoy, Owen (1811–64), representative from Ill., 1856–64; Lincoln called him "my most generous friend." (131, 132)

Lyons, Lord, British minister. (9)

McClellan, George B. (1826–85), successively commander of Division of Potomac, general-in-chief, commander of Army of Virginia, and in 1864 Democratic candidate for presidency. (25n., 27–39 *passim*, 42n., 45–46, 47, 49n., 51, 67, 85, 86, 143, 144, 151, 167, 176, 200, 212–218 *passim*, 221, 229, 237n., 238, 244, 293)

McClernand, John A. (1812–1900), representative from Ill., 1843–51, 1859–61; entered army as brigadier general and became major general in 1862; after Vicksburg campaign Grant ordered him to Ill.; reputation of being poor teamworker with special dislike of West Pointers. (69, 229)

McDowell, Irvin (1818–85), West Point '38; brigadier general assigned to forces protecting Washington in 1861; made major general of volunteers in 1862. (24n., 25n., 36, 37, 42n., 119, 182n.)

McIlvaine, Charles P. (1799–73), Episcopal bishop of Ohio, 1831–73. (30)

McLane, Robert Milligan (1815–98), representative from Md., 1847–51; after the war senator from Md. (18)

MacVeagh, Wayne (1833–1917), lawyer in West Chester, Penn.; chairman of the Republican state committee; made major of cavalry in 1863. (54, 91–92, 119, 120, 121, 129–130, 153)

Harmony; representative from Ind., 1843–47; diplomatic service, 1853–58. (105)

Patterson, Mrs. David T. (Martha), daughter of President Johnson. (264)

Perry, Horatio Justice (1824–91), of N. H.; appointed secretary of legation, Madrid, 1849, after service in Mexican War. (14)

Petherbridge, U. S. Colonel. (3, 4)

Piatt, Donn (1819–91), of Ohio; colonel and chief of staff under Schenck at Baltimore; ordered Gen. Birney to recruit negro brigade. (106)

Plumley, Benjamin Rush (1816–87), Quaker abolitionist of Penn., who entered army as major; member Baltimore convention, 1864. (200)

Pomeroy, Samuel Clarke (1816–91), senator from Kan., 1861–73. (1, 79, 138, 153, 167, 177, 181, 203, 280, 320, 323)

Pope, John (1823–92), major general volunteers, Mar. 21, 1862, and, July 27, placed in command of a new "Army of Virginia," with Frémont, Banks and McDowell. (40, 41n., 43, 45, 46, 47, 167, 176)

Porter, David D. (1813–91), rear admiral in command N. Atlantic blockading squadron. (30, 240, 241, 242, 260)

Post, Philip S. (1833–95), brigadier general of volunteers; consul, Vienna, 1866–74. (287–289, 292, 312, 314)

Powers, Hiram (1805–73), sculptor; made the busts of Franklin and Jefferson placed in Capitol in 1863. (79)

Price, Sterling (1809–67), governor of Mo., 1852–56; president of state convention, 1860; joined Confederacy, 1862. (32, 189, 190)

Quantrell, W. C., Confederate guerrilla. (82)

Raymond, Henry J. (1820–69), established *N. Y. Times*, 1851; entered politics and was representative from New York, 1865–67. (15, 82–83, 213, 223, 236, 239, 269, 270, 280, 283)

Reid, Whitelaw (1837–1912), war correspondent for *Cincinnati Gazette;* subsequently with the *N. Y. Tribune* of which he became editor upon the retirement of Greeley. (114, 138, 220, 297, 328)

Rolla, Lt. (190)

Rosecrans, William Starke (1819–98), West Point '42; volunteer aid to McClellan, 1861; promoted rapidly; relieved of command of Army of the Cumberland and assigned to St. Louis, October 19, 1863. (65, 77, 78, 86, 87, 90–94 *passim,* 101–106 *passim,* 109, 110, 111, 115, 138, 140, 168, 187–192, 194)

Rousseau, Lovell H. (1818–69), Louisville lawyer, rising to rank of major general. (24, 170)

of Vermont. (174, 183, 217–218)

Spinner, Francis Elias (1802–90), representative from N. Y., 1855–61; treasurer of U. S., 1861–75. (9, 47, 53, 130)

Sprague, William (1830–1915), governor of R. I., 1860–63; senator, 1863–75; married Kate Chase. (12, 13, 119)

Stanton, Edwin M. (1814–69), of Ohio; replaced Cameron as secretary of war, Jan. 11, 1862. (37–38, 41, 45–46, 70, 78, 93, 95, 116, 138, 167, 168, 191, 193, 206, 208, 220, 221, 225, 227, 228, 232, 233, 236, 244, 267, 284, 297)

Stanton, Henry B. (1805–87), lawyer, reformer, journalist; m. Elizabeth Cady, 1840. (100, 119, 120)

Stedman, Edmund Clarence (1833–1908), war correspondent early in Civil War; poet and banker. (299)

Steedman, James B. (1817–83), major general. (109)

Stephens, Ann Sophia (1813–86), wife of Edward Stephens who had an appointment in N. Y. Custom House; novelist and editor; wrote "Pictorial History of Civil War." (2, 6–7)

Stockton, Thomas Hewlings (1808–68), chaplain of the senate; pulpit orator. (121)

Stoddard, William Osborn (1835–1925), journalist; served in U. S. volunteers, 1861; attached to White House secretarial staff, 1861–64. (26, 44, 90, 112, 182, 297)

Stone, Robert K., White House physician. (43, 106)

Stone, William L., graduate of Brown; editor of the *College Review*. (308)

Stover, Mrs. Dan (Mary), daughter of President Johnson. (264)

Stuart, John Todd (1807–85), Lincoln's first law partner; representative in Congress, 1863–65. (213)

Sunderland, Dr., pastor of First Presbyterian Church, Wash., D. C. (74)

Taney, Roger Brooke (1777–1864), chief justice of U. S. Supreme Court. (53, 230, 231)

Taylor, Bayard (1825–78), traveler, author; war correspondent for *N. Y. Tribune*, 1862; secretary of legation, St. Petersburg, May 1862. (105, 139)

Thomas, George H. (1816–70), West Point '40; became major general. (74, 92, 102, 105, 106, 110, 125, 127, 179, 192)

Thompson, C. G., artist. (55)

Tilton, Theodore, N. Y. journalist, 1850–71; on staff of *The Independent*, of which he became editor-in-chief. (111, 130)

Tod, David (1805–68), governor of Ohio, 1860–63; lawyer who had made fortune in coal and iron. (98, 99, 198, 199, 200, 201)

INDEX OF PERSONS

343

Wood, Fernando (1812–81), mayor of New York City, 1861–62; representative, 1863–65. (4, 17, 87, 130, 193, 194, 217, 218)

Young, John Russell (1840–99), journalist; war correspondent for Forney, 1861; managing editor for Forney, 1862; managing editor, *N. Y. Tribune,* 1866. (121, 147)

Index

Africa, 89
Alexandria, Va., 8, 13
Ancient. *See* Lincoln, Abraham.
Annapolis, 6, 8, 9, 12, 28
Antietam, battle of, 218
Arkansas, 1 n., 73, 250
Army of the Cumberland, 115, 192
Army of the Potomac, 36, 47, 102
Army of Virginia, 47
Ashley's Bill, 244
Aspinwall case. *See Lloyd Aspinwall* case.
Atlanta, 94, 128 n., 209
Atlantic Monthly, 15, 310, 328
Austria, 280

Ball's Bluff, 30, 32, 36 n.
Baltimore, 3, 6, 7, 13, 16; Convention,
  1864, 73 n., 177, 185
Banking system, 144
Bermuda, 88
Blockade, 2 n., 13, 16, 27, 33, 59, 103, 104,
  157, 219 n.
Boston, 328
Bristow, Va., 101
British Legation, 6-7, 74, 88
Brown University, 83 n., 90
Buchanan, 79
Bull Run, first battle of, 24 n., 26, 36 n.;
  second battle of, 45, 47 n., 176 n. *See
  also* Manassas.

Cabinet, 13, 40, 50, 57, 93, 111 n., 134, 222,
  244
Cairo, Ill., 5, 18
Campaign contributions, 223
Canada, 88
Capitol, 4, 79, 118
"Castilian Days," 328
Cavalry, 88
Cedar Mountain, battle of, 43
Chain Bridge, 45

Chambersburg, 211 n.
Chancellorsville, 68; Campaign, 64 n.
Charleston, S. C., 11, 12, 23, 29 n., 55, 56,
  58, 60, 68 n., 106
Chattanooga, 87, 90-91, 92, 102, 103, 105,
  113 n., 125, 179
Chicago Convention, 1860, 28, 124; 1864,
  189, 193, 211, 238
Chickamauga, battle of, 92 n., 102, 106,
  109, 192
Chirique, 203 n.
Christian Commission, 55
Cincinnati, 98 n.
Clay's Armory, 8
Cleveland Convention, 1864, 180, 184
Colonization, 69, 203
Committee on Foreign Relations, 262
Confederacy, 1 n., 10
Congress, 10, 20, 81, 105, 200
Constitution, 69, 81, 135, 205
Contrabands, 22, 37, 85, 149, 172, 210, 241
Copperheads, 87, 94, 109, 117, 135, 194,
  211, 260
Corinth, Miss., 67
Cotton, 19, 33, 203, 219, 220
Courts martial, 45, 68, 116, 169
Cuba, 302, 306-307, 308, 312, 319, 324, 327
Currency, 51, 99

Dahlgren gun, 22
Davis Bill, 204 n.
Delaware, 9, 237 n.
Democratic party, 116, 117
Department of the Mississippi, 115 n.
Deserters, 39
Donelson, Fort, 36
Draft, 74, 75, 76, 78, 81, 145, 211 n.; riots,
  71

Election, Nov., 1863, 116; Nov., 1864, 233,
  242
Elections, Oct., 1864, 225, 226, 227

Other DACAPO titles of interest